THE QUR'AN
IN
99
QUESTIONS

THE QUR'AN

IN

99

QUESTIONS

Muhittin Akgül

Translated by Abdullah Erdemli

TUGHRA
BOOKS

New Jersey

Originally published in Turkish as *Kur'an İklimine Seyahat*

27 26 25 24   3 4 5 6

Published by Tughra Books
335 Clifton Avenue
Clifton, New jersey 07011, USA

www.tughrabooks.com

Library of Congress Cataloging-in-Publication Data

Akgul, Muhittin.
  [Kur'an iklimine seyahat. English]
  The Qur'an in 99 questions / Muhittin Akgul ; translated by Abdullah Erdemli.
    p. cm.
  Translated from Turkish.
  Includes bibliographical references and index.
  ISBN 978-1-59784-130-6 (pbk.)
  1. Koran. I. Erdemli, Abdullah. II. Title. III. Title: Qur'an in ninety-nine questions.
  BP130.A3313 2008
  297.1'2261--dc22

                                                                2008039724

ISBN: 978-1-59784-130-6 *P*

CONTENTS

INTRODUCTION

The Qur'an is the final Revelation sent by God to humanity. The Holy Scripture, which guides humanity to being prosperous in both this world and in the Hereafter, has numerous distinctive features, such as its universality, inimitableness, power of expression, its preservation from the time of the Revelation to the present time, and the Divine promise that it will be guarded until the end of time.

The Qur'an has reached us today without the least change since the time of its revelation fourteen centuries ago. The Companions of the Prophet and the following Muslim generations were devoted to their Book more than any other people being devoted to their own, and they preserved it without the smallest alteration. They committed the Qur'an in its entirety to memory and compiled Qur'anic manuscript as a single volume so that it could be soundly transmitted to following generations. The later generations employed the same precision, meticulous care, and dedication in studying, reflecting upon, and committing the entire Qur'an to memory.

Peculiar only to the Qur'an is that fact that it is actively taught for memorization to thousands and thousands of people. Muslim girls and boys are taught to read and memorize the passages of the Qur'an, and throughout different stages of life, people recite the Qur'an on various occasions and in their day-to-day life. The endeavor to memorize the Qur'an in its entirety is such a widespread practice among Muslims that there are many people, from young to old, all over the world who can recite the whole Qur'an from memory without any errors.

God's Messenger had more than forty scribes of Revelation who were responsible for recording the Qur'an. The Prophet summoned his scribes and carefully dictated the Revelations to them in the presence of the Companions. In addition, the Companions exerted great efforts to have the revealed portions of the Qur'an written down for their personal copies. They also recited the coming Revelations in the presence of the Prophet so that they would be able to commit them to memory with no errors.

It is possible that some people may attempt to speak against the Qur'an, thus casting doubt on its authenticity; this is something that has been done since the first Revelations. However, when one contemplates the verses of God's Message, as they understand it better, and become acquainted with how it has been preserved with the same care and dedication after the Prophet passed away, remaining exactly the same as it was revealed, then they are better to understand how the Qur'an we hold in our hands today is no different from the texts the Companions held in their hands.

There is no difference between the Qur'an that was recited during the earliest period of Islam and any Qur'an that is printed and recited today. In addition, a great number of studies and resources are available on the Qur'an, and there are practically no subjects about the Qur'an that have not yet been talked or written about. However, many people have little or no time to free themselves from their doubts and search for that which they want to learn from or about the Qur'an, particularly with the hectic pace of modern daily life. Taking into account the use of the media to feed the flames of anti-Islamic prejudice and to spread false information about the Qur'an, it is absolutely necessary that there are publications that provide answers to questions and which present practical information that will help gain easy access to the Qur'an.

God willing, I hope that the answers to the questions discussed in the book are accessible to everyone, regardless of their cultural or religious background, including those who are interested in exploring the fundamentals as well as the different aspects of the Qur'an. The references used in this work, directly or indirectly, except verses from the Qur'an and the hadiths, have not been included so as not to distract the reader; they are given as shared sources in the bibliography. I humbly submit this work, hoping that it will be of benefit to the readers and pray that it may become a means for Divine blessings.

CHAPTER 1

What Is the Qur'an?

DESCRIPTION AND NAMES OF THE QUR'AN

| 1 | How can the Qur'an be defined? |

The Qur'an is the proper name of the Divine Word which God, may His Majesty be exalted, revealed to Prophet Muhammad, upon him be peace and blessings. Literally, the word *Qur'an* can be approached in various ways. According to the most widely accepted view, it is a verbal noun from the Arabic verbal root *Qa-Ra-A*, and means *reading* or *reciting*.

Terminologically, the Qur'an is defined as "the miraculous Divine Word revealed to Prophet Muhammad, upon whom be peace and blessings, written down on sheets and transmitted from the Prophet to succeeding generations via numerous reliable channels, and which is used for worship by means of recitation."

As we examine the above description, we should note the following:

The Qur'an is the Divine Word revealed to Prophet Muhammad: This means that, no matter how excellent a word is, no word other than that which was revealed by God can be described as the Qur'an. And even if a word was recited by Prophet Muhammad or by any other person, if it is not the Word of God then it cannot be described as the Qur'an.

The Qur'an has been written down on sheets (mus'hafs): This is a feature peculiar to the Qur'an; it was written down by the scribes of the revelation at the time of the revelation on a variety of writing materials of the time, with utmost care and dedication. It was then gathered and copied with the same care and dedication after the Prophet had passed away. It has reached us today without the smallest alteration and this is a distinctive feature of the Qur'an among all the Holy Books.

The Qur'an has been transmitted to succeeding generations through numerous reliable channels: A great number of people who were known to be so reliable that they could never agree on falsehood or untruth or make a mistake in conveying the Qur'an transmitted it. This sound transmission is valid both in its revelation from God to the Prophet and in its transmission from the Prophet to all of humankind. This is also a feature found only with the Qur'an and not with other Heavenly Books, which have been subject to change. The Almighty Creator has made the Qur'an easy to memorize, as He pointed out in Sura Qamar: *"Indeed We have made the Qur'an easy to understand and remember. Then, is there any that remembers and takes heed?"* (54:22).[1] This is a feature which has not been given to any other book. There are numerous people who have memorized the entire Qur'an, learning it from the beginning to the end by heart, without any errors even in the letters. The fact that the Qur'an is actively instructed for memorization to thousands and thousands of young children throughout the world is the distinguishing feature. And, the number of people who have committed the entire Qur'an to memory, instead of decreasing, increases day by day.

The reading or recitation of the Qur'an is regarded as a form of worship: The recitation of the Qur'an is itself an act of worship. Moreover, a person who is performing daily prayers is obliged to recite some verses from the Qur'an, in order for the prayer, which is one of the fundamental pillars of Islam, to be accepted.

The Qur'an is the peerless miraculous Word of God: The most striking characteristic of the Qur'an is its inimitableness; human beings are incapable of creating any word that is even similar to the Qur'an. The entire Qur'an, be it even the shortest chapter, has this feature; this is the greatest evidence that the Qur'an is the Word of God, as emphasized in the following verses:

> Say: "Surely, if humankind and the jinn were to come together to produce the like of this Qur'an, they will never be able to produce the like of it, though they backed one another up with help and support." (Isra 17:88)

> If you are in doubt about the Divine authorship of what We have sent down on Our servant (Muhammad), then produce just a sura like it and call for help to all your supporters, all those (to whom you apply for help apart from God), if you are truthful in your doubt and claim. If you fail to do that – and you will most certainly fail – then guard yourselves against the Fire whose fuel is human beings and stones, prepared for the unbelievers. (Baqara 2:23-24)

2 | What are the names of the Glorious Qur'an?

The Glorious Qur'an has a number of names and the most commonly used ones are:

a. *Al-Kitab (the Book):* The Qur'an has been given this name as it gathers letters and sentences and as it also contains various rulings of Islamic law, narratives, and tidings, in a style peculiar to itself.

b. *Al-Nur (the Light):* The Qur'an has been given this name as it emanates light upon the truths in its unique style, and as it provides evidence to establish important issues that pertain to religion and faith which cannot be perceived by mere reasoning, shedding light on lawful and unlawful matters as well as on commands and prohibitions.

c. *Al-Furqan (the Criterion):* The Qur'an has been given this name since it clearly differentiates truth from falsehood, faith from blasphemy, what is allowed from what is not allowed and goodness from evil.

> **d.** *Al-Dhikr (the Remembrance):* The Qur'an has been given this
> name since it reminds us of God, His Names and Attributes,
> His true path, the law and the fact that our final destination
> will be to God, Who will call us to account.
>
> **e.** *Al-Shifa' (the Healer):* The Qur'an is a cure and remedy for
> both physical and spiritual illnesses such as disbelief, poly-
> theism and hypocrisy. It is the cure-all for suspicion in the
> heart, which is a spiritual illness.

In addition to the above names, the Qur'an has other titles,
each of which reflects one of its various aspects; the following
are some of these names: *Rahma* (the Mercy), *Huda* (the
Guidance), *Maw'iza* (the Instruction and Advice), *Hikma* (the
Wisdom), *Muhaymin* (the Guardian, the Witness), *Hablullah* (the
Rope of God), *Ahsan al-Hadith* (the Best of Words), *Tanzil* (the
Book gradually sent down), *Ruh* (the Spirit), *Wahy* (the
Revelation), *Bayan* (the Declaration), *Haqq* (the Unchanging),
Urwat al-Wuthqa (the Firm Handhold), *Tadhkira* (the Reminder),
'Adl (the Justice), *Sidq* (the Truth), *Qasas* (the Narrative), *Bushra*
(the Glad Tiding), *'Aziz* (the Mighty), *Bashir* (the Herald of Glad
Tidings), *Balagh* (the Sufficient and Clear Message).

3	Though the Qur'an was revealed in parts, why does it refer to itself as the Book from the very first revelation, from a time before it was bound between covers?

The term *al-Kitab*, or the Book, is used when we speak of
the Qur'an. The word *al-Kitab* is derived from the Arabic
root word *kitab*, the infinitive of the verb *Ka-Ta-Ba* which
means to write, to judge, prescribe, ordain or decree in writing.
The equivalent to the word *al-Kitab* refers to a document that not
only is written down or recorded, but also one that has been
judged, established and determined. In this sense, the Qur'an speaks
of itself as *al-Kitab* (the Book), being God's most comprehensive
judgment. The phrase al-*Kitab* is used when referring to the record-

ing and compilation of the Qur'anic text as a book, much as the word *al-Qur'an* is used when referring to its reading or recitation by heart. Only the Qur'an is referred to with the expression *al-Kitab*. Thus, the traditions of the Prophet, in this regard, are called as Sunna, not *al-Kitab*. So, *al-Kitab,* or The Book, refers not only to the whole, but any part of the eloquent, inimitable Word of God which was revealed to Prophet Muhammad, peace and blessings be upon him, and compiled as a single volume between covers to be soundly transmitted to the following generations.

CHAPTER 2

What Is the Revelation?

WHAT IS THE REVELATION?

4 | What does Revelation (*wahy*) mean?

The Arabic word *wahy* literally means to communicate secretly, to decree, to reveal, indicate, to inspire, speak through inspiration or revelation, to suggest, to make signs, to call, to whisper, to write, to hasten.

As a term, *wahy* means God's communication of His Messages to His Prophets in a special way, the exact nature of which we cannot know. The term *wahy* is used in the Qur'an in both its specific and general senses. In its specific sense, *wahy* is God's Revelation to the Prophets and, in its general sense, it is God's assigning all existing things with their forms and functions, as the sole Creator, and guiding them to the fulfillment of the aim and purpose of their existence.

We may describe revelation, or *wahy*, in its specific sense as God's conveyance of His guidance and commandments to His Prophets, who were chosen from among all human beings. As for the means of the Revelation, the word passes from God to the human being in one of the following three ways: By way of revelation through inspiration of the heart or dreams during sleep. God Almighty sent His message to the mother of Prophet Moses by inspiration and Prophet Abraham was inspired with the sacrifice of his son through a dream. Another kind of revelation is when God spoke to a Prophet from behind a veil without the mediation of an angel. Prophet Moses was addressed in this way for instance. God's third way of communicating with human beings is that He sends an angel to convey His Revelation to a Prophet.

Revelation is evidence for the prophethood of not only Prophet Muhammad, but for all the Prophets. To each and every Prophet the Almighty Creator revealed:

> We have revealed to you (O Messenger) as We revealed to Noah and the Prophets after him; and We revealed to Abraham, Ishmael, Isaac, Jacob and the Prophets who were raised in the tribes, and Jesus, Job, Jonah, Aaron, and Solomon; and We gave David the Psalms. And Messengers We have already told you of (with respect to their mission) before, and Messengers We have not told you of; and God spoke to Moses in a particular way. (Nisa 4:163–164)

The clearest difference between the Prophets and other human beings lies in the divine reality of Revelation.

5 | Is there any Revelation other than the Qur'an?

The Revelation is not only the Qur'an; Prophet Muhammad received Revelation in addition to the Qur'an. God's Messenger said, "Beware, I have been given the Qur'an and its like together with it."[2] This is clear proof of the fact that God's Messenger received the Revelation from God in addition to what is contained in the Qur'an, and he acted according to it. What is meant by the "like of the Qur'an" in the hadith is the Sunna, or practices of the Prophet. This clearly shows that God's Messenger was given Revelation in addition to the Qur'an which was not recited to him as the Qur'an. Thus, in the same way that the Qur'an is a Revelation sent to the Prophet, the Sunna was also revealed to him. The only difference is that while the Qur'an was revealed in recited (*matlu*) form, the Sunna was the non-recited Revelation (*wahy al-ghayri matlu*). This is why it is obligatory to imitate and follow the example of the Prophet when performing acts of worship, like the daily prayers and the pilgrimage to Mecca, which have not been explained in detail in the Qur'an. Therefore, it is necessary to depend upon the Sunna in order to understand the Book and to practice it in daily life correctly and completely as God Almighty commands in the Qur'an: *"And We have not sent down the Book on you except that you (O Muhammad) may explain to them all (the questions of faith and law) on which they differ, and as guidance and mercy for people who will believe and who have already believed"* (Nahl 16:64).

It is the Prophet's mission to present and also represent the religion in its pristine purity and truth. The Sunna, which is a combination of the sayings, actions and tacit approval of the Prophet, is sanctioned by God and relies on the guidance of Divine Revelation. Thus, if we look for information on a particular subject in the Qur'an but are unable to find it, we then have to refer to the Prophet's practices, or his Sunna, which is a commentary and explanation of the Qur'an. Pertaining to this subject, the Prophet once asked Muadh ibn Jabal, whom he was sending as an envoy to Yemen: "'With what will you rule?' 'With God's Book' Muadh replied. 'What if you cannot find the ruling in the Qur'an?' the Prophet asked. 'Then with the Sunna of God's Messenger' Muadh replied. 'What if you cannot find it there either?' asked the Prophet. 'Then I would rule with my own opinion (with my own understanding and interpretation)' Muadh finally replied. Upon this response, the Prophet put his hand over Muadh's chest and said, 'All praise be to God for He has rendered the envoy of God's Messenger successful and guided him to that which pleases God's Messenger.'"

In particular, the Prophet warned those people who follow only the Qur'an and who reject his Sunna with the following words: "Let me not find one of you reclining on his couch when he hears something that I have commanded or forbidden, saying: 'We don't know (any such a thing as Sunna. God's Book is at our disposal.) We follow what we find in God's Book.'"[3]

There are many Qur'anic verses that act as evidence that Prophet Muhammad, peace and blessings be upon him, received

Revelation from God in addition to the Qur'an. The following two verses, for instance, are of this type: "*...Whatever the Messenger gives you accept it willingly, and whatever he forbids you, refrain from it. Keep from disobedience to God in reverence for Him and piety. Surely God is severe in retribution*" (Hashr 59:7) and "*... And on you (O Muhammad) We have sent down the Reminder so that you may make clear to humankind whatever is sent down to them, and that they may reflect*" (Nahl 16:44). All the above-mentioned factors clearly indicate that the Revelation which was sent to God's Messenger was not only composed of what is found in the Qur'an, but includes non-recited Revelation in Sunna form. As a matter of fact, it is not possible for us to know or understand completely the various aspects of the religion without referring to the practices of the Prophet.

6 | How was the Revelation conveyed to the Prophet?

The Revelation was delivered to Prophet Muhammad in the following ways:

a. The commencement of Revelation to the Prophet took the form of reliable dreams (*ru'ya al-sadiqa*). Whatever he dreamed happened the following day, in exactly the same way that he had dreamed.

b. Coming in the form of a human being, Archangel Gabriel conveyed the Revelation to the Prophet.

c. Archangel Gabriel approached the Prophet in his own angelic form and thus delivered the Revelation to him. It was reported that such Revelation happened only two times; first, during the first stage of the Revelation and second, in the cave of Hira, following a period of temporary cessation of Revelation.

d. Without appearing to the Prophet, the angel put the Revelation straight into the Prophet's heart when he was awake.

e. Archangel Gabriel conveyed the Revelation to the Prophet during his sleep.

f. Sometimes, the Qur'an was revealed like the ringing of a bell. This form of Revelation was most severe for the Prophet. When this state of Revelation passed the Prophet had memorized what had been revealed.

g. Delivery of the Revelation to the Prophet when he was awake, directly by God Almighty Himself. It was reported that such Revelation was delivered to the Prophet during the *Mi'raj* – the Prophet's night journey from Mecca to Al-Aqsa Mosque in Jerusalem and his ascension from there to Heaven.

7 | **Why could other people who were in close vicinity to the Prophet not see Archangel Gabriel when he was delivering the Revelation to the Prophet?**

There are living creatures as well as sounds that exist in different dimensions of the universe. We, as human beings, are capable of seeing, hearing or perceiving only some of these. There are, for instance, thousands of sounds and species around us that we have never heard or seen. Our being totally unaware of them does not mean that they do not exist. Moreover, we are able to see certain species only with the help of special devices, for instance, microscopes. Likewise, the one who delivered the Revelation to the Prophet was an angel, and the angels are luminous, spiritual creatures, invisible to the human eye. It is impossible for us to be aware of them with our senses. It was possible, however, for people to witness certain manifestations of the Revelation while the angel was delivering it to the Prophet; when the Companions were in the presence of the Prophet they were occasionally able to witness such manifestations and thus knew that the Prophet was receiving a Revelation.

8 | Can we understand the true nature of Revelation?

I t is impossible for human beings to fully understand the true nature of the Revelation. Only the Messengers to whom the Revelation was made can know its true nature. The attempt of ordinary people to define the Revelation process is like a blind man trying to describe colors. However, depending on the forms and times of the Revelation, the people in the Messenger's close vicinity would witness certain manners and attitudes, such as his body trembling, a change in facial color, sweating despite cold weather, the emission of certain sounds, or feeling heavier than usual. All of these were evidence that a Revelation was descending. Also, as the angels are able to take different forms by God's will, the Archangel would sometimes appear to the Companions in the disguise of Dihya, one of the Companions of the Prophet, and sometimes the angel came to the Prophet in the form of an unfamiliar person, as the angels that were sent to Prophet Abraham and Virgin Mary had done.

The world of creatures (the universe) is not composed of only those things that are visible to us. There are many things that we can feel but cannot see. Intelligence, love, fear, and grief are just some of the realities which exist that we can never see with our eyes. Thus, it would not be wise to deny that they exist just because we are unable to see them.

9 | Why was the Qur'an revealed to Prophet Muhammad but not to people who were better-known or better-off?

P rophethood is not a quality that can be gained or acquired with effort; rather all Prophets were divinely appointed. If God appointed a person as Prophet, that person was a Prophet even if the people did not believe in him or refused to obey him. Indeed, unbelievers made objections and protests to every

Prophet for various reasons. Prophet Muhammad, peace and blessings be upon him, too was subjected to such treatment, and the question "Why was prophethood given to him but not to others?" was asked. The polytheists asked to be given the like of what God's Messenger had been given, as they wanted to be followed instead of being the followers and to be served instead of being the servants. God Almighty responded to what the nonbelievers wrongly claimed as follows: *"When a Revelation is conveyed to them, they say: 'We will not believe unless we are given the like of what God's Messengers were given.' God knows best upon whom to place His Message. Soon will an abasement from God's Presence befall these criminals and a severe punishment for their scheming"* (An'am 6:124). It was reported that this verse was revealed to the Prophet when Abu Jahl said: "We will neither obey him nor be contented with him unless revelation is sent down to us as it has been sent down to him" and when the polytheist Meccan chieftain, Walid ibn Mughira, said to the Prophet: "If there were such thing as 'prophethood,' I would be more deserving of it than you, as I am older and richer than you."

According to the Meccan polytheists, prophethood should only have been given to those who had wealth, position and posts in Mecca or in Taif, the major cities of the region. According to their standards of importance, the Meccans did not perceive of the Prophet as being equal to them in wealth or status and they therefore claimed that the Revelation should not have been sent to him. As such reasoning is fundamentally wrong, God warned those who were, with their false and baseless reasoning, trying to direct the Divine Revelation and trying to nominate persons for such a mission on God's behalf:

> They also say: "If only this Qur'an had been sent down on a man of leading position of the two (chief) cities!" Is it they who distribute the mercy of your Lord (so that they may appoint whom they wish as Messenger to receive the Book)? (Moreover, how do they presume to value some above others only because of their wealth or status, when) it is also We Who distribute

their means of livelihood among them in the life of this world, and raise some of them above others in degree, so that they may avail themselves of one another's help? But your Lord's mercy (in particular Prophethood) is better than what they amass (in this life). (Zukhruf 43:31-32)

So, prophethood is a matter that belongs to God; He appoints whomever He deems fit to this mission. While granting the Prophet the mission of Prophethood, God did not consult anybody about this matter. Nor did the Prophet receive this mission due to his hard work or because of any worldly possessions. God conferred a great favor on Prophet Muhammad, peace and blessings be upon him, when He granted him this mission of prophethood.

| 10 | What is the significance of the Qur'an descending on the Night of Power (*Laylat al-Qadr*)? |

The time of the descent of the Qur'an is mentioned and referred to in three places in the Qur'an:

The month of Ramadan (is the month) in which the Qur'an was sent down as guidance for people, and as clear truths of the guidance and the Criterion (between truth and falsehood).... (Baqara 2:185)

We have surely sent it (the Qur'an) down in the Night of Destiny and Power. What enables you to perceive what the Night of Destiny and Power is? The Night of Destiny and Power is better than a thousand months. The angels and the Spirit descend in it by the permission of their Lord with His decrees for every affair; (it is) a sheer mercy and security (from all misfortunes, for the servants who spend it in devotions in appreciation of its worth). (It is) until the rising of the dawn. (Qadr 97:1-5)

By the Book clear in itself and clearly showing the truth. We sent it down on a night full of blessings.... (Dukhan 44:2-3)

According to these verses, the Qur'an was sent on the Night of Power, which falls in the month of Ramadan. The month in which the Qur'an was sent down is stated in the first verse above, and the name of the specific night within this holy month of Ramadan is given in the latter. This night, a night on which the single most important event in history unfolded, with the Archangel Gabriel descending with the blessed Book to reveal it to God's Messenger, is alluded to in the third Qur'anic reference above as the most blessed night.

One of the meanings of the word *Qadr* is Destiny, i.e., this is the night on which God commands His angels to fulfill and implement what is to happen - all the affairs predestined by God in the pre-time (*azal*). Another meaning of *Qadr* is veneration and honor, that is, it is a magnificent night that is venerated and honored because of its great value. The Night of Power is a night on which angels come down to the earth; so many angels come down with such a strong desire and in such a rush that they have great difficulty, as if they were passing through a turnstile in one mass; this descent lasts until the break of dawn. According to the majority of Islamic scholars, this blessed night is any one of the odd-numbered nights in the last ten days of the month of Ramadan, and is most likely to be the 27th night of Ramadan.

What we can understand from the above is that the night on which God's angel delivered the very first Revelation to the Prophet was a night in the month of Ramadan and this was the Night of Power. The fact that the Qur'an was revealed on this night may be understood in either of two ways:

Firstly, the whole Qur'an was delivered to the angels of Revelation on this night, and later Archangel Gabriel conveyed its chapters and verses to the Prophet, by God's command, in stages throughout his Prophethood.

Secondly, this is the night on which Prophet Muhammad, peace and blessings be upon him, started to receive the first Revelation. Both of these meanings indicate that the Qur'an began to be sent down on this night, as the descent of the Qur'an began on the Night of Power with the Revelation of the first five verses of Sura al-'Alaq.

It is clear that all things and events have, in God's Knowledge, an eternal existence and the Revelation of the Qur'an to the Prophet in stages have not been decided upon and arranged by God Almighty, just prior to or in time of their descent. The creation of the entire universe and every thing in it was designed and made ready by God in the pre-time. All plans of creation for humankind, the appointing of prophets from among humans, guiding them with the Books and finally sending the Prophet and the Qur'an were all prepared by God and the implementation of the last part of this eternal plan started on the Night of Power.

| 11 | How long did it take for the Qur'an to descend to the Prophet? |

The Qur'an was not sent down to the Prophet all at one time; the descent of the Qur'an lasted over a period of twenty-three years. Prophet Muhammad, peace and blessings be upon him, started to receive the Revelation from the very first moment of his prophethood and this continued until shortly before his death; the Revelation was sent down to him day and night, in times of war and peace, at home or abroad.

| 12 | What would you say to the allegation that the Qur'an was taught to the Prophet by a priest or by other people? |

This is an idea that modern orientalists put forward; it is interesting, however that no one raised such objections at the time when Prophet Muhammad, peace and blessings be upon him, was alive. Unlike the orientalists, no one at that time suggested that when the Prophet met with the monk Bahira during his childhood he had received certain religious information from him, and no one alleged that he had received religious information from Christian monks or Jewish rabbis during journeys he made with caravans.

Moreover, if he had received all his knowledge from the monk Bahira and during the journeys he made later when he was 25, then it could justifiably be asked why did Prophet Muhammad, peace and blessings be upon him, not claim Prophethood until he was forty years old? The people of Mecca did not raise any such absurd or baseless allegations regarding the era prior to the Prophethood; rather their objections were only concerned with the era of the Prophethood.

The people in Mecca who made objections put forward arguments like: "This fellow does not know how to read or write, and thus he could not have obtained any knowledge from books. He has been living among us for 40 years, but we have never heard any of the things that he is now communicating from him before. Therefore, someone must be helping him when people were at home and giving him secretly expressions from the scriptures of the past. He is quickly learning and reciting these to other people as divine revelations during the day. This is nothing more than deception." The names of the three people who were alleged to be helping him are even mentioned in some reports. These people who were of the People of the Book were such unlettered Meccans as Addas, who was the freed slave of Huwaytib ibn Abdul Uzza, Yasar, who was the freed slave of Ala ibn al-Hadrami, and Jabr, who was the freed slave of Amr ibn Rabia.

The fact that the Qur'an directly rejected this, rather than responding to the polytheists' claims can be better understood if the following points are taken into consideration:

a. The polytheists in Mecca did nothing at all to prove their allegations. They would certainly have acted if their allegations had been true. They would often have raided, for instance, the houses of the Prophet and any one whom they thought might have been helping them, seizing anything used in such a deceit to prove that the claim of prophethood was a "lie." It would not have been difficult for the

Meccan polytheists to do such a thing, as we can see that they did not hesitate to apply or implement all sorts of actions, including torture; they were not bound by any sort of moral obligation.

b. Those who were thought to be helping the Prophet were not unknown in the city. The fact that they were uneducated was known well in Mecca. The polytheists themselves knew very well that such illiterate people could not have provided any help in producing a glorious book like the Qur'an, which is an extraordinary marvel of the highest literary skill. Thus, even those who did not know these emancipated slaves very well were aware that such an allegation was nonsensical and meaningless. In addition, why did such so-called helpers not claim the prophethood for themselves if they had such abilities?

c. Moreover, all the so-called helpers were former slaves still bound to their masters, even though they had been emancipated, according to Arabian traditions. Thus, they would not have wanted to help the Prophet in his claim as their masters would have put pressure on them with no tolerance on their existence in Mecca if they had done so.

d. Above and beyond all else, these so-called helpers all converted to Islam. Is it possible to conceive that those who helped Prophet Muhammad, peace and blessings be upon him, would be deceived by his "trick," thus binding themselves to him? Let us even presume for a moment that they helped the Prophet, then, why was not one of them, at least, not given a higher position or status in return for his services or help? Why were Addas, Yasar or Jabr not given higher status than Abu Bakr, Umar or Abu Ubayda?

If the prophethood was a deception staged with the help of these so-called assistants, we must ask why this help stayed secret even from the closest and most devoted Companions of the Prophet, for example, Ali ibn Abu Talib, Abu Bakr, or Zayd ibn Haritha. Thus, not only is such an accusation nonsensical and false, God did not even deem it worthy of a reply in the Qur'an. Rather the Divine origin of the Qur'an is proclaimed:

> Those who disbelieve say: "This (Qur'an) is but a fabrication which he (Muhammad) himself has invented, and some others have helped him with it, so they have produced a wrong and a falsehood." They also say: "(It consists of) only fables of the ancients which he has got written. They are being read to him in early mornings and evenings (while people are at home)." Say: "(It is a Book full of knowledge revealing many secrets such as no human being could in any wise discover by himself:) He Who knows all the secrets contained in the heavens and the earth sends it down (to teach you some of these secrets and guide you in your life so that you may attain happiness in both worlds). He surely is All-Forgiving, All-Compassionate." (Furqan 25:4-6)

There cannot be a worse lie than that of Quraysh polytheists, as they themselves knew much better than anyone else that such expressions were nothing more than baseless claims. The chieftains who spread such ideas among the public would certainly have been aware that the Qur'an, which was recited by Prophet Muhammad, peace and blessings be upon him, could not have been a "human word;" their linguistic and esthetic sensibilities were too developed not to be aware of this reality. In addition, before he was called to Prophethood, Muhammad was recognized as an upright and trust-worthy person, one who never lied or cheated anyone. Why would such a person invent a lie against God or attribute to Him some-thing that was not His?

But, such deceit and rumors were spread among the people; these powerful people were not only blindly stubborn, they also feared losing their social status which was connected to their being seen to be the religious leaders of society. The poor and illiterate people were not able to differentiate esthetically perfect literary works from those which were not. Hence, the status-seeking chief-tains tried to take advantage of the people's illiteracy, and said:

"This is but a fabrication which he himself has invented, and some others have helped him with it" (Furqan 25:4).

The polytheist Quraysh chieftains were speaking of the three non-Arab emancipated slaves when using the word *"others."* The Qur'an goes on to speak of their nonsensical allegations with respect to the Prophet and the Revelation he received: *"They also say: '(It consists of) only fables of the ancients which he has got written. They are being read to him in early mornings and evenings'"* (Furqan 25:5). Such arguments and allegations were dependent on the stories of ancient nations found in the Qur'an. The Qur'an related stories connected to earlier nations, offering them as deterrents for the readers. The polytheists claimed that these factual stories were *"fables of the ancients"* recited to him secretly by these non-Arab emancipated slaves that he subsequently conveyed them to other people. They were trying to claim that Prophet Muhammad, peace and blessings be upon him, was forging the Qur'an with the help of these foreign slaves. They were well aware that such a claim was ridiculous, for how could such a book have been invented by a person, even if others were to help him? If this had been the case, then what was stopping others from inventing something similar? Why could they not make an effort like the Prophet had and invent a book similar to it, helped by others? There were plenty of people who would have been willing to back up each other with help and support. Prophet Muhammad, peace and blessings be upon him, challenged them to do just this, but the polytheists were unable to respond to the challenge.

13 | Did the Prophet write the Qur'an himself?

It would not have been possible for Prophet Muhammad, peace and blessings be upon him, to have written the Qur'an. If this had been possible the people who lived in his era would have made such a claim. The Qur'an clearly states that he was unlettered; he was also known to be illiterate in the community. The verse, *"You did not (O Messenger) read of any book before it (the revelation of this Qur'an), nor did you write one with your right (or left) hand"*[4] shows this clearly. This verse is clear proof that the Prophet was illiterate and did not know how to read or write. It is also mentioned in the Qur'an that the earlier books originally contained mention of the Prophet's illiteracy:

> They follow the (most illustrious) Messenger, the Prophet who neither reads nor writes (and has therefore remained preserved from any traces of the existing written culture and is free from any intellectual and spiritual pollution), whom they find described in the Torah and the Gospel with them." (A'raf 7:157)

Prophet Muhammad, peace and blessings be upon him, had lived among the Meccans a whole lifetime of forty years prior to his Prophethood. The Meccans were well aware of how he had spent his life and with what he had been occupied. He was not by himself even when he went on expeditions outside of Mecca. No moment of his life was unknown to the people around him. Despite this, they refused to believe in the Prophet or his message. The Qur'an states, *"Say: If God had so willed, I would not have recited it (the Qur'an) to you nor would He have brought it to your knowledge. I lived among you a whole lifetime before it (began to be revealed to me). Will you not reason and understand?"* (Yunus 10:16). This verse was trying to tell them the following: I have lived among of you and with you for a lifetime prior to my Prophethood and the revelation of the Qur'an. You are well aware that I did not read anything in these years, that I did not relate anything to you similar to the miraculous verses or meanings of the Qur'an, that I did not deal with any sort of literary work, be it in verse form or in prose form, nor did I pretend to be a poet or a preacher or an author; I did not prepare myself to challenge or invite people to compete against me, and I did not try to dominate, oppress or offend anyone.

Those who were accusing Prophet Muhammad, peace and blessings be upon him, could not say that "he wrote the Qur'an," for they knew that this could not have been the case; rather they said that "Muhammad had someone write it for them." In fact, his illiteracy was accepted even by his enemies. Such slanders and allegations were for the most part put forward at a latter date by orientalists. In order to achieve their primary goal, these orientalists tried to suggest that the Prophet was not illiterate. By establishing such a case they would have been able to strengthen their allegations that the Revelation was produced by the Prophet and that he had put the Qur'an together with summaries of the Old and New Testaments.

As a matter of fact, we can understand that the religion introduced by Prophet Muhammad, peace and blessings be upon him, is both perfect and universal, even though there were no schools or books available in Mecca during the Prophet's lifetime from which he could have benefited. In addition, the number of people at that time who could read and write was very few, while those who knew how to read and write were well-known to the entire community. Had the Prophet taken lessons from any tutor in his childhood or later, this would certainly have been known. In addition, the names and identities of the revelation scribes were recorded, yet no one ever alleged that the Prophet was one of them. If he had not been illiterate, he would have written the Revelation himself and his name would have been mentioned with the names of the other scribes.

The works that relate the story of the life of the Prophet are examples of the Companions' love for him. Even the minutest details from his lifetime have been preserved with utmost care for centuries. If there had been any page or letter written by Prophet Muhammad, peace and blessings be upon him, then it would certainly have been preserved and have survived until today, or at the very least there would be some record of it.

We can understand the Prophet's position with respect to the Revelation that he received, both from the Qur'an itself and the narrations of those who were with him when the Revelations came. These narrations show us that the Prophet did not have any control over the Revelation, rather his submission to the Revelation was definite. The verse, *"And to you (O Messenger) the Qur'an is being conveyed from the Presence of One All-Wise, All-Knowing"*[5] clearly states that the Qur'an is the word, not of any one person, but rather that of God alone and that the Prophet had no share in it.

In the Qur'an we can understand the status and position of Prophet Muhammad, peace and blessings be upon him, with respect to the Revelation in the following contexts:

I. The Prophet is obeying what is being revealed to him

The following verses are clear indications that Prophet Muhammad, peace and blessings be upon him, obeys only the Revelation that was sent to him:

> Say (to them, O Messenger): "(You want me to do miracles. However,) I never tell you that with me are the treasures of God, or that I know the Unseen; nor do I tell you that I am an angel. I only follow what is revealed to me." (An'am 6:50)

> When you (O Messenger) do not produce for them a verse, they say, "Were you unable to make one up?" Say: "I only follow whatever is revealed to me from my Lord. This (the Qur'an) is the light of discernment and insight (into the truth) from your Lord, and guidance and mercy for people who will believe and who have already believed." (A'raf 7:203)

> When Our Revelations, clear as evidence and in meaning are recited (and conveyed) to them, those who have no expectations to meet Us say (in response to Our Messenger): "Either bring a Qur'an other than this or alter it." Say: "It is not for me to alter it of my own accord. I only follow what is revealed to me. Indeed I fear, if I should rebel against my Lord, the punishment of an Awful Day." (Yunus 10:15)

Prophethood is the reception of Revelation from God and obeying the same. Receiving the Revelation, the Prophet conveys the Revelation to people. Some people in the time of the Prophet believed that he was reciting Qur'anic verses according to his own desire and thus would demand verses from him; they questioned him why he did not produce what they wanted. To bring a verse is not something that was under the Prophet's control, for the verses were not his words. God revealed the verses to the Prophet as and when He willed and the Prophet had to obey them. He was only a mortal appointed as the Messenger, and he never claimed to be anything more than a man who had received Revelations from God. The fact that he was not able to bring a verse when it was demanded, but rather that he had to wait for it is in keeping with the fact that he could only relate these words at the behest of God, not according to his own desire or initiative.

From the fact that all the aforementioned verses contain the order "*say*" we can understand that Prophet Muhammad, peace and blessings be upon him, is being ordered to relate whatever is sent to him. Moreover, the Prophet is not speaking out of a selfish desire, but rather is obeying what has been revealed to him. The verb "*say*" is repeated more than 300 times in the Qur'an, clearly indicating that the Prophet did not have the ability to interfere with the Revelation nor were the words his; rather they had been taught to him by God. The Prophet was not the actual speaker, but was God's Messenger who was relaying what he had been told.

II. The Revelation was not from the Prophet's own knowledge

Prophet Muhammad, peace and blessings be upon him, was totally unaware of the things he was to be taught through the Revelation before it came. He did not think about such matters at all. The Qur'an clearly states that the Prophet knew nothing about the stories of past Prophets before the Revelation. The following verses are clear indications of this:

> (O Muhammad,) you were not present on the spot lying to the western side (of the valley) when We decreed the Commandment

(the Torah) to Moses, nor were you a witness (to what happened there). But (after them) We brought into being many generations and long indeed were the ages that passed over them. (The information you give about them is also that which We reveal to you, just as what you tell about what happened concerning Moses in Midian is also a Revelation. For) neither did you dwell among the people of Midian so that you are conveying to them (the Makkan people) Our Revelations (about what Moses did in Midian). Rather, We have been sending Messengers (to convey Our Revelations). And neither were you present on the side of the Mount Sinai when We called out (to Moses), but (We reveal all this to you) as a mercy from your Lord so that you may warn a people to whom no warner has come before you, so that they may reflect and be mindful. (Qasas 28:44-46)

Those are accounts of some exemplary events of the unseen (a time and realm beyond any created's perception) that We reveal to you, (O Messenger). Neither you nor your people knew them before this. Then (seeing that there is no substantial difference between the conditions in which the Messengers carried out their missions and the reactions they encountered) be patient (with their reactions and their persistence in unbelief). The (final, happy) outcome is in favor of the God-revering, pious. (Hud 11:49)

We should not forget the fact that when mentioning past peoples or Prophets, the Qur'an itself states that the sole source of information for Prophet Muhammad, peace and blessings be upon him, is the Divine Revelation. The following verses are clear indications of this:

This is of the tidings of the things of the unseen (the things that took place in the past and have remained hidden from people with all their truth), which We reveal to you (O Muhammad), for you were not present with them when they drew lots with their pens about who should have charge of Mary; nor were you present with them when they were disputing (about the matter). (Al Imran 3:44)

This is an account of some exemplary events of the unseen (a realm and time beyond the reach of any created being's per-

ception) that We reveal to you, (O Messenger). You were not
with them when those agreed upon their plans, and then were
scheming (against Joseph). (Yusuf 12:102)

The repeated descriptions of such events and the stories of
other Prophets in the Qur'an is a clear indication that the source of
information for an illiterate Prophet was the Revelation; indeed it is
only the Revelation that enabled the Prophet to explain in details
historical events that happened thousands of years before he lived.

The Revelation was sent to the Prophet in stages, and in this
way historic and sociological information as well as the knowledge
on the universe which had not been previously known by the
Prophet or by others at that time accumulated in his mind.
Moreover, such information was not an abstract sort of general or
indefinite information; on the contrary, it was concrete information with numerous details and was connected to the history of
monotheistic faith. All this supports that the Revelation could not
and was not something that the Prophet developed himself.

When we look at the details provided by the Qur'an about past
nations and Prophets, we can see that they are sometimes very
detailed. Some of this information is just the opposite of what the
society understood, while other parts they were not even aware of.
In particular, many of the details that pertain to the stories of the
Prophets are completely different to those found in the Old and
New Testaments. The Prophet's disclosure of the histories of bygone
nations without any hesitation is a challenge to all ages and peoples
and is one of the undeniable proofs of both his Prophethood and
the Divine origin of the Qur'an.

III. The Prophet employed haste with respect to the Revelation

When the Revelation first began to be sent to the Prophet he
showed so much concern in receiving and committing to heart the
Qur'an that he used to repeat the Revelation that had been sent to
him and his lips would move impatiently in fear that he would for-

get the words. This manner of the Prophet's moving his tongue to hasten for safekeeping the Revelation in his heart was not a habit he used to do before being called to Prophethood. The Arab poets did not have such a custom either; when preparing a poem they used to come up with the phrases in their minds. If the Qur'an had been something that Prophet Muhammad, peace and blessings be upon him, had created, then he would have prepared and recited it in the way that was customary in his society; that is, he would have had long periods of silence and meditation in order to crystallize his thoughts so that his ideas would be clearer and more understandable. But he in fact did just the opposite. The following verses depict the state of the Prophet during the Revelation:

> Absolutely exalted is God, the Supreme Sovereign, the Absolute Truth and Ever-Constant. Do not show haste (O Messenger) with (the receiving and memorizing of any Revelation included in) the Qur'an before it has been revealed to you in full, but say: "My Lord, increase me in knowledge." (Ta.Ha 20:114)

We can understand that during the Revelation the Prophet's tongue moved quickly and he was in a rush to read it. Thus, he was commanded to listen to the Revelation silently, without trying to repeat, until the coming verses were revealed to him in full. That is to say, the Qur'an ordered the Prophet to just listen to the Revelation in his heart, and to keep his tongue from moving, as its compilation and gathering were the responsibility of God:

> (O Prophet!) Move not your tongue to hasten it (for safekeeping in your heart). Surely it is for Us to collect it (in your heart) and enable you to recite it (by heart). So when We recite it, follow its recitation; thereafter, it is for Us to explain it. (Qiyama 75:16-19)

The above verses warned Prophet Muhammad, peace and blessings be upon him, that he was forbidden to read the revealed parts in haste or to allow his tongue to move, repeating the Revelation that had not yet been completed. This is powerful proof that indicates that the Prophet was aware that what was being revealed to him was the Qur'an, as he was impatient to repeat it, fearful that he might forget even a small part of it. These verses clearly assure the Prophet that God will enable him to memorize the coming Revelation and understand its meaning.

IV. Revelation came suddenly

Before the commencement of the prophethood, Prophet Muhammad, peace and blessings be upon him, did not say anything about the fact that he would one day receive Revelation. He also did not expect to witness such an incident. The Revelation came to him suddenly the first time and also on all subsequent occasions. The following verse clearly indicates that the Prophet did not expect anything like the Revelation in advance:

> You did not expect that this Book would be revealed to you;
> but it is being revealed to you as a mercy from your Lord, so
> do not lend any support to the unbelievers. (Qasas 28:86)

When we examine the accounts that relate the early Revelations, the following becomes clear: The Revelation first occurred to the Prophet as dreams that were later realized. After these dreams the Prophet sought solitude. He would go to the Hira cave in retreat, and then return to his family; after taking with him provisions for a couple of days he would return to the Hira cave, and this cycle would be repeated. Archangel Gabriel suddenly approached him while he was in the Hira cave and told him, "Read!" The Prophet replied, "I do not know how to read!" He goes on to tell us: "The angel caught and pressed me so hard that I could not bear it any more. He then set me free and said, "Read!" I replied, "I do not know how to read!" Thereupon he caught me again and pressed me a second time until I could not bear it any more. He then set me free and said, "Read!" "I do not know how to read!" I replied again. He caught and pressed me again for the third time and after releasing me said:

Read in and with the Name of your Lord, Who has created, created human from a clot clinging (to the wall of the womb). Read, and your Lord is the All-Munificent, Who has taught (human) by the pen, taught human what he did not know. (Alaq 96:1-5)

Prophet Muhammad, peace and blessings be upon him, returned home with fear and trembling in his heart; he told his wife Khadija to cover him. When he had recovered he told his wife: "I am frightened of myself." She said to him: "No, do not fear at all. God would never do anything to shame you, for you protect your relatives, help the destitute, clothe the needy. You are always generous to guests, help those who are in strife and are a true friend for the poor."[6]

The Quraysh heard of this incident and their chieftains held a gathering in which they decided that the Prophet should be labeled with a name that would make people wary of him. Some proposed to call him a soothsayer, while others labeled him insane, others slandered him by attributing to him of magic, and yet others called him a separator of lovers, setting man apart from his father, his brother, his wife, children and family. God's Messenger heard about this and he covered himself with his cloak in grief. Archangel Gabriel came to him and said, *"O you enwrapped one!"* (Muzammil 73:1). Similarly, another time when the Prophet was in solitude in his home, the Angel of Revelation came and said, "O *you cloaked one (who has preferred solitude)! Arise and warn!"* (Muddaththir 74:1-2).

The Revelation that came to Prophet Muhammad, peace and blessings be upon him, was not contemplated before hand and the Revelation was not dependent on any specific time and/or place. It could descend during a journey or while conversing with people, or it could come at night.

V. The Revelation was beyond the Prophet's will

As God was the source of the Revelation only He could determine how and when it descended. It was not possible for the Prophet to speak whenever or however he wished, as even the angel who delivered the Revelation came to him with God's permission. Moreover, Prophet Muhammad, peace and blessings be upon him, used to sometimes ask the Archangel Gabriel to visit him more frequently, and the following verse descended in answer to this desire:

> (In response to an interval in the coming of Revelation, Gabriel explained:) We do not descend but by your Lord's command only. To Him belongs whatever is before us and whatever is behind us and whatever is between (all time and space and whatever we do at all times in all places). And your Lord is never forgetful (so do not fear that He forgets you). (Maryam 19:64)

There were times when the Revelation was delayed for the occasions God's Messenger had to await the Revelation in order to establish a legal principle or to make a decision on a matter that had been submitted to his attention. In the early period in Mecca, the Prophet would at times be saddened if Archangel Gabriel did not appear for a considerably long time. He would become upset at such times and his enemies, who were aware that the Revelation had ceased to come, would start to make fun of him. In such instances God would reassure the Prophet by letting him know that God had not abandoned him and He declared that such thoughts on the part of the enemies of the Prophet was nothing more than an illusion: *"By the forenoon, and the night when it has grown dark and most still, Your Lord has not forsaken you, nor has He become displeased with you"* (Duha 93:1-3).

The Sura Duha is one of the earliest Revelations to the Messenger; such breaks in the Revelation occurred at the beginning. The continuance of the Revelation after the early interruption comforted and reassured the Prophet, and this is an indication that these Revelations were not something from his own mind, but something from beyond his control. This is a point that must be taken into consideration when seeking a relationship between the Qur'an and the Prophet. If, as alleged, the Qur'an was something that was connected to the Prophet's own identity, should he not have searched for it within himself? But, on the contrary, he awaited the Revelation to re-start as one who awaits a beloved one; that is, he did nothing actively to try to bring it about.

From time to time the Prophet used to witness developments that forced him to express his beliefs. If the Revelation would have been solely at his disposal, then he would have been able to develop a certain way of talking, due to the serious need for something to be said on such matters. But days followed nights and he did not even have a couple of Qur'anic verses to recite to the public on such subjects. There are numerous examples of such occasions, but here we would only like to mention a few of them, without going into any specific details:

Prophet Muhammad, peace and blessings be upon him, awaited a revelation that would tell the Muslims that they should pray towards the Ka'ba. He was expecting the Archangel Gabriel to arrive from the Heavens and he was eagerly praying to God to be permitted to turn to the Ka'ba, which was the *qibla* (direction of prayer) of his ancestor Prophet Abraham. The following verses finally descended:

> Certainly We have seen you (O Messenger) often turning your face to heaven (in expectation of a Revelation. Do not worry, for) We will surely turn you towards a direction that will please and satisfy you. (Now the time has come, so) turn your face towards the Sacred Mosque. (And you, O believers) turn your faces towards it wherever you are. Surely those who were given the Book (before, no matter if the hypocrites or the foolish among them deny or object to it) do know (the coming of this Prophet and this change of qibla) to be true (commandments) from their Lord. God is not unaware or unmindful of whatever they do. (Baqara 2:144)

Prophet Muhammad, peace and blessings be upon him, in spite of his strong desire for the Ka'ba to be the *qibla* and despite his eager anticipation for the Revelation to come, could not bring himself to turn to the Ka'ba without the Revelation. Thus, is it conceivable that he would have undergone such a situation, if the Revelation had been something that was under his control or that originated from him? His patient waiting in this situation clearly indicates that the Revelation was totally independent of the Prophet's own will; rather its mode and time of descent, as well as its contents were completely dependent on the will of God.

To clarify this matter, let us look at the incident of the slander (*ifq*). The hypocrites had severely slandered the pure and beloved wife of the Prophet, Aisha. The false information rapidly spread and caused much agitation within society. The Prophet and Muslims were very upset, but there was not much they could do. The Prophet could do nothing but say that he had not seen her act in a way that was not honest or decent. He also consulted many of his Companions about this matter. But they could not say anything more than saying that they had not heard of any dishonest or indecent action that might have caused suspicion. This matter stayed on the agenda of the community, unresolved, for quite a long time, and the Prophet turned to Aisha and told her that although he had not heard anything against her that if such a case were true she should turn to God and seek His forgiveness.

This matter remained unresolved for nearly a month. After this time a Revelation arrived that cleared Aisha's name and stated that those who had slandered her would be punished:

> Surely those who invented and spread the slander (against Aisha, the Messenger's wife) are a band from among you. However, do not deem this incident an evil for you; rather, it is good for you. (As for the slanderers:) every one of them has accumulated sin in proportion to his share in this guilt, and he who has the greater part of it will suffer a tremendous punishment. (Nur 24:11)

Now, if the Revelation had been something that was under the Prophet's control, then what prevented him from declaring a judgment from the very first, securing the honesty of his wife and putting an end to all the gossip and slander right away? Indeed, a Prophet could never bring a verse when he desired and attribute to it God:

> If he (the Messenger) had dared to fabricate some false sayings in attribution to Us, We would certainly have seized him with might, thereafter We would certainly have cut his life-vein. Then not one from among you could have shielded and saved him from Us. (Haqqa 69:44-47)

The fact that Prophet Muhammad, peace and blessings be upon him, remained silent and waited for the Revelation, even in such a serious and difficult situation, particularly on such a delicate matter as chastity, plainly indicates that the Revelation was being sent to him and was not under his control.

Through various Qur'anic verses we learn that the Prophet was, from time to time, given Revelations that dealt with matters that were asked about by the polytheists, the People of the Book, the hypocrites and the believers. Only in *Sura Baqara*, for instance, the expression, *"They ask you about..."* is repeatedly used in answer to such questions about spending for the relatives and needy, fighting in the sacred month, intoxicants and games of chance, orphans, and the injunctions concerning menstruation.[7] The common element of all such Revelations is that the Prophet did not answer these questions himself, but, rather the answer was provided by God via the Revelation; quite often the Prophet had to wait a considerable amount of time for the answers.

Had the Revelation been something that had originated from the Prophet's own will he would not have waited when asked such questions, he would have avoided the difficult situation that he sometimes was forced into due to the lack of a prompt answer, rather instantly giving the answer required. All of the above merely indicate that the relation of Prophet Muhammad, peace and blessings be upon him, in respect to the Revelation was like that of an envoy. If, on the other hand, he had himself invented the Revelation, then none of the above-mentioned situations would have occurred.

14   Which angel delivered the Qur'an to the Prophet?

As far as the Revelation of the Qur'an is concerned, the Prophet served as an envoy between the people and the angel, while the angel fulfilled the same role between God and the Prophet. The Messenger, who had a sensitive but reliant character, was one who was equipped with an extraordinary mission to save humankind from lethargy and from immoral tendencies, bringing them to a higher level of consciousness from which they would clearly recognize God as God and Satan as Satan.

As a result of God's mercy He sent Prophets to humankind so that they could find the true path and worship only God Almighty. For the most part the Prophets were sent to humankind in times of moral crisis or decline. The aspects that are the hardest to control and which are the most dangerous are the moral aspects of human behavior. The Prophets who were sent for this purpose received Revelations from God. In the Qur'an it is stated that the angel who delivered the Revelation to Prophet Muhammad, peace and blessings be upon him, was Archangel Gabriel:

> Say (O Messenger): "(The Lord of the worlds, my and your Lord, declares:) 'Whoever is an enemy to Gabriel (should know that) it is he who brings down the Qur'an on your heart by the leave of God, (not of his own accord), confirming (the Divine origin of and the truths still contained in) the Revelations prior to it, and (serving as) guidance and glad tidings for the believers.'" (Baqara 2:97)

Some members of the Jewish community in Medina came to the Prophet and asked him a number of questions. He answered all their questions. They found no fault with his answers and later asked him about who delivered the Revelation to him. When the Prophet told them that Archangel Gabriel delivered the Revelations to him, they said: "He brings earthquake, disaster, violence, war and death.

So, he is our enemy. But Michael is our friend. Thus, we would have believed in you if it had been Michael who had brought you the Revelation." God Almighty states that the Qur'an is not the word of Gabriel, but rather that it is the Word of God; the verse goes on to state that Gabriel comes to the Prophet only with God's permission and that he brings the Revelation from God to the Prophet.

In another verse, the name of the Angel of Revelation is given as the Trustworthy Spirit (*Ruh al-Amin*):

> This (Qur'an) is indeed the Book of the Lord of the worlds being sent down by Him (in parts). The Trustworthy Spirit brings it down on your heart, so that you may be one of the warners (entrusted with the Divine Revelation). (Shuara 26:192-194)

God Almighty calls Gabriel "*the Trustworthy Spirit*" as he serves to save all of humankind in religious matters. He is called the Trustworthy (*Amin*) because he has been entrusted with a mission to deliver certain things to the Prophets and to others.

Another name given to the Angel of Revelation is "the Spirit of Holiness" (*Ruh al-Qudus*):

> Say (to them, O Messenger): "(My Lord affirms): 'The Spirit of Holiness brings it down in parts from your Lord with truth (embodying the truth and with nothing false in it), that it may confirm those who believe (strengthening them in their faith and adherence to God's way), and as guidance, and glad tidings for the Muslims (those who have submitted themselves wholly to God).'" (Nahl 16:102)

The Spirit of Holiness implies a spirit that is pure, a spirit that cannot become blemished, one that is sacred, trustworthy and ever-purified. This is Gabriel, who is described as the *Ruh al-Qudus* in the Qur'an. In other words, Gabriel is called by this name because he brings Divine enlightenment and wisdom in the form of the Qur'an from God; this will serve until the Day of Judgment to purify humankind.

According to another Qur'anic definition, the angel who acts as an envoy to the Prophet has the following features:

> This is the Word (brought) by an honored messenger (Gabriel), endowed with power, with high rank and esteem before the Lord of the Supreme Throne; one obeyed (by his aides), and trustworthy (in fulfilling God's orders, most particularly conveying the Revelation). (Takwir 81:19-21)

Prophet Muhammad, peace and blessings be upon him, the Messenger of God, saw and communicated with Archangel Gabriel, who is also an envoy of God, and received the Revelation from the angel on different occasions. When the Prophet stated that he was receiving the Revelation from Gabriel, the polytheists of Mecca protested. The verse, *"Indeed he saw him (Gabriel) on the clear horizon"* (Takwir 81:23) was revealed in connection with this objection of the polytheists. It can be clearly understood that there is an angel who delivered the Revelation from God to the Prophets. This angel is Gabriel, who is entrusted with the Revelations and who is sincere in this mission.

CHAPTER 3

Verses of the Qur'an

VERSES OF THE QUR'AN

| 15 | What does the word *ayat* (verse) mean? |

This word literally means "clear proof," "sign," "evidence," "warning," "extraordinary event or people." As a Qur'anic term a verse is composed of one or more sentences, has a clear beginning and a clear end, and is a constituent part of a Qur'anic chapter. The meaning of the word *ayat* that occurs in the Holy Qur'an can be given as follows:

a. **Miracle**: The word *ayat* is used to mean clear proof of miracles in verse, "*Ask the Children of Israel how many clear proofs We gave to them...*" (Baqara 2:211). Indeed, all Qur'anic verses are miracles, as no one has been able to come up with anything similar to them.

b. **Sign**: The word *ayat* is used to mean a sign in verse, "*Their Prophet added: 'The sign of his kingdom is that the Ark will come to you, in which there is inward peace and assurance from your Lord, and a remnant of what the house of Moses and the house of Aaron left behind, the angels bearing it. Truly in that is a sign for you, if you are (true) believers'*" (Baqara 2:248).

c. **Verses of the Qur'an:** In the verse, "*It is He Who has sent down on you this (glorious) Book, wherein are verses absolutely explicit and firm: they are the core of the Book...*" (Al Imran 3:7), the term *ayat* is used to refer to each of the individual units (i.e. verses) of the Qur'an that have definite beginnings and endings.

d. **Warning or lesson:** In the verse, *"the (shocking) punishment seized them. Surely in that (which took place between Salih and his people) there is a sign (a great, important lesson). Most of them were not believers"* (Shuara 26:158), the term *ayat* is used in connection with the punishment meted out to the people of Prophet Salih to indicate a lesson or warning that should be taken.

e. **An unprecedented thing that amazes people:** In the verse, *"We made the Son of Mary and his mother a miraculous sign (of Our Lordship and Power)…"* (Mu'minun 23:50), the term *ayat* is used in connection with the creation of Mary and her son Jesus to mean something that is unexampled and marvelous to people or extraordinary events.

f. **Proof and evidence:** In the verse, *"And among His signs is the creation of the heavens and the earth, and the diversity of your languages and colors. Surely in this are signs indeed for people who have knowledge"* (Rum 30:22), God Almighty draws our attention to the signs and proofs in both the created world and one's self through which humans can have knowledge of the Creator of all universe; here the term *ayat* is used for proof and evidence that leads humans to recognize God.

In fact, all the meanings of *ayat* that are used have close connections with Qur'anic verses; this is because each Qur'anic verse is a miracle, a proof of Prophethood and a declaration of the honesty of God's Messenger, evidence of the power and might of God Almighty, guidance to and knowledge of God, as well as a lesson and reminder to be reflected upon.

16 | How were the Qur'anic verses gathered?

T he words and meanings of the Qur'an, as well as their revelation and conveyance to people have all been realized with God's guidance. The intervention of any entity,

including the Prophet, is not relevant in this context. The same is
also true for the order of the verses in the Qur'an. The present
sequence and arrangement of the Qur'anic verses as they are
found today were made by divine decree, not according to the
opinion of others or achieved by comparison. This is something
that the Islamic community as a whole is in agreement on; all the
Qur'an *mushafs* that were compiled both during and after the life
of Prophet Muhammad, peace and blessings be upon him, have
had the same sequential order and there have been no differences
since that time. Whenever Archangel Gabriel delivered a
Revelation, he would dictate it to the Prophet and instruct him to
place it in its exact sequential position within the chapter it
belonged to. Prophet Muhammad, peace and blessings be upon
him, read the verses to his Companions immediately upon their
revelation and had them placed in their exact position among the
chapters and verses that had been revealed at an earlier date.
God's Messenger followed the same sequential order of verses and
suras when reciting during the prayers, while speaking and advis-
ing his Companions, and on various other occasions; he also
recited all the *suras* that had been revealed up until that time with
Archangel Gabriel once a year. In his final year on the earth
Prophet Muhammad, peace and blessings be upon him, met with
Gabriel twice; their recitation in this year is known as "the final
presentation." Each time the Prophet recited the Qur'an with
Gabriel it was carried out in the same sequential order that is
found today in the Qur'an.

Today there are a number of reliable narrations concerning
Gabriel's dictation of the place, position and order of each revealed
portion, as well as narrations about God's Messenger's dictation of
the Revelation to his scribes and his orderly recitation of the chapters during the prayers. All these plainly indicate that the sequence
of the Qur'anic verses were determined by God.

17 | Why are there different figures mentioned with respect to the total number of verses and what is the actual number?

The general accord is that the total number of verses is 6,200-odd verses in the entire Qur'an. According to differing ways of reciting the Qur'an, there are differing opinions on what the odd numbers exactly are. Considering these variant readings of the Qur'an, the exact number of total Qur'anic verses is 6220 according to the reciting of Meccans of the period, 6236 according to the reciting of the people of Kufa, 6216 according to the reciting of the people of Damascus, 6210, 6214 or 6217 according to the reciting of the people of Medina and 6204, 6205 or 6219 according to the reciting of Basrans of the time.

As for the disagreements over where certain verses begin and end, this is due to the differences in narration that the scholars of *qira'a* received but this is not a matter of interpretation. (*Qira'a* is the method of recitation, punctuation and localization of the Qur'an, and there are seven main *qira'at*, or readings, of the Qur'an.) The differences in *qira'a* narrations are due to the fact that Prophet Muhammad, peace and blessings be upon him, stopped in different places in the same verses on different occasions. When the Prophet recited verses for the first time he would stop at the end of each verse so that the Companions would know where the verse began and ended. When he was sure that this detail had been understood, he would sometimes pass onto the following verse without halting between, to ensure continuity in meaning. Thus, if someone were to hear this second type of recital of two consecutive verses for the first time, it would be possible that they would consider these verses to be one single verse and they would recite it to others accordingly.

Another reason for variance over the total number of verses depends on whether or not the *basmala* that is found at the beginning of every chapter, the Qur'anic initials (*muqatta'at*) that can be found at the beginning of certain chapters, some words at the beginning of certain chapters, or some short Qur'anic verses are considered to be independent verses or not.

Finally, such differences of opinion does not by any means indicate any interpolation in the verses; rather the numerical variations are nothing but a different understanding of the same text by different people.

18	What were the first and last verses or chapters to be revealed in the Qur'an?

a. **The first verses to be revealed:** There are different opinions about the early Revelations to the Prophet. The best-known and mostly widely accepted opinion is that the first five verses of Sura Alaq were the first to be revealed. There are a number of narrations that support this opinion; one of these is as follows:

According to the narration of Aisha, the commencement of the divine inspiration to God's Messenger was in the form of good dreams that came like bright daylight (i.e. true) and then the love of seclusion was bestowed upon him. Gabriel, the Angel of Revelation, descended upon him while he was in seclusion in the Cave of Hira and revealed him the first five verses from Sura Alaq.

After this first visit of Archangel Gabriel, Revelation ceased for a certain period (*dawr al-fatra*) and then resumed. Revelation came regularly after this cessation period with the revelation of the first five verses from Sura Muddaththir. On the other hand, many hold that the verses to be revealed first were the verses of Sura al-Fatiha. According to others, the *basmala* was the first verse to be revealed.

b. **The last verses to be revealed:** There are differing narrations about which verse was revealed last. Neither the

Qur'an nor the Prophet give any definite information on this matter. The only narrations on this matter are from the Companions. Bayhaqi says: "If they are all true, the only way to abolish the differences between them is to understand that every one replies to the question according to their own understanding." Qadi Abu Bakr says: "None of these narrations are invalid. Every one has spoken according to their opinion or their comprehension. They are presumably speaking about the last words they heard from the Prophet just before he passed away. Some of them might not have even heard them directly from the Prophet, but perhaps heard them later." The most widely accepted opinion is that the 281st verse of Sura Baqara was the verse to be revealed last.

19 Was each and every verse or chapter of the Qur'an revealed in connection with a certain occasion?

As previously explained, the Qur'an was revealed in parts to Prophet Muhammad, peace and blessings be upon him, over a period of 23 years. Each verse that was revealed had a certain aim and purpose. The sum total of all these reasons and purposes was to secure the happiness and prosperity of humanity both in this world and in the Hereafter. Although this was the general and overall purpose of the Revelation, there were also verses and/or chapters that were revealed for particular reasons, in connection with certain cases, questions or to remove doubts, solve problems etc. However, it must be clarified that the entire Qur'an was not revealed in connection with the above-mentioned reasons. Even the first chapters and/or verses to be revealed were not connected with similar causes. Many such verses were concerned with the relations of various Prophets with their communities, certain events in the remote past or in the distant future, the Day of Judgment, Heaven and Hell or other similar subjects.

On the other hand, many of the verses pertain to judgments and morals that were revealed in connection with the circumstances leading up to a revelation or in which particular verses were revealed, known as the *asbab al-nuzul* (causes of revelation); such verses are directed towards the transformation of social life. With such verses one must be aware of the circumstances of revelation in order to understand the legislative principles accurately. The time and location of revelation in other verses, for the most part consisting of the stories of bygone nations, are not so important and it is not necessary to be aware of the circumstances of their revelation to understand them correctly.

20 | How are the circumstances of the revelation of the verses to be understood?

It is not permissible for one to express an opinion of their own; i.e., one that has not been narrated by someone who witnessed the Revelation of the relevant verse, without knowing the circumstances or having a thorough knowledge about them. Pertaining to this subject Muhammad ibn Sirin states: "I asked Ubayda about a verse in the Qur'an and he said to me: 'Fear God and speak the truth! Those who knew the circumstances of Revelation have all passed away.'"

Only the Companions of the Prophet were able to know the circumstances of the Revelation. If they were not very well acquainted with the circumstances they would not give a definite opinion on the matter. An example of this can be found with the matter of some verses in Sura Nisa. Abdullah ibn Zubayr narrated that a dispute arose between Zubayr and a person from the Ansar over an irrigation channel and they turned to Prophet Muhammad, peace and blessings be upon him, for a solution. After evaluating the issue, the Prophet said: "O Zubayr! You water your land first and later let your neighbor water his!" The man from the Ansar said: "O God's Messenger! What can one say? He is your cousin!" The Prophet's face changed at this serious allegation. Zubayr said: "I think the following verses were revealed upon this incident: *"But no! By your Lord, they do not (truly) believe unless they make you the judge regarding any dispute between them, and then find not the least vexation within themselves over what you have decided, and surrender in full submission"* (Nisa 4:65).

This incident shows that only a few of the Companions, not all, would be aware of the circumstances in which particular verses were revealed. Therefore, it would not be right to determine one event as the circumstance of Revelation only through guess-work or supposition.

21	Is the *basmala* a verse and why is written at the start of every chapter?

It is considered proper Islamic manners to begin to read or to do any action with the name of the Supreme Creator. This can be seen in the following verses:

> Read in and with the Name of your Lord, Who has created, created human from a clot clinging (to the wall of the womb). Read, and your Lord is the All-Munificent, Who has taught (human) by the pen, taught human what he did not know. (Alaq 96:1-5)

These are the verses which most people think are the earliest revealed verses. This is in keeping with the basic Islamic principle that is emphasized in the verse, *"He is the First and the Last, the All-Outward and the All-Inward. He has full knowledge of everything"* (Hadid 57:3). God is the Unique One to Whom every creature owes its existence and from Whom the beginning of everything originated. Every beginning, every action and every operation is achieved only with His Name. Due to this, God willed the *basmala* (the expression of *Bismi'llahir-Rahmani'r-Rahim*, meaning "In the Name of God, the All-Merciful, the All-Compassionate") to be the key to the 113 chapters, as well as an independent verse within another chapter.

There are many narrations that emphasize the importance of the *basmala*. Some of them are as follows: Prophet Muhammad, peace and blessings be upon him, said: "I have been revealed such a verse that has been revealed to no one but Prophet Solomon, the son of David and myself. This is *'Bismi'llahir-Rahmani'r-Rahim.'*"[8]

As reported the Prophet said, "Any action that is not started with *Bismi'llahir-Rahmani'r-Rahim* has no divine gift in it, it will not last long and it is without foundation."[9]

In another narration, the Prophet said: "Satan would certainly regard any meal that is not started with *Bismi'llah* as his own."[10]

The fact that the *basmala* is repeated at the beginning of every chapter and in various hadiths indicates the importance of this phrase. It is regarded as a summary of the Qur'an. God has revealed universal realities through various Prophets since humankind first came to the earth. These realities are also included in the Qur'an, which is the last Divine Book. The Qur'an is summarized in Sura al-Fatiha, while the chapter is summarized in the phrase *Bismi'llah*. Hence, the *basmala* can be regarded to be a spiritual connection between all Prophets and Books.

There is some debate about whether the *basmala* is an independent verse in every chapter or whether it is a single Qur'anic verse that is repeated at the beginning of every chapter. Here we will briefly examine the discussions and arguments of the different opinions: According to Shafi'i and Hanbali Schools, the *basmala* is an independent verse in Sura al-Fatiha and in all other chapters. According to the Maliki School "the *basmala* is neither a verse of Sura al-Fatiha nor of the other chapters."

According to the Hanafi School, the *basmala* is considered to be a verse of the Qur'an. However, the fact that it is written at the beginning of every chapter does not necessarily mean that it is an independent verse in every chapter. So, the *basmala* is, as a verse, a part of the Qur'an and it was revealed for the purpose of separating the chapters. According to the Hanafis, there are various narrations that indicate that the *basmala* was not recited along with Sura al-Fatiha in the prayers; this indicates that it is not a verse of Sura al-Fatiha. As a matter of fact, the Companions said: "We did not know before when a sura would end until the *basmala* was recited."[11] This is considered to indicate that the *basmala* was not an independent verse in every sura, but rather was recited to separate the *suras*.

The *basmala*, whether it is used for purposes of separating chapters or for making a chapter blessed or to seek God's help to thoroughly understand the contents of a chapter, is something like a spiritual lifeline that has been extended to humanity for their salvation.

It would be useful to give a summary of all these discussions and narrations: The *basmala* is an independent verse in Sura Naml, but it is not a verse in other chapters, nor was it revealed only to separate the chapters. Thus, the differences in opinion are not related to the essence of the issue, but rather to its details. That is, none of those who voice an opinion have any doubts that the *basmala* is a verse. Their only hesitation is about whether this is a verse in every *sura*. Additionally, there is no question that the *basmala* was written at the beginning of every chapter during the lifetime of Prophet Muhammad, peace and blessings be upon him, and that this was done on his order; it has been the same ever since.

There is much rational and narrative evidence that the *basmala* is a part of the Qur'an:

a. The Companions were in agreement about the Qur'an from its beginning until its end. There is not even one narration from the Companions that suggests any doubts about the Qur'an we use today. The *basmala* is part of the Qur'an and they had no hesitation or doubt about its existence at the beginning of every *sura*; therefore it is obvious that the *basmala* is a part of the Qur'an.

b. The Companions were able to recognize the beginning and end of the *sura*s after the Revelation by the *basmala*.[12] Before the *basmala* was revealed, the Muslims did not know where a chapter ended. They were only able to understand where a chapter ended after the revelation of the *basmala*.[13] Ibn Abbas said: "We used to learn the Holy Qur'an when God's Messenger was alive and only after the revelation of the *basmala* could we understand that a *sura* had ended." All the above narrations indicate that the *basmala* at the beginning of the chapter is a verse.

c. The following narration from Ibn Abbas also confirms that the *basmala* is a verse: "Whoever refrains from beginning to read the Qur'an with the *basmala* leaves out a verse from God's Book."[14]

d. The fact that the *basmala* is not included only at the beginning of Sura Bara'a and that it is written at the beginning of all other chapters indicates that the *basmala* is a verse.

e. If we review the history of the Qur'an, we can see that there were various reactions to undertakings, such as the naming of the chapters, carrying out of punctuation and *ta'shir* (division of the Qur'an into sections, each of which contains 10 verses for purposes of recitation). But there is no argument about the *basmala*. If there had been any, we certainly would have heard of it. Thus, the *basmala* is a part of the Qur'an and God's Messenger expressed this.

Meticulous care and dedication has been employed to prevent any non-Qur'anic elements from being inserted into the Qur'an from the earliest times; this was so much so that when Umar heard that a man had been writing some explanatory notes in the margins of the *sura*s, called this man and had him severely punished.

The same reaction can be observed not only with Umar, but also with all other Companions. Ibn Mas'ud, for instance, said: "Protect the Qur'an from everything." He even once saw some non-Qur'anic writing on the copy of a person's Qur'an (probably a commentary pertaining to that verse); he took the copy, erased the writing and said: "Do not add anything to the Qur'an."

Thus, all these and similar narrations indicate that the copies of the Qur'an which were compiled and gathered by Uthman, the third caliph, were copies of the Book that had been revealed to Prophet Muhammad, peace and blessings be upon him. If the *basmala* at the start of every *sura* had not been per the Prophet's instructions, or if it had not been part of the Qur'an, then the Companions would have raised serious objections, as they had in other matters and the *basmala* would not have been included.

In addition, in such matters as the *ta'shir* and the writing of chapter names and verse numbers, permission was given during the time of the *tabi'in* (the second generation of Muslims) and later generations. However, they never used the argument of Uthman's approach to the *basmala* to support their views, although they justified their opinions in many different ways. This shows that the *basmala* found at the beginning of all chapters was there because Prophet Muhammad, peace and blessings be upon him, had so instructed, and no one saw any objections or problems with it appearing there.

In Sura Naml the *basmala*, which we have briefly examined and dealt with here, is an independent verse. The *basmala* is put at the beginning of every *sura*. We cannot understand the Divine reason for this. However, essentially there is no difference between the *basmala* being mentioned because it was revealed by God for each and every chapter or it being only revealed once, and the Prophet was told to recite and mention it at the beginning of every *sura*. Such differences in opinion on the *basmala* do not focus on its essence, but rather they are related as to whether or not it was a verse that was repeatedly revealed for every chapter. Obviously, none of the Companions had the least hesitation or suspicion about why the *basmala* was placed at the beginning of every chapter during the lifetime of the Prophet.

22 | Qur'anic verses are divided into two groups, known as *muhkam* or *mutashabih*. What is the difference?

These two categories of Qur'anic verses are concerned with their meaning; *muhkam* means established, decisive, while *mutashabih* means allegorical.

a. The meanings of the terms *muhkam* and *mutashabih*: The term *muhkam* literally means "to make something firm and perfect, or to preserve something against defects or errors." In connection with the Qur'an, this term is used for those Qur'anic verses that are easily understandable, which do not need much exegetical effort, and which have one clear meaning. Whereas, the term *mutashabih* literally has the meaning of "things that are comparable and consistent with each other, or which have mutual resemblance or which are alike," while in relation to the Qur'an, this term means "those verses that have more than one meaning, that need exegetical effort for elucidation, or whose true nature cannot be conceived by mere reasoning or narration."

There are three verses in the Glorious Qur'an that are related to this subject. According to the first of these, the entire Qur'an is *muhkam*: "*Alif. Lam. Ra. (This is) a Book whose Revelations in verses have been made firm (absolutely free of doubt, alteration, or annulment) and full of wisdom, and arranged in sequence and distinctly detailed. It is from One All-Wise, All-Aware*" (Hud 11:1). The term *muhkam* here has the meaning of "something far removed from annulment and doubt in all aspects, which is firm and well-established, which is durable and resilient at all times, and is orderly and full of supreme virtues."

According to the second verse, the entire Qur'an is *mutashabih*: "*God sends down in parts the best of the words as a Book fully consistent in itself and whose statements corroborate, expound and refer to one another...*" (Zumar 39:23). The term *mutashabih* here means "Qur'anic verses which resemble each other in beauty, wisdom, authority and soundness, which verify one another and which are founded on ultimate truth and honesty; verses that contain words and meanings that are in full concordance and harmony." The term *mathaniya* in the above verse means "that in which the decrees, admonitions or narratives are repeated, the reading, promises and challenges of which is repeated, or that in which something is mentioned and afterwards something opposed to it is mentioned (as the mentioning of believers or unbelievers, or of Heaven and Hell)."

According to the third verse, some Qur'anic verses are *muhkam* and some others are *mutashabih*: "*It is He Who has sent down on you this Book, in which there are verses explicit in meaning and content and decisive: they are core of the Book, others being allegorical...*" (Al Imran 3:7). The terms *muhkam* and *mutashabih* in this verse have been used with meanings that are different to that above. These two terms have contrasting meanings here. Accordingly, there are certain verses which are *mutashabih* and can thus be grasped only by those who are firmly grounded in knowledge; the meanings of such verses are only known by God.

b. Types of *mutashabih* verses: The reason why there are *mutashabih* verses is that Divine Wisdom is a mystery and can never be known exactly. There may be something hidden in words or meaning, or sometimes hidden in words and meanings both.

1. *Mutashabih* **only in words:** The quality of being *mutashabih* can be contained in a single word or in a sentence. That is, a single word may occur either because that word is a *gharib* (uncommon) word, because it has more than one meaning, or because it is in a sentence which has an intricate meaning or which is not totally clear. Now, let us examine these in more detail in order to understand better:

   a. **Uncommon words:** The verse, "*And fruits and herbage*" (Abasa 80:31) may be regarded as an example of this category. The meaning of the term *abban* in this verse (which can be transliterated as "*Wa fakihatan wa*

abban") was not known as it was not a commonly
used word at that time. There is a narration that when
preaching from the pulpit, Caliph Umar read this verse
and said, "We all understand these, but what does this
abb (in the verse) mean?" He said: "O God! I swear
that it is a hardship and an onerous task to try to
understand this." Talking to himself, he continued and
said, "O Umar! So what if you do not know the meaning of *abban*?" Recognizing the limitations of human
beings in the face of Divine Knowledge, Umar went
on to say, "Look into what is explained in the Qur'an
and act in accordance with it; leave whatever you do
not understand to (the All-Knowing) God."

b. **Words with multiple meaning**: A word can be
   mutashabih in some instances if it has more than one
   meaning. For instance, the term *yamin* has more than
   one meaning in the verse, "*Then he fell upon them, striking them (the idols) with his **right hand (with all his
   strength**)*" (Saffat 37:93), meaning right hand,
   strength or oath.

c. **Being *mutashabih* due to brevity of the sentence**:
   Another reason for a sentence being *mutashabih* is that
   some words may not be clearly mentioned in the sentence, but rather are implied by the text. For instance,
   the phrases *law tazawwajtumuhunna*, meaning "when
   you marry" and *min ghayrihinna*, meaning "other (than
   them)" are implied by the context, even though they
   are not clearly mentioned in the verse, "*If you fear that
   you will not be able to observe their rights with exact fairness
   when you marry the orphan girls, you can marry, from
   among **other** women (who are permitted to you in marriage
   and) who seem good to you...*" (Nisa 4:3).

d. **Being *mutashabih* due to word order**: Another reason for a word or phrase being *mutashabih* could be

the structure of the sentence. For instance, if the word *qayyiman*, or unerringly straight, in the verse came earlier in, "*All praise and gratitude are for God, Who has sent down on His servant the Book and has put no crookedness in it, - unerringly straight, to warn of a stern punishment from Him and give the believers who do good, righteous deeds the glad tidings that for them is an excellent reward*" (Kahf 18:1-2), there would not be a lack of clarity or case of *mutashabih* here. When the word *qayyiman* is put in a different place in the sentence, the meaning would be more direct and easier to understand, "All praise and gratitude are for God, Who has sent down on His servant the Book and has made it a flawless guide (for human beings)...."

2. *Mutashabih* **caused by meaning:** Sometimes the phenomenon of *mutashabih* can happen through the meaning. There are a number of examples in the Qur'an that are related to this. For example, the attributes of God, Judgment Day, life after death, the rewards of Heaven, and the hardships of Hell are metaphysical matters which the human intellect cannot fully comprehend. The Islamic scholars adopt two distinct approaches in this regard; according to the first, the *mutashabih* verses in connection with the Divine attributes, for instance, do not refer to God's Self, Who cannot be known in His Essence. Thus, they choose to refer the true nature of such attributes to God. The second is that these attributive words, which outwardly seem inconceivable, should be interpreted in accordance with God's Divinity. For instance, in connection with the Divine attribute mentioned in, "*Those who swear allegiance to you (O Messenger), swear allegiance to God only. God's "Hand" is over their hands...*" (Fath 48:10), the *Salafis*[15] consider that God is far above the literary meanings of these attributes. They do not make any com-

mentary on such attributive words; rather they believe in them as they are mentioned and thus refer their true meanings to God. But, later scholars have felt that it is possible to interpret such attributes so long as one can ascribe a sound meaning to these words that is both reasonably appropriate to God and which is in accordance with Islamic Law. They give two important meanings to the aforementioned verse. One meaning they give to this *mutashabih* word is that the Messenger's hand is over the hand he grasps in allegiance as it represents God's Hand; that is, obedience to the Messenger means the same as obedience to God. The other meaning is that God helps those who swear allegiance to the Messenger. So, here "Hand" signifies "Power." Similarly, for God "Hand," "Face," or any other such term is metaphorical.

3. *Mutashabih* **verses in both words and meaning:** The *mutashabih* state in certain verses arises both from the word and its meaning. The following verse may be an example for this:

> They ask you (O Messenger) about the new moons (because of the month of Ramadan). Say: "They are appointed times (markers) for the people (to determine time periods) and for the Pilgrimage." (Do not link them to superstitions and superstitious behavior like entering dwellings by the back rather than the front.) It is not virtue that you enter dwellings from the backs of them, but virtue is (the state of) one who (truly believing in God) strives to attain righteousness and piety (by carrying out His commandments and refraining from His prohibitions). So come to dwellings (in the normal way) by their doors. (Do everything according to the rule and establish relations with your leader and among yourselves in proper terms.) And strive to obey God in due reverence for Him and piety so that you may prosper. (Baqara 2:189)

This verse uses the occasion of people asking the Prophet about the new moons and demands that people not connect such events to superstitions or superstitious behavior, like entering dwellings by the rear entrance rather than the front. The Arabs at that time would, when dressed in *ihram* (a special two-part apparel put on for pilgrimage purpose), enter and exit their houses from the rear entrance, through an opening in the back wall of their houses. God Almighty expressed in the above verse that such behavior does not entail good behavior, and thus no righteousness is derived from it. The verse, thus, invites them to true piety and godliness. Obviously, it is difficult to understand what is meant by this verse without knowing the tradition of the Arabs at that time. The verse, thus, clearly shows that both its words and meaning are *mutashabih*, or intricate.

To sum up, the aspect of *mutashabih* can be divided into three parts: One is the category of *mutashabih* from which no one can comprehend the true meaning. There are many *mutashabih* matters about which only God can know their true meanings, such as God's Divinity, the Truth (essence) of His attributes and the time of the Day of Judgment.

Secondly, there are verses that any one can comprehend with a little study or by some exegetical effort. The quality of *mutashabih* in this category arises either from the brevity of the words or from the word order.

Finally, there are certain *mutashabih* verses which can be grasped only by those who are firmly grounded in knowledge. These are concerned with matters that only the scholars who study the commentaries and explanations of the Messenger and who are experts in the Arabic language, linguistics, literature, and other relevant fields of science, can comprehend. The prayer that the Prophet made for Ibn Abbas indicates this third category: "O God! Make him (Ibn Abbas) a learned scholar in religion and teach him the exegesis of the Qur'an."[16]

23 | What is the reason for the mutashabih verses in the Qur'an?

The Qur'an is not a book that addresses the people of a particular area at a particular time. On the contrary, it is universal, speaking to all people at all times. Accordingly, whatever principles and messages it has brought are able to be grasped and understood by all people, no matter where or when they live. Such intelligibility can only be achieved with the expressions that the Qur'an employed in its approach to and introduction of matters; that is, people at all times should be able to perceive the implications of the expressions used in the Qur'an to the degree of comprehension that they have reached at the time in which they live. Such a condition is secured and maintained by the existence of the *mutashabih*, or intricate, verses of the Qur'an.

The following example might help to make the matter clearer: Suppose that you are to explain the radio to an audience that has a scientific understanding from many centuries earlier. Naturally, such a people are unaware of even electricity, let alone information about electro-magnetic waves, transistors, transmitters, receivers, or studios, all of which are required for radio technology. Therefore, it would be best to tell them, for instance, that the radio is a speaking box. Such a description is, in fact, not even 1% of the facts inherent in radio technology. Since it is impossible to present to such an audience all the facts in all their aspects, the best way to tell them about the radio is to compare it to things they know, using certain words that are suitable for their level of comprehension. This comparison of the radio, on the one hand, makes it more easily understandable, while, on the other, people are better able to understand that the radio is a complicated piece of machinery which is difficult to explain. What is expected of such an audience is to believe in the ideas and knowledge they can glean from the description without having any overly detailed or complicated explanations. Otherwise, they might be inclined to unrealistic or wrong deductions and may end up saying: "The radio should have a mouth if it speaks and it should have a tongue if it has a mouth. It should also feed itself." Likewise, interpreting *mutashabih* verses according to one's own preconceptions, and contrary to their context, would result in the same unrealistic deductions that God reproaches in the Qur'an.

Because of the realities of human life, people place, in most cases, more importance on relative truths than on absolute ones. For instance, largeness and smallness, abundance and scarceness, beauty and ugliness, nearness and distance, or heat and cold are all relative concepts and may vary from person to person or from situation to situation. Human life continues its existence dependent on these relativities. What's more, time progresses, conditions change, human information increases, and there are as many levels of understanding as there are people. The Qur'an is a treasury of realities that addresses all humanity – present and future generations – until the Final Day. It is full of lessons, and it speaks to all levels of understanding. Such addressing to different understanding levels with the very same words is attained with the *mutashabihat* (plural for *mutashabih*) in the Qur'an.

The creation, like a tree, has a tendency toward maturation and perfection. Humanity also has the same tendency toward advancement. To carry on with the metaphor, the tendency for progression is like the seed that gradually develops as a result of many experiences. Arts and sciences develop and mature when the seed is nurtured by various ideals and thoughts.

The Divine wisdom of the Absolute Sovereign willed His Supreme Book to contain *mutashabihat* in various categories. Through these *mutashabih* expressions the Qur'an becomes the source of countless and limitless meanings. God Almighty has not made it possible for His servants to be able to understand such matters in only one way with one single meaning; rather, He has kept the doors open for the human mind and intellect to exercise personal efforts and judgment (*ijtihad*) so that we can benefit from the blessings of the God-given faculty of understanding and perception. As a result of this incentive to study the Qur'an, people are invited to reflect on the Book and scholars are prompted to discover the hidden beauties of the Qur'an.

Let us not forget that God Almighty has clearly explained in the *muhkam* (perspicuous) verses all the basics of faith, acts of worship, interrelations of human beings and moral principles for which human beings are accountable. Although the genuine purposes of the Qur'an have been laid out by these *muhkam* verses which convey a firm and unequivocal meaning, it would be neither right nor proper to expect each and every verse of the Qur'an to be understood and comprehended by everybody all at the same level.

God Almighty speaks to human beings in a way that they can understand. The Qur'an does not contain any words that are entirely incomprehensible for human beings. According to their levels of understanding and the scientific knowledge of the time, God's servants can perceive the implications of the *mutashabih* verses, but they cannot fully encompass them in their knowledge. Accordingly, it is possible to derive meanings even from the verses that pertain to God's Attributes, which are from the *mutashabih* verses. Obviously, as we cannot grasp His Attributes in all their reality, we abstain from likening God to His creatures. It should also be noted that we must take the *muhkam* verses as criterion and understand the *mutashabih* verses in the light of the *muhkam* ones, as we cannot perceive their true nature fully or the divine purpose behind them. We believe in whatever meaning God Almighty intended in those verses that have more than one dimension and which are known by God alone in all their reality. This inadequacy of knowing everything in full in the Book is evidence that it was revealed by God Almighty, Who is the only Owner of the absolute knowledge.

CHAPTER 4

Chapters of the Qur'an

CHAPTERS OF THE QUR'AN

24 | What does the word *sura* mean?

T he word *sura* (chapter of the Qur'an) literally means rank, high position, honor, high and beautiful building, city-wall, floors or the upper parts of a building. The plural form of the term is *suwar* (chapters). When applied to the Qur'an it means the separate parts of the Qur'an that have a beginning and an end and which are made up of verses. The Glorious Qur'an is composed of 114 chapters. In the same way that floors or upper parts of a building are called *sura* in Arabic, the various parts of the Qur'an are also called *sura*. The Qur'anic chapters most probably have been referred to with this term because each of them contains divine words and thus holds a high rank. Just like high city-walls built from bricks, the chapters of the Qur'an are built of verses that have a unique meaning and wording, each phrase standing in a specific place, supporting each other. Each *sura* of the Qur'an is like a castle of truths; it is a high and strong building that is easily distinguishable from other *suras*, with a definite cooperation between the verses, each one elucidating the other.

25 | Where do the names of the Qur'anic chapters come from?

T he Qur'anic chapters take their names either from the personalities included in them, for example, the stories of Prophets Noah, Abraham, Joseph, Mary, or the family of Imran, or from the communities included in them, for example, the civilization of Sheba or the Children of Israel, or from the first word of the chapter like *najm*, *asr*, or *kawthar*, or from an unusual word used in the chapter, like *ra'd* or *nahl*, or from the *huruf al-muqatta'at* (Qur'anic initials of different letters of the alphabet), like the individual Arabic letters of "*qaf*" and "*sad*," found at the beginning of the Sura Qaf or Sura Sad, or sets of letter, for example "*ta ha*" and "*ya sin*," found at the beginning of Sura Ta. Ha and Sura Ya. Sin. While sometimes a chapter has more than one name, for example, Sura Insan is also called Dahr, Sura Fatir may also be called Malaika, or Sura Isra is also Banu Isra'il, two or more chapters sometimes share a name. For instance, Sura Baqara and Sura Al Imran are called together Zahrawan, which means "two bright chapters." Similarly, the Qur'anic chapters of Falaq and Nas are known as *Muawwizatayn*. When Sura Ikhlas is included, they are given the title of *Muawwizat*, which means "*suras* of refuge or shelter."

26   Why is the Qur'an divided into chapters?

The following are just some of the reasons why the Qur'an is made up of various chapters. It should be noted however, that more important than these is that the Almighty Creator Who sent down the Qur'an has so willed.

The fact that the Qur'an is divided into chapters facilitates its memorization, since attempting to commit the whole Qur'an to memory would be more difficult than memorizing it in smaller parts. Each chapter of the Qur'an in general deals with a particular subject. These subjects are given in different chapters in such a way that the reader can better understand them and so that the main idea can be better emphasized.

When writing any book the division of the text under certain headings or chapters is more helpful for readers than if the book was presented as a whole. Readers know, by experience, that they can understand the content better, and the book is more approachable and easier to read when it is divided into chapters.

Chapters of the Qur'an vary in length. Of its 114 chapters, the shortest is Sura Kawthar, with only 3 verses, while the longest is Sura Baqara with 286 verses. However, there is no difference between the long and short chapters as far as the miraculousness of the Qur'an is concerned, for humankind are absolutely unable to produce the like of even its shortest chapter, no matter how many people come together, helping and supporting one another. This challenge of the Qur'an, which goes to prove the human's inability to produce the like of just one Qur'anic chapter, is an indication of the Divine authorship of the Qur'an.

27   Who gave the chapters their names?

The present names of the Qur'anic chapters were conveyed by Prophet Muhammad, peace and blessings be upon him, under God's direction. Accordingly, neither the Companions nor the following generations were authorized to change or replace them.

28   Why is the story of Prophet Joseph in Sura Yusuf, which is named after him, called "the best of stories"?

Unlike the accounts of other Prophets, different elements and aspects of which are related in different *suras*, the astonishing story of Prophet Joseph begins and ends in the very same *sura* which is named after him. This *sura*, which exhibits its amazing beauty from the very beginning, relates his story as "*the best of stories*" (Yusuf 12:3). We can mention the following reasons for the Qur'an describing his story in the *sura* as the most beautiful of stories:

a. There is no other story in the entire Qur'an that contains lessons and principles at a similar level of magnitude than this story. While all the other stories of Prophets are scattered throughout different *suras*, the story of Prophet Joseph is given in its entirety and with great detail in this *sura* alone; his life history, in full chronological order, is provided. Just like this best narrative of Prophet Joseph, the Qur'anic accounts of the Prophets provide lessons with which one may take a warning and deduce various lessons. As a matter of fact, the following verse at the end of the *sura* clearly expresses this: *"Indeed, in their exemplary life-stories there is a significant lesson for people of discernment"* (Yusuf 12:111).

b. Revealing the manners of a Prophet in all his words and actions, Prophet Joseph showed patience and forbearance when treated badly by his brothers and he even forgave them, without leaving them feeling any guilt for their former misdeeds. He tells them, *"No reproach this day shall be on you. May God forgive you; indeed He is the Most Merciful of the merciful"* (Yusuf 12:92). So, the story, with such aspects, gives the best lesson and is the manifestation of godly acts.

c. In this chapter, not only are the manners of people from all walks of life – from the Prophets and God-revering, pious people, from the king and the courtiers to the servants and ordinary people, from scholars to the ignorant, from the destitute to merchants and beautiful temptresses mentioned, but also those of a variety of other characters, including angels, devils, jinn and animals. In this chapter also, the Oneness of God, Islamic jurisprudence, narratives of the Prophets, the dream episodes in Prophet Joseph's life and his ability to interpret them, politics, human interrelations, economic life and many other subjects, which are important for both religious and worldly aspects of the lives of human beings, are dealt with. It could be for this reason that this *sura* is called the most beautiful of stories.

d. What is meant by the expression *"the best of stories"* here is that this is the most striking, the most surprising, the most beautiful description, and also that the Qur'an has described all matters in the best and most striking style. That is to say, the beauty of the words, expressions and their meanings has attained a miraculous level of eloquence.

e. Whoever is mentioned in this chapter obtains happiness in the end; Prophet Joseph, his father Prophet Jacob, and all his brothers. Indeed, all the persons involved in the events described in the *sura* come to understand their mistakes and find the truth, including Joseph's brothers who jealously harbored murderous intentions toward Joseph. It is also narrated that the king believed in Prophet Joseph, embraced Islam and became a devout Muslim. The prisoner who dreamed that he served wine to his lord again and asked Prophet Joseph to interpret his dream as well as the courtier who witnessed Joseph's shirt being torn from his back all obtained happiness in the end. While almost all of the other narratives in other *suras* contain elements of destruction, the way the lives of people unfold in this *sura* proves that everyone can attain goodness and prosperity by finding the truth in the end.

f. Stories can be both realistic and imaginary. And certainly, the most beautiful stories are the ones that are realistic. That is, stories in which a real event has been depicted with a refined sense of aesthetics that refers to a permanent beauty and is expressed in a full and eloquent style. Real beauty is always ahead of the imagination. Ideal beauty gains importance only when it becomes a symbol or a sample of real beauty.

Sura Yusuf eloquently lays before us the life of innocent beauty and at the same time it also tells how an eye that witnessed the reality of eternal beauty, belittlingly perceived the manifestations of a temporary physical beauty; Sura Yusuf is obviously a beautiful narration of the reality that disclosed its manifestation with a *mutashabih* (parabolical, allegorical) symbol from the unseen world. Also, as the dream of Prophet Joseph is the symbol and indication of his spiritual beauty, reflected in his physical beauty and his representation of such important virtues as chastity and devotion to doing good, so too is Sura Yusuf, in all its details, an invisible reality that is revealed as an introductory symbol of the highest level of spiritual beauty. Thus, Sura Yusuf is the most beautiful of all stories.

g. The story deals with all the religious, social, economic, political and literary aspects of this worldly life and is full of lessons and reminders. Probably the most significant lessons it gives are patience and forgiveness at a time when one is able to repay cruelty and torture in kind. With all these elements, this is the best of stories.

29 Certain chapters and verses are said to be more virtuous than others. What does this mean, as all are divine words?

We firstly have to be aware that the degree of perfection for every creature has been determined by God's will and we do not have even the smallest role or share in this determination. Accordingly, we do accept that which Almighty God teaches us to be superior as superior.

No two things are identical to each other in the universe. There are differences and degrees of superiority among them. For instance, the month of Ramadan is superior to other months, and *Laylat al-Qadr* (the Night of Power) is better than a thousand months. Similarly, Friday is more worthy of reverence than other days of the week, and even within a day, the time just before dawn is superior to other times, and hence the morning prayer, which is performed at this time, is more blessed and more likely to be accepted. The Ka'ba has superiority over all other places in the world. Likewise, not all our conducts are evaluated in the same way and certain behaviors and acts are regarded by God as being more righteous and some pious deeds more worthy of reward.

The four grand angels, Archangel Gabriel, Michael, Israfel and Azrael, the angel of death, are superior to other angels. Prophets are superior to all humankind. The five great prophets – Prophet Muhammad, Prophet Noah, Prophet Abraham, Prophet Moses and Prophet Jesus, peace be upon them all – whom are distinguished by Muslims as highest in rank, are superior to all other Prophets. And Prophet Muhammad, peace and blessings be upon him, is the best of all creation.

Thus, certain chapters and verses are more superior to others. What is most important is that if their superiority has been stated by God, then we have to accept this and act accordingly.

The entire Qur'an is the Word of God. All its words and letters have been revealed in Arabic and there is no difference among any of them. However, the fact that certain chapters and verses are superior to others is due to certain divine reasons. In the same way that breathing, eating food and eating fruit are all requirements for human beings, but with different levels of necessity, so too are certain chapters and verses of the Qur'an different. There are certain Qur'anic verses and chapters whose importance in comparison to others is like the importance of breathing compared to other bodily functions. There are also certain Qur'anic verses and chapters whose superiority to others is equal in rank to that of eating food several times a day. And finally, there are certain Qur'anic verses and chapters whose superiority to others is equal in rank to that of our occasional eating of certain luxury fruits.

If, for instance, we examine Sura Ikhlas in this respect, we notice that this chapter is of primary importance, declaring God's Oneness and Absolute Unity. Prophet Muhammad, peace and blessings be upon him, expended great effort to inform the Muslims of the importance of this chapter, encouraging them to read it and teach it to others. This chapter describes *tawhid*, or the absolute unity of God – the very core of the religion – in a way that instantly establishes the concept of the deity in the human mind. Throughout the Qur'an, every verse aims to establish and confirm four basic, universal truths, that is, the existence and Oneness of the Maker of the Universe, the Prophethood, the bodily Resurrection, and worship. God's Messenger describes the short Sura Ikhlas as being equivalent to one-third of the entire Qur'an, as pure *tawhid* is described in this chapter. *Ikhlas* means purity of faith, sincerity in religion, and the observation of the principles of Islam for the pleasure of God. This *sura* is the most precise and meaningful description of *tawhid*, or Oneness and Unity of God. In just six sentences, three positive and three negative, the *sura* proves and establishes various aspects of Divine Unity and rejects and negates all forms of association of partners with God. The superiority of this chapter is obvious as the recognition of God and His attributes is, more or less, equal to the importance of respiration for human beings as life would be meaningless without truly recognizing God Almighty.

Another important *sura*, Sura Fatiha, is recited in all *rak'ats*, or cycles, of the prayers. Sura Fatiha is the greatest prayer and the most internal supplication to God. A number of facts, such as God deserves to be worshipped, that only God provides help, being guided to the right path or being deviated from the right path is dependent only on God's will and that goodness and evil are all created only by God are all clearly mentioned in this chapter. The Qur'an has been revealed for the purpose of providing ultimate guidance for humankind and all the basic principles contained in the Qur'an are also outlined in Sura Fatiha. Because, the existence of One God, Who deserves all praise, recognition and worship,

Who has Sovereignty over all and on Whom everyone relies and depends, is explained in this *sura*, and our request to God to be pious, righteous people is stated. Thus, Sura Fatiha has a different status in comparison to the others; it balances praise in its first four verses with petition in the remaining, thus establishing the aforementioned four basic purposes of Qur'anic guidance in a marvelously succinct yet comprehensive way.

30 | Why is there no *basmala* at the beginning of Sura Tawba while there is one at the beginning of every other chapter?

This is the only *sura* in the Qur'an that does not begin with the *basmala*, the usual opening formula of *Bismi'llahir-Rahmani'r-Rahim*. Among the numerous reasons that have been narrated about this, the first reason is that God's Messenger did not order that the *basmala* be put at the beginning of this chapter. Therefore, neither his Companions nor the following generation put the *basmala* at the start of this *sura*. This feature is another proof that the Qur'an has remained without the least alteration, with utmost care being given to preserve and transmit it in its full and authentic form.

This chapter, which contains 129 verses, was revealed in Medina in the 9th year of the Hijra. The name *Tawba* is derived from one of the topics included in the verse. Another name for the chapter is *Bara'a*, which is the first word of the *sura*, meaning "to cut relations, give a warning or ultimatum." Sura Tawba deals with almost the same topics as those dealt with in Sura Anfal, and therefore is like a continuation of this preceding chapter.

Sura Tawba deals with the hypocrites, who are, indeed, more dangerous than polytheists, and who are willing to cooperate with the aggressors against their own community, and about their establishing the Masjid al-Dhirar (the mosque that was demolished on the command of the Prophet as it had been built by the hypocrites near Medina to distract the Muslim community and destroy unity of Islam.)

Like the Islamic salutation *Salaam Alaykum*, or "Peace be upon you," the *basmala* of "In the Name of God, the All-Merciful, the All-Compassionate" expresses security and the giving of quarter to those addressed. This *sura*, however, begins with an ultimatum to the polytheists. As it deals mostly with the polytheists, who were frequently violating their agreements and the intrigues of the hypocrites in Medina, it therefore is thought that it did not begin with the *basmala* that reminds the addressee of God's mercy and compassion.

CHAPTER 5

Compilation and Duplication
of the Qur'an

COMPILATION AND DUPLICATION
OF THE QUR'AN

31	How was the compilation of the Qur'an realized during the time of Caliph Abu Bakr?

Following the death of Prophet Muhammad, peace and blessings be upon him, it was realized that many of those who had died in military campaigns had been memorizers of the Qur'an, with around 70 dying in the Battle of Yamama alone; Umar ibn al-Khattab suggested to Caliph Abu Bakr that the entire Qur'an be compiled and written down. Abu Bakr entrusted this task to Zayd ibn Thabit, who had worked as a scribe for Prophet Muhammad. Zayd ibn Thabit was a leading scholar and memorizer of the Qur'an.

After carrying out this task meticulously, Zayd ibn Thabit prepared the official compilation of the Qur'an; however, he did not depend solely on his own memory, but rather searched for written texts from two separate persons as two proofs of each verse. Abu Bakr also openly demanded that every person in the city who had a portion of the Qur'an that had been written down bring it to Zayd ibn Thabit. At the same time, Umar first verified whether the Qur'anic portion in hands of the Companions had been written in the presence of Prophet Muhammad, peace and blessings be upon him, and then checked that such a revelation had been committed to memory by the Companions. Zayd ibn Thabit showed great care and dedication in this sacred task, and required two independent witnesses before accepting that a certain Qur'anic portion had been written in the presence of the Prophet. The main aim in this undertaking was not only to confirm the Qur'anic portion with one that had been memorized but also to ensure that it had been written in the Prophet's presence.

In connection with this precision, utmost care and dedication, it is impossible not to see the manifestations of Divine will and God's help, as mentioned in the verse, *"Indeed it is We, We Who send down the Reminder, and it is indeed We Who are its Guardian"* (Hijr 15:9).

The pages which were compiled during the time of Caliph Abu Bakr were known as a *mushaf*. This word literally means a manuscript that is bound between two covers as a single volume. After Abu Bakr, this *mushaf* was transferred to Caliph Umar and stayed with him during his lifetime; later being transferred to his daughter Hafsa. As a matter of fact, this was not the first time the Revelation had been recorded. Prophet Muhammad, peace and blessings be upon, had himself done the same thing when he was alive. But, the difference between the two undertakings is that during the Prophet's lifetime the Revelation had been written on sheets of various materials, whereas it was written and compiled between two covers during the period of Caliph Abu Bakr.

32 | How was the duplication of the Qur'an realized during the time of Caliph Uthman?

The Qur'an, in the form compiled during the time of Abu Bakr, was constantly in use during the rule of Caliph Umar and until the beginning of the era of Uthman, the third Caliph. During the rule of Uthman, the borders of the Islamic state became much greater and Companions were sent to various places for the purpose of conveying the message of Islam and enlightening the people. In every new destination, the people learned how to read the Qur'an as taught by the Companions. For instance, the people of Kufa learned the *qira'a*, or the style of reading of Abdullah ibn Mas'ud, while the people of Basra learned the *qira'a* of Abu Musa al-Ash'ari and the people of Damascus learned the *qira'a* of Ubayy ibn Ka'ab. In this way differences in the reading started to appear among the Muslims. The *mushaf* which was compiled during the time of Abu Bakr had been written by taking the "seven words" (dialects) into consideration; certain words were pronounced differently according to the local dialect. Although the spellings of words were the same, the way of reciting certain words was different. Caliph Uthman decided that the *mushaf* should be duplicated to meet the needs of the newly converted Muslims in provinces and to prevent any changes being made to the Qur'an. Caliph Uthman gathered and consulted with the Companions. He asked Hafsa for the *mushaf* that had been compiled during Abu Bakr's time and later transferred to her by her father Umar. Hafsa gave him the *mushaf* and Uthman selected Zayd ibn Thabit, Said ibn al-As, Abdurrahman ibn al-Harith and Abdullah ibn Zubayr to produce new copies of the *mushaf* and ordered them to write according to the dialect of the Quraysh.

The new copies of the Qur'an, after having been bound, were sent to various cities and provinces, including Medina, Damascus, Kufa, Basra, Mecca, Bahrain and Yemen. The Qur'an that we have now is the one which was originally prepared in the era of Caliph Uthman. It has remained exactly the same over the last fourteen centuries and there is not the slightest difference between the Qur'an that was recited during the earliest period of Islam and any other Qur'an that is printed and recited in any part of the Muslim world today. As for attempts by those who wish to cast doubts on the authenticity of the Book, especially unfounded accusations made against the Shiites of possessing a *mushaf* other than the one which is unanimously recognized by all Muslims throughout the history of Islam, Abu Jafar, a scholar of the Imamiyya group of Shiites explains their belief about the authenticity of the Qur'an as follows: "Such is our belief about the Glorious Qur'an which God Almighty revealed to Prophet Muhammad, peace and blessings be upon him: This Qur'an was no different than the one which is in

the hands of Muslims today. Its number of chapters, as accepted
by the majority of Muslims, is 114. But, in our opinion and belief,
a couple of the *suras* of Dukha and Sharh as well as the *suras* of Fil
and Quraysh and the *suras* of Anfal and Tawba are one chapter
rather than each of these being an independent *sura*. Any one who
attributes us the so-called belief that the Qur'an was more than it
is now lies about us."

In short, the authenticity of the Qur'an has been well preserved
in various ways. As far as the writing and copying of the Qur'an,
there are certain differences in the activities carried out during the
times of the Prophet, Abu Bakr and Uthman. During the lifetime
of the Messenger of God, Prophet Muhammad summoned his
scribes of the Revelations, and he carefully dictated the text of the
Qur'an to them, instructing them to write the Revelations on sheets
of various materials of the time. What was done during Caliph Abu
Bakr's time was the gathering of Qur'anic verses by careful collecting of the Revelations that had been written on surfaces of various
writing materials of the time. During the era of Caliph Uthman the
seven accepted variant readings of the Qur'an were replaced by the
dialect of the Quraysh, in which the Qur'an was revealed. This way
the unification of Muslims was ensured with a single *mushaf* in a
single dialect.

33   How and when were the diacritical marks and vowel symbols introduced in the Qur'an?

According to Islamic sources, there were not many literate
persons in Mecca during the time of the Prophet, and the
Arabic of the period did not use vowel symbols or diacritics to distinguish between the consonants that are similar in
form. When Islam had spread over vast territories and lands and
various non-Arab nations had converted to the Islamic faith, the
vowel symbols and diacritical marks were introduced in order to
ease the reading of the Qur'an.

Punctuation and vowel indicators in the *mushaf* was first introduced in response to a serious and urgent need at the time of Abdul Malik ibn Marwan in the 65th year of Hijra. In the beginning, dots were used instead of vowel symbols. A dot over the letter instead of *fatha* (vowel sign for "a"), a dot under the letter instead of the *kasra* (vowel sign for "i"), a dot in front of the letter instead of *dhamma* (vowel sign for "u"), and two dots instead of a *sukun*, (a stop) were being used. Even though the first usage of diacritics is said to have begun with Abu al-Aswad al-Dualy (D. 688), Hasan Basri (D. 728), Nasr ibn Asim (D. 707) or Yahya ibn Ya'mur, it seems more likely that Abu al-Aswad began this usage and the rest played important roles in its development. As a matter of fact, Nasr and Yahya were both students of Abu al-Aswad and were nominated to carry out this task on the order of Hajjaj.

The following is one of the most obvious and gravest cases of the need for the introduction of punctuation and vowel indicators. It is narrated that Ziyad, the governor of Basra, sent a message to Abu al-Aswad asking him to put some marks in the Qur'an so that the Word of God could be read correctly. Abu al-Aswad was reluctant to do such a thing. But, someone was reading the Qur'an one day and they mispronounced the word *rasuluhu* in the third verse of Sura Tawba as *rasulihi*, and thus made a grave mistake in meaning. This error changed the meaning in the verse from: *"God disavows those who associate partners with Him and His Messenger likewise disavows them"* to "God disavows those who associate partners with Him and disavows also His Messenger." So, Abu al-Aswad said: "God forbid! God cannot disavow His Messenger!", thus accepting the Governor's suggestion. Consequently, he put a dot over the letter for the vowel sign for "a", a dot under the letter for the vowel sign for "i" and a dot in front of the letter for the vowel sign for "u".

Later on, during the time of Abdul Malik (D. 705), the *i'jam* (the dotting of letter(s) in the Arabic alphabet) was needed in order to distinguish between those consonants that are similar in form. However, this use of the dotting system led to confusion with the aforementioned use of vowel indicators. Instead of using dots for vowels, the vowel symbols that we use today started to be used.

Manuscript copies of the *mushafs* were improved and beautified by the third century after the Hijra. Sura names, numerical verse indicators to separate the verses, the Arabic letter "م" (mim) to indicate a pause, the letter "لا" (lam'alif) for places where there was no pause, and letters like "ج" (jim) for cases where one can either pause or pass, have all been introduced to enable the correct recitation of the Qur'an.

In the beginning, many people were not pleased with such diacritics and vowel symbols that were seen as foreign elements to the *mushafs*. But, over the course of time, the necessity of such elements has become clear and their use has become common.

CHAPTER 6

Language of the Qur'an and Characteristics of Its Style

LANGUAGE OF THE QUR'AN AND CHARACTERISTICS OF ITS STYLE

34 | What are the stylistic characteristics of the Qur'an?

In each and every verse of the Qur'an there is an inimitable and eloquent style; this is apparent in the reminders, admonitions, narratives of bygone nations and in the more prosaic presentation of the truth. This eloquence is a distinctive feature of the Qur'an which renders it unique among all other books and also renders it incomparable in human communication. Therefore, it is not correct to compare it with any other word, literary style or work; rather it should be regarded as having a unique and individual style.

The style of the Qur'an is strikingly different from that of other books in both the choice of words and sentence construction. However, this style does not appear strange to us, even though each and every word has a style unique. By saying that the Qur'an has a unique style, this does not mean that it was revealed in a different language from that the Arabs were using. Although the same language that the Arabs were using every day is used in the Qur'an, the language of the Holy Book differs from that of the Arabs in many aspects. It may help to make a comparison here: Every tailor uses fabric to sew clothing. Even if they use the same fabric, the clothing that they create can all appear different to one another. That is, the clothing differs in accordance with the style and expertise of the individual tailor. In a similar way, the skill in using a language does not lie in the letters or words; that is, the same Arabic letters and words that are used everyday are employed in the Qur'an, but the style and eloquence of the Qur'anic text is inimitable, and nothing can even begin to compare to the language of the Qur'an.

Briefly if we are to mention only the literary aspects of the difference in style we can say the following:

The language of the Glorious Qur'an is so perfect, with its vowel sounds and pauses, with its elongated vowels and abrupt stops, that it is not possible to find the same in any other verse or poem. Everyone, even if they do not know Arabic, receives pleasure when listening to the Qur'an on some level. The words in the Qur'an take on completely different characteristics to all other words, and everybody, from the illiterate to scholars, receive a share from it.

Those who are well-versed in Arabic are amazed by the beauty of just one page of the Qur'an when compared to any other poem or work in Arabic. The Qur'an has a breathtakingly beautiful style with an authentic and unusual eloquence; anything like this has not been seen before or since. If a verse from the Qur'an is included within the works of famous literary figures, it is instantly noticeable, just like the voice of an angel can be detected among the melodies and fresh fruit among vegetables.

The Qur'anic verses can be distinguished among countless works in any language by their uniqueness. The language of the Qur'an is recognizable without any doubt, for it comes from a source that is different from any other source we know. While reflecting on the reasons why the Qur'an was sent down in Arabic, we should keep in mind the fact that, more than any other language, the pronunciation of the words and the conjugation of verbs in Arabic call to mind deeper meanings.

The Qur'anic verses are not only distinguished by their rhythm and inner harmony, but also by their grandeur. For example, if only a verse about the Flood is studied carefully, it is impossible not to feel this grandeur in the words that have a style so unique and wonderful: *"It was said: 'O earth, swallow up your waters! And, O sky, cease (your rain)!' And waters were made to subside, and (by*

God's will) the affair was accomplished..." (Hud 11:44). These are words of incredible majesty that fill the human soul with awe and dread. The word in the verse that has been translated as "swallow" is *abla'iy*, a word associated with the act of swallowing. The pronunciation of the word in Arabic is in keeping with its meaning. Each word in the verse carries the weight of mountains and has the influence of thunder. Then there is a sudden silence, a calm and a serenity as it ends, the raging storm ceases, and the story comes to a conclusion: "*...Then the Ark came to rest on al-Judi, and it was said: 'Away with the wrongdoing people!'*" (Hud 11:44).

By indicating this, which is only a mere drop in the sea of Qur'anic eloquence, we can understand from this verse that both the sky and the earth are under God's dominion and they obey Him alone, working under His absolute rule like the commander who says "Cease fire!" to the army. The Lord of the Worlds, to whom belong "*the hosts of the heavens and the earth,*" issued the command to the sky and the earth to annihilate the people of Noah; the sky and the earth reacted as if they were conscious beings angry at the unbelief and rebellion of the human beings. When they had carried out their duty, God Almighty decreed: "*Swallow up your waters, O earth! And, cease your rain, O sky! It is finished.*"

One can be aware of almost supra-human sentiments in these words, each one of which is as magnificent as if it has been carved out of hard rock, making apparent the weight and grandeur of each word of alpine magnitude. This important historic event of the Flood is described, with all its consequences and truths, in a concise, miraculous, and succinct manner; it would be impossible to replace any word or even any letter, or to formulate any other (similar) sentence of equal intensity and impact. If you like, try to replace one letter or word in the apparently simple sentence, made up of only ten words. But, the result will never be anywhere as powerful as the original. Just imagine the devastating impact that the Qur'anic verses of such magnitude had on the Arabs of the pre-Islamic era, a people who prized eloquence and rhetoric greatly.

The following event that took place in the early period of the Revelation also clearly indicates the wonderful beauty of the Qur'anic style: Walid ibn Mughira, one of the chieftains of the Quraysh, came to Prophet Muhammad, peace and blessings be upon him. He was greatly moved when the Prophet recited some parts from the Qur'an to him. He later went to his close relatives from the Banu Makhzum tribe and told them: "By God, I listened to some words from Muhammad a short while ago; these were not the word of a human or a jinn. What he said does not resemble any of these; it has such sweetness, such beauty. This speech is so sweet that its branches are fruitful, its roots are deep and productive! It is certainly bound to prevail and not be defeated."

Upon understanding that Walid was inclined towards the Message, the people of Quraysh said: "Walid has deviated from the path of his forefathers. By God, all the people of the Quraysh will follow him and will deviate from this path." Abu Jahl heard of this and he said: "Do not worry, I will dissuade him, and bring him back." Abu Jahl went to Walid and said sadly: "O Uncle! Your tribe has mobilized and is collecting money and property." When Walid asked the reason for this Abu Jahl replied that they were collecting money to give to Walid. He again asked the reason for this and Abu Jahl said: "Because they have heard that you went to Muhammad hoping for something from him." Walid responded: "The Quraysh certainly know that I am one of the richest among them." Abu Jahl then told Walid that he should speak against Muhammad so that they could hear and understand that he was not supporting Muhammad and that he denied the Message. Walid responded: "I do not know what to say! There is no one among you who knows poetry better than me. Nor is there anyone who knows the poetry of the jinn better than me. What Muhammad said does not resemble any of these!" But, Abu Jahl insisted and told Walid: "Your people will never be pleased with you unless you say something against him." Walid asked for some time to think. He thought for a while and then stood up and went to the gathering of his people; they demanded that he declare Muhammad crazy. But Walid said: "No, by God, he is not insane. We have seen insane people; the way one talks disjointedly and behaves foolishly in that state is known to all. Who would believe that what Muhammad presented was the incoherent speech of a madman?" Some people then stated that he should be called a soothsayer. Walid said, "He is not a soothsayer. We have seen the soothsayers. What they murmur and what they utter has no resemblance whatsoever to the Qur'an." Some other people said they should call him a poet. In return Walid said, "No, he is not a poet, for we know poetry in all its forms, and what he presents conforms to none of those forms." Some said they should call him a liar. Walid asked, "Have you ever heard him lie?" The people had to answer in the negative, but this left the problem of what they should call him. Walid asked for some more time to think. He finally said: "This is bewitching magic which could have been learned only from masters. This cannot be the words of a human being." These words made Walid's people happy, and they were all in agreement. The following verses were revealed concerning this incident and Walid:

> Leave Me (to deal) with him whom I created alone, and I enabled for him abundant wealth, and children around him as means of power; and I have granted him all means and status for a comfortable life. And yet, he desires that I should give more. By no means! Surely he has been in obstinate opposition to Our Revelations. I will oblige him to a strenuous climb. He pondered and he calculated (how he could disprove the Qur'an in people's sight). Be away from God's mercy, how he calculated! Yea, may God preserve him from the evil eye! How he calculated! Then he looked around (in the manner of one who will decide on a matter about which he is asked). Then he frowned and scowled. Then he turned his back and (despite inwardly acknowledging the Qur'an's Divine origin), grew in arrogance. And he said: "This is nothing but sorcery (of a sort transmitted from sorcerers) from old times. This is nothing but the word of a mortal." (Muddatthir 74:11-25)

35 | What is the divine wisdom behind the frequent repetitions in the Qur'an?

Human beings dislike repetition, no matter what is being repeated, whether it is the reiteration of words or having the same kind of food every day, even if it is something that they are very fond of. Likewise, people do not enjoy reading texts that are repetitious. If something is repeatedly mentioned in a poem, story, or novel it causes weariness and even makes the reader fed up. If the repeated thing is composed of the same sentences, then, it becomes inevitable that one will become very bored. However, this is not the case with the repetitions in the Qur'an.

Important matters which require our serious attention are repeated frequently in the Qur'an in such a way that they penetrate the life of all sorts of people, from those who are arrogant to the more retiring; these repetitions make them feel connected with the Qur'an, thus producing a feeling of peace and serenity on the reader. One of the best and most beautiful examples of this is that the Qur'an frequently utilizes repetitions, speaking of the same matter sometimes with a clear expression, sometimes with allusions, sometimes briefly, or sometimes in great detail; this repetition emphasizes and produces acceptance of the belief in the Divine Oneness and cures the spiritual illness of polytheism. Certain sentences, words and stories have been mentioned repeatedly in different parts of the Qur'an. All such instances of repetition are made with a definite aim and target, and they are never boring to the reader. With each repetition, the reader or listener is aware of different sentiments. The oneness and unity of God, for instance, is repeatedly mentioned, sometimes even in the very same verse; however, each time a different aspect of it is taken into consideration. Sometimes a certain aspect is dealt with in length while another is only mentioned briefly; sometimes we are presented with proof of the true faith, while at other times we are given a parable. The repetitions in the Qur'an have different styles in keeping with the purpose they are intended to serve. One such aim is to reinforce or intensify the message that is being conveyed and to influence the listener. In order to provide reinforcement, for instance, the same expression is repeated twice in, *"No indeed! You will surely come to understand (when death comes to you). Again, no indeed! You will surely come to understand it (when you are raised from the dead)"* (Takathur 102:3-4).

The Qur'an also deters with warnings. By repeating the same expression twice in the verse, *"What enables you to perceive what the Day of Judgment is? Again: What is it that enables you to perceive what the Day of Judgment is?"* (Infitar 82:17-18), the Qur'an intends to indicate that the Day of Judgment is such a serious subject, that the magnitude and horror of the doomsday is so great, that a feeling of awe is instilled in the heart of those who are being addressed. The following verse may be given as a further example of this: *"The sudden, mighty strike! What is the sudden, mighty strike? What enables you to perceive what the sudden, mighty strike is?"* (Qari'a 101:1-3).

The term *qari'a*, after which Sura Qari'a is named, is one of the names of the Day of Resurrection and is repeated here in the verse to raise a sense of awe about the dreadful occurrences on the Day of Resurrection. Another aim of such repetitions is to amaze and astound the reader/listener. The following verse is an example of this: The repeated words in, *"He pondered and he calculated (how he could disprove the Qur'ān in people's sight). Be away from God's mercy, how he calculated! Yea, may God preserve him from the evil eye! How he calculated!"* (Muddatthir 74:18-20) are, in fact, depicting the actions of a person, and it is as if a picture or even a snapshots has been made. First, this person pondered and then he plotted. He is afterwards cursed by divine ordinance: *"Be away from God's mercy"* and is ridiculed by the description, *"Yea, may God preserve him from the evil eye!"* The original of the initial phrases in these last two sentences, namely *"Be away from God's mercy"* and *"Yea, may God preserve him from the evil eye!"* is *qutila*, which has the meaning of both being removed from something and being protected against something. Its usage in the second case is figurative and derisive, and is telling us how badly this action was preformed to demonstrate how deserving this person was of the divine curse.

Another aim of the repetition in the Qur'an is to openly warn people and to receive a favorable response from the addressee. The Qur'an sometimes repeats certain words in the very same sentence or in two related sentences to heighten the awareness of its audience.

We can mention the verses, *"And the one who believed said (continuing his warnings): 'O my people! Follow me so that I may guide you to the way of right guidance. O my people! The life of this world is but a (passing) enjoyment, while the Hereafter – that is indeed the home of permanence'"* (Mu'min 40:38-39) as an example of this. The expression, *"O my people"* is repeated twice at the beginning of both verses, attracting the attention of the audience so that they will carefully listen to the message.

Another aim is to remind us of the core idea if the preceding sentences are lengthy. In such cases it is possible for the reader/listener to have forgotten what was mentioned before or their attention or focus may have wandered. Certain words are repeated in the middle or at the end of sentences to avoid this case, as in the following verses:

> Then **indeed your Lord is** – to those who do evil in ignorance (as a result of failing to counter the prompting of the evil-commanding soul), and then repent (soon as they realize what they have done is wrong) and mend their ways and conduct – **indeed your Lord is** All-Forgiving, All-Compassionate (with special mercy toward His penitent servants). (Nahl 16:119)

> (Remember) when God took a covenant from those who were given the Book: "You shall make clear to the people (the whole truth of all that is in) the Book (including mention of the Last, promised Prophet), and not conceal it." But they paid no heed to it, flinging it behind their backs, and sold it for a trifling price (such as worldly advantage and position, status and renown).

> How evil a bargain they made! **Never suppose that** those who rejoice in what they have thus contrived, and who love to be (famed and) praised for what they have not achieved (such as being devout and pious and defenders of God's law) – **never suppose that** they have saved themselves from the punishment: for them is a painful punishment. (Al Imran 3:187-8)

Another aim of such repetitions is to re-express the meaning that is related to the repeat. We also see that certain sentences or verses in the Qur'an have been repeated at certain intervals within the same chapter. Such repetition is neither unnecessary nor purposeless; rather, each one has a different goal. Each and every instance of repetition relates itself to a situation that is different to that of the previous one. For instance, the expression: *"Then, (O humankind and jinn) which of the favors of your Lord will you deny?"* is repeated 31 times in Sura Rahman. Each repetition is mentioned after a divine favor is described, and the intention is to remind both human beings and jinn of these divine favors and that they should show their thanksgiving to their Almighty Creator and not forget their duties as God's servants.

Likewise, in Sura Mursalat, the expression: *"Woe on that Day to those who deny!"* is repeated ten times. The meaning of each matter that is explained prior to the repetition of this expression should be taken into consideration to better understand the context. For instance, the first repetition is speaking of the Day of Judgment, the second repetition is associated with the torment that sinners will receive, the third repetition is concerned with God's Knowledge and Power, while the fourth tells us that humankind is needy and has limited power whereas Divine Power encompasses everything, and so on.

As has been clearly set out and explained until now, certain expressions are repeated in the Holy Qur'an. Such repetition might consist of words or sentences, but in all cases, the repetitions are made with a certain aim or purpose, not because there is a paucity of alternative words or sentences. Moreover, repetition influences the listener/reader to a greater degree. With this method the Qur'an aims to perfectly instruct and educate those whom it corrected, to train its students with the affection of a guide and to better convey the information that they need.

36 Oaths are sworn upon different things in the Qur'an. What is the divine wisdom of such oaths?

There are a number of things that are sworn on in the Qur'an. Such oaths may have been taken on something due either to the virtue of that thing, due to its usefulness, or because it is a glorious proof. Also, such oaths emphasize the importance of the thing that is sworn on, exalting it or drawing people's attention to the advice, lessons, benefits or losses that are contained in it. Some scholars state that the reason God swore upon His creatures is because they provide evidence for what is being discussed.

37 Is an accurate translation of the Qur'an possible?

Translation is the rendering of the exact words of an original text into another language. For a translation to be accurate it should be in keeping with the original language, expressing all the subtleties of the words, meanings, indications, allusions, fine points and reflecting its style, eloquence, concision, explicitness, impact and distinctness exactly; in short, a translation should be in keeping with the original text both syntactically and artistically. Otherwise, the translation cannot even approach the forms of the source language. On the other hand, although there are many similarities and common features between languages, there are also many different and distinctive features. Thus, it is possible to translate technical works that do not possess much literary value or artistry and which address only simple logic and the mind. But, success in translations of vivid and beautiful works which address the heart, sentiments, the mind and aesthetic pleasures and which also have literary value and art is quite a difficult task and sometimes may even be impossible.

As we look at the Qur'anic expressions, we can notice that they have been miraculously brought together in a vivid harmony that cannot have been achieved by anyone but God. The Qur'an challenges everyone if they do not believe that the Qur'an is the Word of God, openly inviting them to *"produce the like of it."* Even though the text appears to be simple and plain, it is beyond human power to imitate or produce anything similar to it. The Qur'an is miraculously inimitable; even listening to the recitation of the Qur'an gives pleasure to those who do not understand Arabic. Someone who knows a little Arabic instantly understands one meaning when they read or hear a verse and may think that he or she can also say similar things. But, once they attempt to imitate it, they see that the Qur'anic words have a range of meanings that are dependent on the context, making a true translation even more difficult. At the level of verses, it becomes even more elevated, profound, and immeasurable as they realize that a number of meanings spring up in every part of every verse.

No matter how lofty and unattainable the style of a human being may be, it can be imitated to some extent. Starting from the time of the revelation of the Qur'an, all the great literary figures and masters of Arabic eloquence have taken its style and eloquence as the ultimate example to follow and have so advanced themselves in Arabic language and literature. But no one who has dared to imitate the Qur'an has been capable of doing so. Therefore, not only is it impossible to produce any imitation or anything like the Qur'an in Arabic, it is also impossible to create something like it in another language. In the Qur'an, there are words that have extremely profound and deep meanings and words for which there are a number of diverse meanings, and there are expressions that have different nuances; understanding which one is meant is dependent on comprehension and interpretation. Although it is possible to produce some of these aspects in a translation, it would be impossible to include all of them.

A translation of the Qur'an reflects the degree to which the translator has understood all the meanings of the Qur'an. The end result therefore cannot be thought to be the same as the Qur'an, nor can it have the same value. The richness of the Qur'an is inexhaustible and its meanings are infinite; therefore it can never be fully understood. One meaning is given for a word, phrase or verse; but then yet another meaning if found, and another. While addressing the believer, the Qur'an hurls words to frighten the non-believer. While frightening the non-believer, the Qur'an alludes to some good news for the believer. While addressing the average person, it provokes thought among the refined. While speaking to educated people, it attracts the attention of the illiterate. While speaking to the ignorant, it arouses the learned. While mentioning the past, it points to the future. While depicting today, the Qur'an explains tomorrow. It leads to the highest realities from the simplest observations. While disclosing the *ghayb*, or the unseen of the past or future, to the believers, it leads the unbelievers to become wearied with the present. Moreover, the Qur'an relates all this with the most appropriate and the most beautiful words, in keeping with the situation, place, time and subject. For instance, when it relates how a rock cracks and water emerges, the Qur'an does not remain content with mere description, just using the Arabic terms, *yanshaqqu* or *yatashaqqaqu*, but rather uses the expressions, "*lama yash'shaqqaqu*" thus emphasizing the rushing and cracking sounds of the splitting of the rock and the subsequent flow of liquid. In this way in the same verse the Qur'an brings together many different meanings and many different numerous aspects.

Thus, a translation of the Qur'an is not the Qur'an and can in no way be considered to be the Qur'an, which is the miraculous

Word of God. It is not possible that people can have the power to reproduce that miracle.

The grandeur and elegance of the expressive style of the Qur'an diminishes in translation. Translators who have attempted to make the Qur'an accessible in their native languages admit that the translations of the Qur'an are incapable of conveying the rich meanings, indications and subtleties of the Word of God, rather only being able to express part of the meanings comprised in the verses. The French Professor Edouard Monted, honorary rector of the University of Geneva, explains this in his preface to the translation of the Qur'an, saying: "Whatever the judgment be about our explanations of the many subjects of the Qur'an, all those who can understand the Arabic Qur'an will agree on admitting the beauty of this religious book and the ultimate perfection of its expressive style. All its translations in the European languages are, unfortunately, unable to express or sense this beauty."[17] Georges Sale, another translator of the Qur'an, says: "Even though I have tried to make an impartial translation of the Qur'an, my readers will notice that I could not stay loyal to its text."[18]

In his preface, Muhammad Marmaduke Pickthall writes and expresses how impossible it is to translate the Qur'an: "The Koran cannot be translated. That is the belief of the old-fashioned Sheykhs and the view of the present writer. The Book is here rendered almost literally and every effort has been made to choose befitting language. But the result is not the Glorious Koran, that inimitable symphony, the very sounds of which move men to tears and ecstasy. It is only an attempt to present the meaning of the Koran – and peradventure something of the charm – in English. It can never take the place of the Koran in Arabic, nor is it meant to do so."[19]

The famous Brahman poet of India, Rabindranath Tagore, during his visit to Egypt, replied to those who asked him to translate those works he had written in his native language into English, replied: "Even though the works in my native language reflect my own views, I am unable to translate them into English, for, the

English language is unsuitable for such a translation." Thus, this example of a person who knows a language well admits the difficulty in translating their own views into that language makes it easier for us to understand the difficulty of translating the ideas of others into another language. If a person is incapable of reproducing the rich meanings and artistry of their own work in another language, the translation of the inimitable miraculous Word of God, which surpasses all human composition, is, naturally, all the more difficult.

38 | Is it possible to use the translations of the Qur'an during the recitation of the daily prayers?

It is a must to refer to the verses of the Qur'an and the practices of Prophet Muhammad (*Sunna*) to see whether a certain action is permissible or not. Reciting the Qur'an while performing the daily prayers, which is one of the five pillars of Islam, is an obligatory component that is laid down by the Qur'an and the Sunna.

God described the Qur'an as an Arabic Qur'an, and Prophet Muhammad, who was commissioned with following and practicing it, showed us how to perform the prayers. Throughout his life he performed his prayers with the Qur'an which had been revealed to him in Arabic. The Four Rightly-Guided Caliphs also performed their prayers with the Arabic Qur'an. Therefore, reciting the Arabic Qur'an in the prayers is obligatory (*fard*) for us. The following hadith is clear proof of the necessity of obeying the first four caliphs. Irbaz ibn Sariya tells us, "God's Messenger led us in prayer one day. Later, he turned his face to the crowd and made such a sublime and eloquent speech that the eyes of the listeners were full of tears and the hearts were full of excitement. A man from the crowd stood up and said: 'O God's Messenger, you speak as if you are giving a farewell speech. What advice can you give us?' 'I advise you to fear God, to listen to the orders of your leader, and to obey him, even if he is an Abyssinian slave. Those of you who survive will witness many disputes after me. So, I remind you of my Sunna and of the practice of the future Rightly Guided Caliphs, who will be on the right path. Obey them and hold to them firmly. Be alert and take care against things that are later invented, for, every invented thing (that is, that which is contrary to my practices) is an innovation (*bid'at*) and every innovation is a corruption and a perversion.'"[20]

The Companions of the Prophet who closely followed his example did not recite anything other than the Qur'an in their prayers. So, reciting some verses from the Arabic Qur'an is obligatory (*fard*) for us while performing the prayers. In addition, the entire community of Muslims has, since the beginning of Islam until today, performed their prayers, in all corners of the world, with the Arabic Qur'an. The Islamic community is unanimously agreed on this matter.

A person who reads the translation of the Qur'an in another language cannot be said to have recited the Qur'an. God Almighty says in the Qur'an:

> This (Qur'an) is indeed the Book of the Lord of the worlds being sent down by Him (in parts). The Trustworthy Spirit brings it down on your heart (O Prophet), so that you may be one of the warners (entrusted with the Divine Revelation) in clear Arabic tongue. (Shuara 26:192-195)

The Qur'an is a miracle both in its word and its meanings. If any alteration is made on it, its word harmony and order, which have been divinely determined, become disordered; it is no longer the Qur'an. Muslims are commanded to recite the Qur'an in their prayers. As no translation of the Qur'an can be considered to be the Qur'an, one cannot recite it in place of the Qur'an in their prayers. Muslim scholars are unanimously agreed that it is not permissible for the Qur'an to be recited in anything but Arabic while performing prayers.

39 | Why is the Qur'an in Arabic? How can the Qur'an have a universal nature if it was revealed in Arabic?

The guidance from God comes through the Prophets and the Messengers; they brought with them the Book from God in the language of their people. The fact that the Qur'an was revealed in Arabic is clearly referred to in the following verses:

> *Alif. Lam. Ra.* These are the Revelations of the Book clear in itself and clearly showing the truth. We send it down as a qur'an (discourse) in Arabic so that you may reflect (on both its meaning and wording) and understand. (Yusuf 12:1-2)

> We have sent no Messenger save with the tongue of his people, that he might make (the Message) clear to them. Then God leads whomever He wills astray, and He guides whomever He wills. He is the All-Glorious with irresistible might, the All-Wise. (Ibrahim 14:4)

> This (Qur'an) is indeed the Book of the Lord of the worlds being sent down by Him (in parts). The Trustworthy Spirit brings it down on your heart, so that you may be one of the warners (entrusted with the Divine Revelation), in clear Arabic tongue. (Shu'ara 26:192-195)

The divine reason why God sent Messengers from among human beings and why He revealed His Books to them was to guide His servants to the right path via the same Messengers and Books. God sent every Messenger to communicate in the language of his people. Prophet Moses and Prophet Jesus, peace be upon them, appeared among the Jews, the Books sent to them were revealed in Hebrew. In the same way God's Messenger appeared among the Arabs as the last link of the chain of Prophets and was sent with God's final Revelation to all humanity, which was in Arabic. The Divine reason why the Qur'an was revealed in Arabic is that the people, to whom the Qur'an was initially addressed, would better understand God's commands and prohibitions. If the Prophet had been sent revelations in different languages then his people would have been confused and would not have understood anything; they would have demanded an explanation. Accordingly, one of the purposes of the Qur'an being revealed in Arabic is that the Arab community was expected to understand the perfection of the Qur'an which was clear evidence to its being a divine Revelation. It was revealed to the Prophet in his own language and therefore, they could not hide behind any excuses of not being able to understand the Book. The fact that the Glorious Qur'an is in Arabic does not mean that it was revealed only for the Arabs. In the following verse, God Almighty calls on people to reflect on the fact that He never sent any Messenger but in the language of that Messenger's people so that the Message would be clear to them: *"We have sent no Messenger save with the tongue of his people, that he might make (the Message) clear to them."* (Ibrahim 14:4). This verse is does not mean that the Message brought by Prophet Muhammad, peace and blessings be upon him, is not binding for all to whom it is conveyed. God says in the Qur'an: *"We have not sent you but to all humankind as a bearer of glad tidings (of prosperity for faith and righteousness) and a warner (against the consequences of misguidance). But most of humankind do not know (this, nor do they appreciate what a great blessing it is for them)"* (Seaba 34:28). God's Messenger said, "Every prophet was sent to their people in their respective language. God Almighty has sent me to both the red-skinned and the dark-skinned from among His creatures." In another tradition, he says: "I have been granted five things which were granted to no one before me: God made me victorious with awe (He caused awe among my enemies) for a distance of one month's journey. The earth has been made for me (and for my followers) as a place for the offering of prayers and as a thing for purification (to perform *tayammum*); therefore anyone of my community can perform the prayers wherever they are at the time of a prayer. The gains of war have been made lawful to me yet it was not lawful to anyone else before me. I have been given the right of intercession (on the Day of Resurrection). Every Prophet was sent to his nation alone, but I have been sent to all of humanity."[21]

It is quite clear that even a Book with a universal nature must perforce use of the words of one of the many languages in the world so that people can understand teachings of the Book and convey its messages to other people, especially to those who are not conversant with the original language. This is the only way by which the Divine Message can become universally widespread. The verse, *"We send it down as a qur'an (discourse) in Arabic so that you may reflect (on both its meaning and wording) and understand"* (Yusuf 12:1) implies that the Revelation is sent in the language of the Arabs. The addressees of the Prophet at the time were unable to make any excuses or to say that they could not understand whether the message was true or not, as they did not understand the language. The words, subject, style and language of the Qur'an are all clear and it cannot be alleged that it was written by the Prophet himself or by any other Arabic speaking person.

God did not send any Prophet to people with a message that was in a different language. He sent them all Revelations in the language of their communities. This is *Sunnatullah*, or practice of God. Indeed, the fact that God sent every Messenger with a Book to their respective communities in their own languages so that the Prophets could easily communicate the religion to these communities and so that these communities could understand God's commands and transmit them to others is one of God's blessings. It is in this way that Almighty God made it easier for them to find and reach the truth. Thus, all Messengers were sent with a Book in the language of their people so that they would be able to explain the message for which they were responsible. They were also reminded that those who know something have a duty to inform others and those who are present must inform those who are absent. The mission of Prophets is to declare their Prophethood to their communities and to invite them to faith in God, whether they were sent to only a particular community or to other communities, or whether this is, as in the case of Prophet Muhammad, peace and blessings be upon him, all of humanity and the jinn. Such a duty is best fulfilled in the language that the community most easily understands. As in the verse, *"And (O Messenger) warn your nearest kinsfolk"* (Shuara 26:214), God's Messenger is ordered to warn first his kith and kin. Starting from his close relatives, the Prophet delivers the divine Message to all of his community and, during the course of such a delivery, those who know Arabic can render the Message into the languages of other communities and thus convey the Message to them. People with knowledge of more than one language thus have the honor of being messengers of the Messenger and heirs of the Prophet. In order to enjoy the same honor, other individuals also learn Arabic and the Message is conveyed widely from one language to another and from one community to another.

It should be noted that there must be other divine reasons for the revelation of the Qur'an in Arabic; some of these we can know, while others we cannot. One of these reasons may be that Arabic could be the most appropriate language in the human realm for Divine discourse. In the Qur'an, God Almighty described it as the *"Arabic Qur'an,"* thus making the Arabic language the vessel for His miraculous Book.

40	Are there words of the Prophet or other people in the Qur'an?

C ertainly their words are quoted and find place in the Qur'an. As we read the Qur'an, we see that the words and thoughts of Prophet Muhammad, other Prophets, peace be upon them all, as well as their people, Satan, the jinn, hypocrites, unbelievers and polytheists and also the sentiments of human self are all expressed in the Qur'an. However, every one of these people, who spoke in their own language, is quoted by God in Arabic in the Qur'an.

What is miraculous in these words is that they are expressed in unique ways by God. An example to make this situation easier to understand is when a number of cooks are given the same ingredients to prepare food. The master cook can prepare delicious dishes which everybody eats with great pleasure. As the skill is not in the ingredients, other cooks can prepare other dishes, but these will not be the same as that of the master cook. The case of the Qur'an is like this.

The Qur'an speaks to all humans and jinn, it gives some orders, places some prohibitions and discloses their and Satan's words. For instance, God Almighty expresses Satan's words verbatim and discloses his secret feelings. The miraculousness of such expressions is achieved not only by the expressions themselves, but by the quality of these expressions, the materials and motives chosen and the unseen character of the information given.

The different methods used in the Qur'an are extraordinary. Humans, jinns nor angels can achieve something similar. However, one must carefully examine the Qur'anic verses to discover their miraculous aspects. In the Qur'an, whether the person quoted is Satan, a jinn, an angel, the Pharaoh, Nimrod or a tyrant, the expressive style is uniquely Qur'anic and it is so wonderful that it is at once demonstrative and allegorical, satisfying all the senses, while still being open for wide interpretations and comments. There is no style that would enable the Qur'an to better be able to express such a goal with the same motives and materials.

41 | Why is the same event mentioned differently in different chapters of the Qur'an?

Certain stories of Prophets or narratives of past nations have been mentioned more than once in different Qur'anic chapters. Such repetition is not simply repetition for the sake of repetition, but it is, each time, the placing of emphasis on a different aspect of the same event; i.e., while some aspects of a story are dealt with in one chapter, other aspects of the same story are referred to in another chapter. When a verse is dealing with a certain matter, it is that aspect of the story that is found in the relevant verse. This is similar to the recording of a football match from more than one camera angle and later discussing the events of the match from the different recordings, choosing that which is most suitable for the aspect that is to be discussed.

An event may be mentioned in one place for a certain purpose in the Qur'an, while the same event is mentioned in another place from completely another aspect. For instance, an incident that is given in connection with an event concerned with the children of Israel during the time of Prophet Moses is given; later, the very same incident is told again, from another aspect, to give a totally different lesson. It can be used to relate their history, to comment on their behavior or to act as a means of giving advice, or all of the above at the same time.

When the different elements of one story that is mentioned in different chapters are brought together we can obtain a detailed but united picture of the same event, taken from different angles. However, if one does not carefully follow the stories it is possible to think that the same event is being mentioned over and over again, but in fact, a different aspect of it is being emphasized and a different scene is being put forth each time.

In these narratives, it is not the details of events that are important; rather whatever the reader needs to have explained is being provided in the right quantity. Even though the accounts of these events are given in different verses and chapters, they contain a freshness and originality each time. These different accounts make it possible to visualize the history of humanity before our eyes and thus we are able to extract the necessary lessons and warnings from these accounts.

42 God is described as "the Lord of the two easts and the Lord of the two wests" in the Qur'an. What does this mean?

In the Qur'an God Almighty is referred to as the Lord of the two easts and the two wests and as the Lord of the easts and the wests. The related verses are as follows:

> He is the Lord of the two easts and the Lord of the two wests. (Rahman 55:17)

> So, I swear by the Lord of the easts and the wests (i.e., the points of sunrise and sunset), that surely We are able to replace them with (others) better than them (in respect of faith in God and in their worship of Him), and We are not to be frustrated (in doing what We will). (Ma'arij 70:40-41)

Thus, according to these verses, there are two ultimate easts and two ultimate wests, and these verses indicate their utmost limits. The point at which the sun rises in the summer or in the winter is different. The sun, on the longest day of summer, rises at the farthest point in the east and sets at the farthest point in the west. On the shortest day of winter it rises at the nearest point in the east and sets at the nearest point in the west. Thus, the sun rises, every day, from a different point. Likewise, every day it sets from a different point, and this means that there are different points of setting. Consequently, the phrase *"the Lord of the two easts and of the two wests"* and *"the Lord of the easts and of the wests"* is used.

The phrases the two easts and the two wests might be referring to the longest and the shortest days of the winter and summer. These verses remind us that the sun rises and sets at the command of God and this happens every day from different angles. Another meaning might be that God, Who has absolute authority and control over the entire universe, is the Lord of both the world and the sun. Such a harmony would never exist if the two had different masters. Also, God is the sole Creator of the east, the west and everything in between. He is the Master and the Owner of the wise order of the universe, and He has full power and authority over every point in space and time and everything that occurs there.

43 | Why is the masculine form of address used in the Qur'an?

First it should be stated that the Qur'an addresses not only men, but all of humanity. There are more than thirty different forms of address in the Qur'an; it addresses the Prophet as "O Prophet," the believers as "O believers," the unbelievers as "O unbelievers," the wives of the Prophet as "O wives of the Prophet" and humanity as "O human beings," "O children of Adam," or "O My servants." Such forms of address as "O humankind," "O My servants," "O believers" or "O unbelievers" are not peculiar to men, but for everybody, man and woman alike. Arabic, like French and Spanish, is based on grammatical gender; even inanimate objects are masculine or feminine. Words like *amanu* or *kafaru* in these forms of address in the Qur'an are masculine forms of the words, but they do not refer only to the males but to both masculine and feminine genders, as in other languages.

44 | Why is Paradise used in a plural form in the Qur'an and sometimes referred to by different names?

The term *janna*, or heaven, literally means "to be covered" or "to cover with." All derivatives of this word have the meaning of being covered or being hidden. Derived from the same root, the term *jinnat* means madness, frenzy while *jann* means to darken or to make something invisible. Similarly, the spiritual beings the *jinn* have been so named because they are not visible. The term *janna* suggests that which is veiled, covered or surrounded; thus an enclosed garden that is luxuriant with foliage. As a religious term, *janna* means the land of happiness that is veiled and hidden in an unseen world and is invisible to our worldly eyes.

The Qur'an mentions not just one heaven, but many heavens when describing it. Therefore we understand that there are a variety of heavens in the Hereafter, not just one. This land of eternal bliss has been described in the Qur'an with the following names: *Dar al-Salaam*, (a place far and free from all hardships, calamities and difficulties), *Jannat al-Adn* (a place where the sources of everything and various blessings exist), *Jannat al-Na'im* (a place where different foods, drinks, clothing and vistas exist), *Jannat al-Firdaws* (the highest place), *Jannat al-Khuld* (a place to abide in forever), *Jannat al-Aliya* (a high, supreme and valuable place), *Dar al-Maqam* (a place to stay and rest in), *Jannat al-Ma'wa* (a place where the Archangel Gabriel and other angels and souls of martyrs permanently abide), *Dar al-Hayawan* (a place where there is a permanent life and there is never death). As we look at the descriptions of these heavens in the Qur'an, we see that God is rewarding the believers with various heavens depending on their deeds and actions; each of these has differing pleasures and rewards.

Heaven is a place where one receives rewards. God will reward His servants with blessings in the Hereafter after being tested and enduring this worldly life. The delights prepared for the blessed are concealed and difficult to imagine in our present state of existence; they will be totally different from those that are available in this world.

45 | What is the divine wisdom in God's referring to Himself sometimes as "I" and sometimes as "We" in the Qur'an?

In the Qur'an, God Almighty employs both the first person singular and plural, i.e., "I" and "We". If we examine the verses in which God uses the first person singular or plural, we see that He uses "I" in cases where only His entity and attributions are involved, or where He particularly addresses someone, or where no interference of any others is involved: *"...he was called by name: "O Moses! Indeed it is I, I am your Lord..."* (Ta.Ha 20:11-12).

God is speaking here to Prophet Moses, who is the only addressee of this speech. On the other hand, whenever God speaks of His own praiseworthy Attributes or whenever He addresses matters to everyone, the first person plural is used in the Qur'an. The following verse is an example of this type of address: *"We have not sent you (O Muhammad) but as an unequalled mercy for all the worlds."* (Anbiya 21:107). The Prophethood of God's Messenger is in everybody's interest. God has sent him as a mercy for all. God's mercy is so wide that it shows guidance and ways of salvation to all beings and explains them as a means of happiness both in this world and in the Hereafter. Even the non-believers have accepted many of his principles and have benefited from them in this world. Thus, the plural form of the divine voice is used in such verses.

Again in the verse, *"We have surely sent it (the Qur'an) down in the Night of Destiny and Power"* (Qadr 97:1) the Qur'an employs the plural form "We." The descent of the Qur'an is in the interest of all times and all places, not of only a particular people or place, and Archangel Gabriel accompanies it, with other angels witnessing its descent. Accordingly, the first person plural, "We," has been used for both God's exaltation and the angels' accompaniment of the Revelation.

Sometimes, by using "We," God Almighty might allow the angels who act as the supervisors in His sovereignty to participate in the process. The plural form "We" is generally used when the creation of the universe and the events that occur in it are mentioned; God has assigned every angel a certain duty and they perform their duties. This does not mean that God has left all the operational responsibility to His angels (God forbid!) and remains distant; rather He appoints them as His envoys in these processes.

CHAPTER 7

The Miraculousness of the Qur'an

THE MIRACULOUSNESS OF THE QUR'AN

46 | Why was the Qur'an revealed at different intervals and not as a whole?

The Qur'an certainly could have been revealed as a complete book in one single revelation. But it was revealed in sections over a period of twenty-three years. There are a number of divine reasons for this, including but not limited to the following benefits for God's servants and the Prophet:

a. To strengthen the Prophet's heart: The people whom the Prophet addressed were living in ignorance of the Unity and Oneness of God. With their tribal polytheistic belief, they indulged in many bad habits which they had inherited from their forefathers. The Prophet came to them at a time when they were practicing misguided customs and invited them to accept the Oneness of God and not to associate partners with God. However, at first the polytheists showed strong resistance to his invitation. They even tortured the believers as well as making things very difficult for the Prophet, labeling him as a "poet," "madman," "soothsayer" or "magician." Their anger against the Prophet and the believers was such that they spent their life immersed in feelings of hatred, cruel plots, and carrying out persecution against others. The tensions grew worse from year to year; after the death of Abu Talib, his most important protector, and his wife Khadija God's Messenger was very alone. At such a time of increasing difficulties, God did not abandon His Messenger, but rather reassured his heart, giving him support against the mischief of others and fortifying him with extra strength and power against all such unfavorable circumstances. This fortification was provided with the gradual revelation of the Qur'an. The Prophet's heart was also strengthened by meetings with Archangel Gabriel and he then felt that he was strong enough to endure all the hardships and tortures he had encountered during his Prophetic mission. The occasional slanders by the unbelievers against the Prophet and their allegations were rejected via the Revelation and in this way the Prophet was not abandoned.

God's Messenger was so concerned about the guidance of the people and so physically pained by their unbelief that God Almighty consoled him with the Qur'an; He informed Prophet Muhammad that the Prophet's role was merely that of a Warner and a Messenger, that embracing spiritual guidance can only be done according to God's will and that the reason of unbelief was (and is) due to their inability to see the truth, therefore this was not a fault of the Prophet.

Despite the heavy weight of the mission of Prophethood on his shoulders and the extreme difficulty he found himself in because of the aggression of the unbelievers, the Prophet was asked to be calm and patient; God reminded him that the Prophets who had previously shouldered the same heavy mission had also faced the same difficulties. The Prophet was further comforted by the good news that he would be under permanent divine supervision and protection, that his enemies would be defeated, and he would certainly be victorious one day.

God's Messenger received the Revelation whenever the need for guidance arouse. Sometimes the Prophet was asked questions to which he could answer only via the Revelations. Basing his decisions on the Revelation, he was also prevented from making any errors. In addition, if the entire Qur'an were to have been revealed all at once, the Prophet, not knowing how to read and write, might have suffered hardships in committing the entire text to memory. We know that he would be impatient until each newly revealed Qur'anic text was memorized. However, this gradual process insured that there was a better understanding and memorization of the Revelation.

The Qur'an was revealed in stages out of consideration for the Prophet; receiving the Revelation was a difficult experience for him. It is not difficult to realize what a strain it would have been for the Prophet if the Qur'an had descended all at once. Among the narrations we learn that the Prophet sweated a great deal, that the color of his skin changed, and that he became physically heavier during the Revelation of certain Qur'anic verses.

b. To provide ease and comfort for people: The believers and the Prophet were exposed to many hardships and troubles. They came face to face with the enemy during battles and were always anxious. The Qur'an rushed to their aid at such difficult times, calming and encouraging them by reminding them of the narratives of bygone communities and the hardships they had gone through:

> God has promised those of you who believe and do good, righteous deeds that He will most certainly empower them as vicegerents on the earth (in the place of those who are in power at present), even as He empowered those (of the same qualities) that preceded them, and that, assuredly, He will firmly establish for them their Religion, which He has (chosen and) approved of for them, and He will replace their present state of fear with security.... (Nur 24:55)

> Most certainly We help Our Messengers, and those who believe, in the life of this world and on the Day when the Witnesses will stand forth (to testify concerning people's response to the Messengers). (Mu'min 40:51)

During the time of the Prophet, the polytheists were indulging in all their misguided customs and behaviors that had existed before the advent of the Revelation and they were not inclined to abandon such bad habits easily or quickly. They had many irrational and absurd beliefs and much time was needed to divert them from such misguided practices. Thus, certain commands and prohibitions were gradually put into practice; it would not have been otherwise possible to attain positive results, in fact it would have been counter-productive to try to put an end to all the misguided customs at once. Aisha, the wife of the Prophet, clearly explains the rationale behind this gradual method. She tells us that in the early days of Islam only verses that sought to change a person's heart and mind were revealed and later the verses that laid down divine law were sent. She said: "People would have said 'We shall never give up alcohol' if the command 'Do not drink alcohol' had been revealed at the beginning. Likewise, they would have said 'We shall never give up adultery' if the command 'Do not commit adultery' had initially been revealed."

This method of gradual change was extremely effective in establishing a society free from evil, and we can detect the principle of gradualism in all the commands and prohibitions of Islam. By using such a method, the people gradually turned from committing bad acts and began to practice Islam with all its commands and prohibitions. In this way the spread of a new religion was made relatively easy.

The Qur'an was revealed first to a people the majority of which were illiterate. During the early period of Islam the number of believers was few, and thus neither writing the Qur'an, nor memorizing it and practicing Islam would have been possible if the Revelation had been sent down all at once. The revelation of the Qur'an in stages, thus, made the understanding, application and memorization of the Revelations easier for the believers.

c. To prove the uniqueness of the Qur'an: The Qur'an, even though it was revealed over a relatively long period of time, has never been proven to contain the least error or defect either in its wording or its meaning. On the contrary, the existence of a perfect consistency can be witnessed among its verses and chapters when a thorough observation is made. The fact that there is not the least inconsistency or defect in the Qur'an although it was revealed over such a long period of time is the best proof that it is not the word of human beings. Such a great diversity in time, place, occasion and context in any teaching would normally cause dissociation and disorder within the segments. But, the Qur'an marvelously attained a perfect and systematic completion, although it was revealed gradually in parts.

| 47 | What is meant by the Qur'anic letters (*huruf al-muqatta'at*) and why are they used at the beginning of certain chapters? |

The Qur'anic term *huruf al-muqatta'at* is used for certain Arabic letters that are found at the beginning of several chapters in the Qur'an. There are fourteen different Arabic letters making up thirteen different sets of Qur'anic initials found in various combinations at the beginning of twenty-nine chapters; these are either in the form of single letters at the beginning of some chapters or are found in different combinations of up to five letters at the beginning of other chapters.

There are basically two different opinions pertaining to the meanings of these letters. According to the first opinion, these letters are considered to be a kind of cipher between God and His Messenger, the exact and complete meaning of which is unknown to anyone but God Almighty and His Messenger. According to another opinion, the Qur'an was revealed in order to be understood and thus, these letters should have some meanings. Nevertheless, there is quite a variety of different views about what is meant by these letters. The different views are basically as follows:

a. These letters refer to the names of certain chapters when used singly like *qaf*, as in Sura Qaf and *sad*, as in Sura Sad.

b. These letters denote certain attributes of God.

c. These are the letters by which God swears, as in: "*Qaf. By the Qur'an most sublime*" (Qaf 50:1).

d. With such letters, God, the Supreme Creator, openly challenges both the Arabs of the time and all future generations about the matter of the revelation of the Qur'an.

God's Messenger was an illiterate person who did not know how to read or write. It is impossible for an illiterate person to recite these letters. As since these letters do not belong to the Prophet himself, the Qur'an does not belong to him either and he is teaching the Qur'an to us after having received it from God, the All-Wise, the All-Knowing.

Secondly, the Qur'an uses the letters of the Arabs. Had the Prophet, as they alleged, learned the Qur'an from a human being, they themselves as well would have been able to produce one chapter like it, as the Meccans of this time were superior in Arabic eloquence and rhetoric. Hence, these letters challenged them and proved their impotence in a style with which they were not familiar.

e. These letters are an indication of the Qur'an's uniqueness which is displayed in the following manner:

1. **The inimitability of the Qur'an:** Evidence for the inimitability of the Qur'an and its divine authorship is presented in the Qur'an in the form of a challenge; it is stated that humankind is not able to produce anything like the Qur'an. God has warned us with these letters, saying, "The Qur'an is composed of letters which you already know well, you who are at the peak of Arabic eloquence. Come and invent a similar book, if you can!" When the Qur'an was revealed, eloquence, oration and poetry were held in the highest regard among the Arabs, and therefore they should have been able to utilize these mere letters with which they were familiar and from which the Qur'an had been miraculously composed of, thus gaining a victory over the Prophet and the Qur'an, both of which they regarded as prime enemies. However, they were unable to produce anything that was even like one of its chapters. This fact clearly shows that the Qur'an is the Word of God, not that of any human.

2. **The authenticity of the Qur'an:** Arabs used to attribute certain meanings to letters and utilize them as abbreviations though this was not a frequent practice. The use of such letters in the Qur'an at the beginning of certain chapters was still a novel practice, and was not in imitation of any poet or preacher. The Qur'an also proves its inimitability in this respect.

3. **The uniqueness of the Qur'an due to the interrelation of these letters with the relevant chapters:** The single letters found at the beginning of some chapters have a close interrelation with the general contents of the related chapters. Such interrelations are valid in both their words and meanings. If we look at Sura Qaf, which starts with the line, "*Qaf: Wal-Qur'anil-Majid,*" ("*Qaf. By the Qur'an most sublime*") for instance, we see that many rhymes are based upon the letter *qaf* and that this letter frequently appears in the words used in the sura.

Likewise, the letter *sad* has been used often in Sura Sad. Also in this chapter another feature of this letter becomes apparent; it has been used for words that imply *khusuma*, or opposition and enmity. This is present throughout the whole *sura*.

First and foremost, the enmity and opposition of the unbelievers towards the Prophet is expressed in the initial verses of Sura Sad. Later, the dispute of two men who came to Prophet David is mentioned in verses 21 and 22 in the same *sura*. Then, the discussions of the people of hell are given in verses 63 and 64. Finally, we see Satan's disobedience to the command of God to prostrate before Adam in verse 76 of Sura Sad.

In addition to all of the above, the letter *sad* is frequently used in this chapter within many other words. In Arabic the letter *sad* is also considered to be a symbol and reflection of patience and self-sufficiency, which are believed to be the Divine Attributes of *As-Sabur*, or the All-Patient, and *As-Samad*, or the Eternally-Besought-of-All Who is in Need of Nothing and on Whom Everyone Relies. But, in the sense of human patience it is the Prophets that hold the highest rank; Prophet Job is presented as an example of such human patience as expressed in the verse, "...*Surely, We found him (Prophet Job) full of patience and constancy. How excellent a servant! He was surely one ever-turning to God in penitence*" (Sad 38:44).

All twenty-nine chapters that begin with Qur'anic initials mention the Qur'an itself or its gradual descent (*tanzil*) or revelation (*wahy*) immediately after these letters. It should be noted that there are 28 letters in Arabic alphabet and half of these 28 letters are used at the beginning of chapters. These 14 letters that are used in different combinations as Qur'anic initials appear more frequently in the Qur'an than the other letters of the Arabic alphabet. These letters seem to be an introduction or indication of something that is important. At first glance their usage may appear meaningless; one reason behind this may be to make any opponents helpless and deprive them of any means to employ. They may be divine passwords or codes which are not able to be solved by human comprehension. It would not be wrong, however, to say that they draw attention to the Qur'an and to its inimitability. These letters also indicate the extraordinary intelligence of the Prophet and make it clear that only he could understand and comprehend the exact meanings of the most secret letters and symbols found here.

48	How can we explain the harmony in both the wording and meaning of the Qur'anic verses?

The words of the Qur'an are in perfect harmony with their meanings. They are free of the least defect and far from excessiveness or any deficiency. This may be something that appears difficult to achieve but it is clear that the Qur'an has succeeded in doing so where other written works fail. Even the most eloquent works of literary masters seem to be lacking something if they concentrate more on the meaning than on the words.

The more details that an author tries to give, the more words they have to use. There is no single page in the Qur'an where it is possible to replace a word with some other and make it "better" nor is it possible to say that even a single letter is superfluous. The following is just one of the striking examples of the miraculous eloquence of the Qur'an: *"And yet, if but a breath of your Lord's punishment touches them, they are sure to cry: 'Oh, woe to us! We were indeed wrongdoers!'"* (Anbiya 21:46).

This verse ironically uses the expression, "If but a breath of punishment" to refer to the slightness of the punishment in order to indicate the power of God's punishment; the entire sentence expresses this slightness and thus reinforces the meaning. The words, *la-in*, or "If but," signify uncertainty and this doubtfulness implies the meagerness of the punishment. The word, *massa* means "to touch slightly" and it also refers to slightness. The word, *nafhatun*, or breath, refers to a mere puff of air. This word is used without the definite article, which in Arabic indicates indefiniteness, again underlining the quality of slightness. The word *min* means "a bit" and thus indicating paucity. The word *'adhab* is a slighter punishment than other Arabic terms such as *nakal* or *iqab*. The use of the word *Rabb*, meaning Lord, Provider, and Sustainer, suggests affection as compared to such other Divine Names, like *Al-Qahhar*, or The Overwhelming, *Al-Jabbar*, or All-Compelling, and *Al-Muntaqim*, or Ever-Able to Requite, and thus also imply a slightness or gentleness. Therefore, if so slight a breath of divine punishment has such an effect, then imagine how severe the grand punishment dealt out by God is! In just this short sentence we can see how the parts are related to each other and complement one another. This example alone is enough to demonstrate how carefully the words in the Qur'an are chosen, the depths of their meanings, and the wisdom inherent in their selection. This is valid and applicable for the entire Qur'an. The verses were revealed by God for human comprehension and are superbly suited for this, but at the same time, they have an inimitably elevated style.

49 How does the Qur'an take the psychology of human beings into consideration while addressing them?

The Qur'an has been revealed for all of humanity so that they may be guided to prosperity in both worlds through the acceptance of faith, the performance of righteous deeds and the purification of the heart; in this way the Qur'an takes all human feelings into consideration. Humanity has a variety of emotions, like fear, love, anxiety about the future, excitement, emulation, desire for eternal life, etc. These feelings do not appear in the same degree or intensity in everyone. In some fear is more dominant, while in some others it might be love, or the desire for immortality. The Supreme Creator, when calling out to humankind, addresses such feelings and invites them all to believe in Him. In the Qur'an there are various psychological portrayals, depictions and narratives which stimulate various aspects of human sentiments and thus be either desired for or feared via these emotions. However, the aim of the Qur'an in presenting these situations is to correct and improve human beings and to convey Qur'anic truths to them, while encouraging them to avoid pursuing fantasies and whims. So that no one will be deprived of the message of Islam the Qur'an addresses all the emotions of all human beings and uses all such methods to influence them more effectively.

In pursuit of such a goal the Qur'an speaks to believers about the rewards of Paradise by focusing on their emotions towards certain things. Details of the Paradise that has been promised to believers and the blessings that will be granted therein are all explained vividly. The following verses are but a few of this type:

> The Paradise promised to the God-revering, pious ones can be likened to a garden through which rivers flow. Its produce is everlasting, and so its shade. That is the ultimate outcome for those who keep from disobedience to God in reverence for

Him and piety, just as the ultimate outcome for the unbelievers is the Fire. (Rad 13:35)

Whereas the companions of Paradise will, on that Day, have appointed for them the best abode and the fairest place of repose. (Furqan 25:24)

On that Day you will be arraigned for judgment, and no secret of yours will remain hidden. Then as for him who is given his Record in his right hand, he will say: "Here, take and read my Record! "I surely knew that (one day) I would meet my account." And so he will be in a state of life pleasing to him, in a lofty Garden with clusters (of fruit) within easy reach. "Eat and drink to your hearts' content for all that you sent ahead in advance in days past (in anticipation of this Day)." (Haqqa 69:18-24)

(They will be seated) on lined thrones (encrusted with gold and precious stones), reclining upon them, facing one another. There will go round them immortal youths, with goblets, and ewers, and a cup from a clear-flowing spring, from which no aching of the head ensues, nor intoxication of the mind; and with fruits such as they choose, and with the flesh of fowls such as they desire, and (there will be) pure maidens, most beautiful of eye, like pearls kept hidden (in their shells), a reward for all (the good) that they used to do. They will hear there neither vain talk nor accusing speech; (They will hear) only speech (wishing) peace and security after peace and security. And the people of the Right (the people of happiness and prosperity who will receive their Records in their right hands): how happy and prosperous are the people of the Right! Amidst cherry trees laden with fruit and banana trees with fruit piled high, and shade long-extended, and water gushing (and flowing constantly), and fruits (of every other kind) abounding, never cut off, nor forbidden. And (with them will be their) spouses ennobled with beauty and spiritual perfection: We have brought them into being in a new creation; and We have made them virgins, full of love for their husbands, and equal in age for the people of the Right (the people of happiness and prosperity). (Waqi'a 56:15-38)

> He will reward them for all that they endure: a Garden (of Paradise) and garments of silk, reclining therein on thrones. They will find therein neither (burning) sun nor severe cold. And its shade will come down low over them, and its clusters of fruit hang down low within their reach. And they will be served with vessels of silver and goblets like crystal, crystal-clear, made of silver – they themselves determine the measure of the drink (as they wish.) And there they will be given to drink of a cup flavored with ginger (of Paradise), (filled from) a spring therein called Salsabil (as it flows smoothly and continuously as they wish). There will go round them youths of perpetual fresh-ness; when you see them you would think them scattered pearls. And wherever you have a look therein, you will see unimaginable delight and a great kingdom. Upon those (ser-vants) will be garments of fine green silk and brocade, and they will be adorned with armbands of silver; and their Lord will favor them with the service of a pure drink. "This is what has been (prepared) for you as a reward, and your endeavor has been recognized and accepted." (Insan 76:12-22)

In the verses above, details of Paradise are vividly explained and human sentiments are delicately touched upon; thus it is almost unimaginable for an ordinary person not to feel a strong desire or interest towards Paradise or to desire to go there.

Likewise, by activating sentiments of fear in human beings, the existence of Hell, its horrifying conditions that will be encoun-tered there and some of the terrible punishments that were inflict-ed on previous nations are all mentioned as lessons to people so that they are mindful of them and carry out their lives in this world accordingly. The following verses are only a few examples of this kind of verse:

> They (both the Messengers and unbelievers) sought a judg-ment (through test of right and might), and in the end every stubborn tyrant was frustrated (made to fail), and Hell is awaiting him, and he is made to drink of oozing pus, sipping it little by little, yet hardly able to swallow it, and death besets him from every side though he cannot die, and a still harsher punishment lies ahead of him. (Ibrahim 14:15-17)

Whoever comes before his Lord as a disbelieving criminal, for him surely there will be Hell: he will neither die therein nor live. (Ta.Ha 20:74)

And We did indeed send Messengers to the communities before you, and We seized those (communities) with trials and tribulations so that they might invoke Us with humility (seeking the truth and forgiveness). If only, when Our trial came upon them, they had invoked Us with humility! But their hearts grew hard and Satan decked out whatever they were doing as appealing to them. Then, when they forgot (the advice and warnings) that they were reminded of, We opened for them the gates of all things, until, even while they were rejoicing in what they were granted, We seized them suddenly, so then they were plunged into despair. (An'am 6:42-44)

The Day when they will come forth (from death), with nothing of them being hidden from God. Whose is the absolute Sovereignty on that Day? It is God's, the One, the All-Overwhelming (with absolute sway over all that exist). On that Day every soul will be recompensed for what it has earned; no wrong (will be done to any) on that Day. God is Swift at reckoning. (Mu'min 40:16-17)

By focusing on the natural tendency of human beings to emulate others, examples of the good behavior of others are encouraged as the aim is to educate future generations with high moral standards.

By nature some people are more sensitive to tidings about Hell and are deterred by such, while others are more influenced by the glad tidings of Paradise and its depictions. Likewise, some people are disposed to avoid being exposed to evil and calamities, while some others enjoy following good and exemplary personalities. In fact, such diverse warnings and lessons could well apply to the same individual at different times. Thus we can understand that such an approach takes into account all aspects of an individual or all of humankind. This is an ideal method for disciplining and improving human characters and the Qur'an carefully implements this method and takes into account all human sentiments.

| What is the significance of the linguistic miraculousness of the Qur'an?

God Almighty granted every Prophet He commissioned miracles in fields in which the people of the time were accomplished. The most miraculous aspect of the Qur'an, revealed at a time when Arab literature was at its peak, was its linguistic perfection. God Almighty employed eloquence as the most notable aspect of the Qur'an, and this was the chief miracle of God's Messenger. It is well-known that eloquent speech and poetry were a major influence that shaped the social life at that time. This love for language was associated with the poets who had developed a poetic heritage over many centuries of oral tradition. Poetry contests, which were frequently held, were part of the tribal code of Arabia.

When the Qur'an was recited to the Arabs, they could not help but notice the brilliant linguistic melody that was contained in the letters that made up the words and in the words that made up the verses. With its inner rhythms, sound patterns, and textual dynamics the Qur'an appeared as a peerless poetic masterpiece, elevating people to the realms of grand meanings. This was a challenging miracle which they could have never coped with and plainly displayed the ultimate helplessness and impotence of human beings.

The Qur'an is the peak of literary art and we clearly witness this fact in the following verse:

> And it was said: "O earth, swallow up your waters! And, O sky, cease (your rain)!" And the waters were made to subside, and (by God's will) the affair was accomplished. Then the Ark came to rest on al-Judi, and it was said: "Away with the wrongdoing people!" (Hud 11:44)

The words above are awe-inspiring and of a magnitude of grandeur for the human spirit. A single word here carries the weight of a giant mountain and roars like thunder. Suddenly once the words have finished and the narrative has ended there is silence, serenity, calmness and a sudden cessation of universal wrath.

One feels the existence and influence of superhuman might in these magnificent words, which appear as if chipped out of a hard rock and one feels the mountainous weight and magnitude of each letter in these words. It is absolutely not possible to change any letter in this verse, nor to replace any word with another or to formulate another sentence that will produce a meaning, magnitude, action or tune that is similar. One can try to replace a letter or even a word with one another in this modest 10-word sentence. If you do so, you will have caused this unparalleled sentence to lose its beauty and eloquence, you will have simplified its style and it will have become as dry as barren land. In short, the Qur'anic verses, due to their magnitude, created an impact, the like of which had never been experienced, among the Arabs of the pre-Islamic era who loved literary eloquence and rhetoric.

The Qur'an, which surpassed all the masterpieces of Arab literature, has caused all to pay heed to it with its style and has inculcated the Islamic faith to men and women of all ages, young and old alike. Thanks to the miraculousness of its elevated style, which is pleasant for all hearts, even its most notorious enemies, like Walid ibn Mughira and Abu Jahl, could not help but listen to it. It was the style of the Qur'an that turned a stern man like Umar ibn Al-Khattab, on his way to kill the Prophet, into the most honorable Umar Al-Faruq (so called by the Prophet after becoming Muslim and declaring the truth of Islam openly); it was the style of the Qur'an that made Utba ibn Rabia say, "I heard words from Muhammad that I have never heard before. It is neither poetry nor soothsaying, and resembles no such thing. O people of Quraysh! Listen to me! Stay away from him, for if he is not successful, you will thus get rid of him, but if he is successful, then his victory will be your victory." Again it was this elevated style of the Qur'an that made Labid, the poet of one of the famous "Hanging Odes," or

Muallaqat, (the celebrated seven odes that were hung on the black cloth suspended from the walls of Ka'ba in the pre-Islamic era) exclaim: "It is not fitting that I should write poetry now."

| 51 | Can the compilation of the Qur'an explain its miraculousness? |

The Qur'an descended over a relatively long period of time, that is, 23 years; it was often revealed upon various occasions or incidents, when there was a need for divine guidance, as a response to either an inquiry, for the solution of an issue, or to correct a misunderstanding, or for a number of other reasons. Despite the length of the Qur'an or that it was revealed for various reasons, at various times or in various places, there are no discrepancies or contradictions in it; this fact clearly proves that the Qur'an is the Word of God and that it brings together all its many elements harmoniously is only a miracle of the Qur'an. If, for instance, we take Sura Baqara, although it was revealed over a long period of time, in total on 80 separate occasions, it appears to have been revealed all at once due to the close interrelation of the subject matter of the verses.

We may consider the same, also, for other chapters and verses of the Qur'an. If the Qur'an is approached from this standpoint, it does indeed appear as if it descended all at once, despite being revealed in parts at different times. This is a feature peculiar to the Qur'an and cannot possibly be attributed in any other literary work.

Whenever a verse or a group of verses was revealed, the Prophet would carefully dictate the contents and instruct the scribes where these were to be placed in relation to other verses and chapters. The arrangement of chapters and verses is not according to the order of their revelation. There are a number of individual chapters that were revealed all at once while others were revealed in stages. Also, in the Qur'an there are verses that were revealed earlier but were put after other verses in accordance with divine instruction. So, the fact that the Qur'an reflects utmost harmony and integrity, as if it were revealed all at once, shows that there was a miracle according to its method of compilation.

52 | It is said that the Qur'an is inimitable (that no one can produce the like). What does this mean?

At the time the Qur'an was revealed, eloquence, oratory and poetry were held in the highest regard among the Arabs. Everybody, from believers to skeptics and nonbelievers, was amazed at the verbal elegance, totality and flawlessness of the Qur'an, as well as by those features which are beyond human capability of expression. The Qur'an challenged first the literary geniuses of the time and then all of humankind until the Last Day; it has challenged all those who doubt its Divine authorship and its authenticity to compose a similar piece of text. This challenge of the Qur'an can be seen in the following:

> And yet, now that the truth has come to them from Us (through a Messenger), still they say (by way of an excuse for their denial of it), "Why has he not been granted the like of what Moses was granted (all at once)?" Did they not previously refuse to believe in what had been granted to Moses? They said: "Both are sorcery, each supporting the other." They also said: "In each we are unbelievers." Say (to them): "Then bring another Book from God which would offer better guidance than either of these two so that I may follow it, if you are truthful (in your claim that they are both sorcery)." If they cannot respond, then know that they are merely following their whims and caprices. Who can be more astray than he who follows his lusts and fancies deprived of all guidance from God? God surely does not guide people given to wrongdoing and injustice. (Qasas 28:48-50)

> Say: "Surely, if humankind and jinn were to come together to produce the like of this Qur'an, they will never be able to produce the like of it, though they backed one another up with help and support. (Isra 17:88)

> Or they say (about the Messenger): "He fabricates it (the Qur'an)"? Say (to them): "Then produce ten invented surahs like it (in eloquence, meaningfulness and truth), and call to your aid whomever you can, apart from God, if you are truthful (in your claim, not deluded or just making up excuses to justify your unbelief). "If they (whom you call to your aid) cannot answer your call, then know that it (the Qur'an) is sent down as based on God's Knowledge, and that there is no deity save Him. Will you, then, submit to God as Muslims?" (Hud 11:13-14)

Here the Qur'an effectively proclaims: "If you are correct in your doubts and allegations that the Prophet invented this Qur'an and then attributed it to God, then put forth at least ten chapters of a thing similar to those in the Qur'an, either by yourselves or seek the help of persons of your choice or the deities you worship." But, the unbelievers were helpless and incapable to rise to this challenge. Then the Qur'an challenges those who claim that the Qur'an is the speech of the Prophet, saying:

> Or do they say: "He forges it (and then attributes the Qur'an to God)?" No indeed. Rather, (they make such claims because) they have no will to believe. (If they really believe such a Book can be forged) then, let them produce a Discourse like it, if they are truthful (in their claims). (Tur 52:33-34)

These verses challenge the unbelievers to bring forth a word that is as beautiful as the Qur'an and which has the same supreme features as it, both in wording and meaning. If the Qur'an was words invented by man, then other men, logically, would be able to create a text similar to it; people who were concerned with oration, speech and poetry, who were experienced in the styles of poetry and prose and who were literate and well-versed in history and phenomena, as they too, like the Prophet, were human. How could they refuse to believe in what God had sent down and become nonbelievers when they were unable to rise to the challenge?

> And this Qur'an is not such that it could possibly be fabricated by one in attribution to God, but it is a (Divine Book) confirm-

ing (the Divine origin of and the truths that are still contained by) the Revelations prior to it, and an explanation of the Essence of all Divine Books – wherein there is no doubt, from the Lord of the worlds. Or do they say that he (the Messenger) has fabricated it? Say: "(If it is possible for a mortal to fabricate it) then produce a surah like it and call for help on anyone you can, apart from God, if you are truthful (in your doubt and the claim you base upon it)." No (they are not truthful in their doubt and claim), but they have denied a thing (the Qur'an) whose knowledge they could not encompass and whose exposition (through the fulfillment of its promises and threats) has not reached them. Even so did those who were before them deny (the Books sent to them). So look! how was the outcome for the wrong-doers (who judged and acted wrongly)? (Yunus 10: 37-39)

This is the ultimate challenge to the unbelievers, and they are asked to bring forth a text similar to just one chapter of the Qur'an.

If you are in doubt about the Divine authorship of what We have been sending down on Our servant (Muhammad) (and claim that it is the work of a human being like Muhammad who is illiterate), then produce just a surah like it and call for help to all your supporters, all those (to whom you apply for help apart from God), if you are truthful in your doubt and claim. If you fail to do that – and you will most certainly fail – then guard yourselves against the Fire whose fuel is human beings and stones (that you have shaped into idols to adore), prepared for the unbelievers. (Baqara 2:23-24)

These verses certainly reinforce the Qur'an's foothold at the peak. With the clear expression of *"You will most certainly fail to do so,"* the Qur'an not only makes clear their humiliation in this world, but also shows them their place in Hell. When faced by this straightforward challenge by the Qur'an, if they had the ability to respond they never would have remained silent or wait, even for one second. But, they were completely unable to rise to the challenge. Instead they took up arms instead of using words to speak on their behalf; they had totally lost hope and had realized their complete impotence in this regard. War is the final refuge of those

who have been defeated and who cannot peacefully defend themselves by pen or through dialogue.

The Qur'an's open declaration about the absolute inability of
the unbelievers in this respect and the fact that this declaration has
remained as the truth since this time is just one of the indubitable
miracles of the Qur'an. It is completely different from all kinds of
human words and this difference is eternal, ensuring that the Word
of God will remain the ultimate truth for all times.

	How should we understand the verse, *"Had the Qur'an*
53	*been from any other than God, they would surely have found*
	in it much incoherence or inconsistency"?

No human being has been able to find a defect in the
Qur'an and they never will be able to do so. Nothing
contrary to pure reason, true science or human psychology has been or will be found in the messages of the Qur'an, in the
excellent and universal legal principles it contains, nor in its commands and prohibitions which it introduces for perfect individuals
and societies. The Qur'an would not be a miraculous, unique Book
if it were not the Word of God. On the contrary, some parts of it
would have been great, some parts defective, some parts would have
been acceptable and other parts objectionable. If we take into
account the numerous explanations within so many different frames
of references then we can understand that the totality and textual
integrity of the Qur'an could not have been achieved in any other
way. The Qur'an would also have suffered from many defects, such
as natural compulsions, idealistic constraints, carnal and selfish
desires and tendencies that were not aimed at any justice or benevo-
lence or any truthful way of thinking.

The non-contradictory style and internal coherence of the
Qur'an constitute a dominant aspect of this uniqueness. Human
words contain many imperfect features, such as meanness, defeatism,
a variety of weaknesses, sloth or a lack of insight and intelligence.
Inconsistency is another important human feature which makes itself

apparent in a number of situations. All such are features, which are obvious in human speech, actions and deeds, whether the person be a literati, an artist, a politician or a military commander, are easily recognizable in any human artistic action, be it practical or artistic. All such features are the result of human inconsistency. In contrast to these we are presented with the miraculous integrity and harmony that are features peculiar to the Qur'an.

The Qur'an carries the seal of divine artistry and thus indicates the Supreme Artist and His works, unchanging from moment to moment, displaying no relativity. There is too great a difference between divine and human art; it cannot be measured. Moreover, there is no human world view, there is no school of teaching that does not suffer from such deficiencies of limited perception, or which is not influenced by worldly problems or the inability to see contradictions in views, teachings or styles of action. Also, there has been no human world view or school of thought that has not been criticized by later generations; the human way of thinking is not capable of taking into consideration all the distinct features of personality, numbering in the hundreds or even thousands, which stem from our capacity to perceive our own needs. Hence, such schools of thought are incapable of taking into account every aspect of human personality. But the Qur'an has none of the above-mentioned defects as it was revealed by God, the All-Knowing.

God Almighty informs us that He has sent down the Qur'an free from conflict or contradiction. This is why God says, *"Do they not meditate earnestly on the Qur'an, or are there locks on the hearts (that are particular to them so that they are as if deaf and blind, and incapable of understanding the truth)?"* (Muhammad 47:24), i.e. would we not have found many conflicts, contradictions, inconsistencies and the like in the Qur'an if it had been produced by a human being? Whereas, the Qur'an is free of all such deficiencies, for it was sent down by God.

As stated above, although the Qur'an was revealed in parts over a period of 23 years, on different occasions at different times and locations, it has perfect harmony; the parts are so united and harmonious with one another that it is as if the Qur'an had been revealed on one occasion all at once. Although the Qur'an was revealed in answer to different questions and upon a variety of circumstances, its parts are so consistent, in agreement with each other and mutually supportive that it is as if it had been revealed in answer to one question and revealed at one time. All these definitely prove that the Qur'an is the Word of God.

The Qur'an depicts the truths of this world and the next without any prejudice, conflict or contradiction. Not only does it realistically explain the past, the Qur'an also astonishingly describes situations of its own time and the inner secrets of people, thus preventing its opponents from effectively denying its authenticity. There is lots of news it provides regarding the future which has been realized. It has brought forth basics of faith, general and specific subjects and many principles that belong to modern international politics and administration which were not known at the time of the revelation. These principles today have more advanced positions than the most modern and established theories or philosophical doctrines that have been attained by humanity after long and instable periods of struggle. It so vividly and sensibly depicts the *ghayb*, or the world of the Unseen, portrays the Judgment Day, heaven and hell that when we read about them we feel as if we are seeing and experiencing them. The effect and feeling these passages leave in our mind never disappears. God Almighty has certainly revealed the best and most beautiful of all words.

54 It is said that five things that only God can know are mentioned in the Qur'an. What are they?

The following verse explains the five things of which God alone has exact knowledge:

> With God alone rests the knowledge of the Last Hour (when it will come). He sends down rain (just at the time and place He alone knows), and He alone knows what is in the wombs. No soul knows what it will reap tomorrow, and no soul knows in what place it will die. Surely God is All-Knowing, All-Aware. (Luqman 31:34)

The first thing is the date and time of the Last Hour; this is known only by God. Nobody can know the time of the end of the world as God has kept knowledge of when certain things will occur to Himself. The time of the Last Hour is just one of these.

The second thing here is the rain sent down by God. The weather forecasts that we have today, achieved by means of modern technology are not actually concerned with this unknowable aspect of rain. Such forecasts are nothing more than predictions and are not certain in any way. This is because those things that are now recognized by means of technology today are indications of only those elements that have become evident to us. They do not describe the unknown, for they can only predict rain after the obvious signs have appeared, much like an advanced form of an elderly person's "feeling it in their bones."

So, being able to know that it will rain within this context and in this form is not knowing the unknown. Giving a forecast of rain is based on certain calculations and is done by taking into consideration such factors as the condition of the clouds, air pressure and certain other atmospheric conditions. Only God has full knowledge of when, where, how much and in what way He will make it rain.

The third thing explained in the verse is the fact that only God knows what is in a woman's womb. Today, we can examine the fetus in the mother's womb and determine the sex with ultrasound technology; we can even determine which sperm will form a male fetus and which will form a female fetus. The same principle outlined above applies here as well; being able to make an identity or determination due to some visible causes is not the same as knowing the unknown. If a sperm is recognized as masculine, this is not foreknowledge. The statement referring to what is in the wombs does not merely relate to the sex of the embryo in the womb, as the word *ma*, or "thing," relates to all the details of that which is in the womb, such as its future physical traits, character, and inborn capacities; these known by God alone.

The fourth thing mentioned in the verse is that one cannot know what they will achieve tomorrow. This achievement should not be understood as only material, but rather as all sorts of good or evil things that can be gained either materially or spiritually. The work of a scientist, for instance, is their achievement and only God knows the scope of such gains. No one can predict their own achievements, that is, what will happen to them in future and whether it will be good or evil.

The fifth unknowable thing is how and where one will die. This is another thing known only by God. The place, date and time at which the Angel of Death will come to us and say "Your time is up!" is unknown to all of us and none of us can object to such a destiny.

By mentioning five things from the Unseen in this verse, the Qur'an proclaims, "O human being! How can you know the time at which the whole universe will come to an end when you do not even know anything about the things you are so familiar with in this life? You enjoy bounties or suffer from famine, totally depen-dent on rain; the control and order of the rain is totally at God's supreme disposal. He allocates and gives the rain when He so desires. You cannot know how much rain will fall in a certain place at a certain time, which country will be deprived of it or which country will suffer damage from too much. You do not know whether the thing being formed in the womb is good or evil. You do not even know what will happen to you tomorrow. A sudden accident might change your destiny, but you are not able to foresee it, even a minute before it happens. You do not know when and where your present life will end. With these five unknowable things, the Qur'an draws our attention to God's absolute, all-encompassing

Knowledge. It is only God Who has full knowledge of everything and has absolute command and possession over all things.

Similarly, there is no option but to await God's command and decision concerning the end of the world, as no one has even the least bit of information about this.

This verse indicates some aspects of unknown and secret matters in order to stimulate God-consciousness in human beings, but does not provide a full list of God's absolute knowledge over them. The realm of the Unseen contains everything that is secret and unknowable to the creatures but which is absolutely and plainly knowable by God; such things are innumerable and infinite.

55	What does the statement the Qur'an guides people to the truest path mean?

T he Qur'an guides people to the truest path and to the most suitable attitudes. The following verse explains this as: "This Qur'an surely guides (in all matters) to that which is most just and right and gives the believers who do good, righteous deeds the glad tidings that for them there is a great reward" (Isra 17:9).

The Qur'an is a book that always orientates, without any limitations in time or geographical location, all nations and generations to the truest of all things. This guidance has in itself every kind of goodness, righteousness, and prosperity in both worlds. The Qur'an guides human beings to the highest level of harmony between body and soul and to the best modes of behavior by maintaining balanced relations between their beliefs and actions and between their emotions, perceptions, and attitudes.

The Qur'an is also a book which shows humanity the truest of inter-human relations. It bases all relations among individuals, spouses, governments, states and races on fixed and firm foundations. These firm foundations cannot be shaken by differences of opinion or fancies or eliminated by human sentiments. Personal interests and selfish tendencies cannot deviate them from their targets, for the All-Knowing God has established them for His obedient servants. He knows best His servants' situation and can best decide what is good for them, no matter the place or the time.

The Qur'an has an open method that covers all aspects of human worldly life. It is such an authentic method that there has never been anything similar to it in the past; this is a system that has brought rewards to humankind unlike that of any other system, materially or spiritually. A Prophet or Messenger was sent to every nation, but this ended with the advent of Prophet Muhammad, the last link in the chain of Prophets; the Qur'an was revealed to him as the culmination of a series of divine messages. Thus, the guidance it provides was of a universal nature.

We can observe the perfect principles that have been laid down by the final revelation of the Qur'an in the following categories:

a. Interpersonal relations: The Qur'an introduced brother/ sisterhood and peaceful relations with others to all humanity. In this respect it emphasizes the fact that human beings were created of various nations so that they would recognize one another, not to fight with each other and it states that all of humanity share common ancestors:

> O humankind! Surely We have created you from a single (pair of) male and female, and made you into tribes and families so that you may know one another (and so build mutuality and co-operative relationships, not so that you may take pride in your differences of race or social rank, and breed enmities). Surely the noblest, most honorable of you in God's sight is the one best in piety, righteousness, and reverence for God. Surely God is All-Knowing, All-Aware. (Hujurat 49:13)

The Qur'an states that believers are nothing less than brothers and sisters who should fulfill their filial duties to one another:

> The believers are but brothers, so make peace between your brothers and keep from disobedience to God in reverence for Him and piety (particularly in your duties toward one another as brothers), so that you may be shown mercy (granted a good,

virtuous life in the world as individuals and as a community, and eternal happiness in the Hereafter). (Hujurat 49:10)

The Qur'an states that sincere believers are those who treat each other with mercy and compassion; it is emphasized that believers should deal with each other on the basis of mutual respect and that God's mercy and help is with a community that has good social relations.

b. Relations with one's own family: God regards the family as one of His signs and draws our attention to this:

> And among His signs is that He has created for you, from your selves, mates, that you may incline towards them and find rest in them, and He has engendered love and tenderness between you. Surely in this are signs for people who reflect. (Rum 30:21)

The importance of harmonious marital relations between the spouses, the kind treatment of children and parental responsibilities are stressed in the Qur'an.

c. Relations with one's own society: The Qur'an also lays down certain irrevocable principles concerning the relations of the individual with society. In this respect, the Qur'an emphasizes some important aspects of human rights, even ordering that the needs of kin and the poor should be met by stressing that these people are entitled to a certain portion of the possessions of the rich. The Qur'an also commands such steps as seeking permission to enter the house of another and greeting people when entering their houses to prevent any possible deterioration in relations among members of society and thus guides us to the best direction, always and everywhere.

56 | How does the Qur'an inform us of the Unseen?

The Qur'an contains knowledge of the unseen, or the *ghayb*, which is beyond any sort of perception; it also presents much of the history of bygone nations and predictions about the near or distant future. As the exact knowledge of the unseen belongs to God exclusively, neither the Prophets nor any other people have knowledge of the future and cannot acquire true knowledge of the past or even of the present except through the Revelation. If we look at such information and knowledge of the unseen in the Qur'an, we can see that the majority is concerned with the people living in the past. Even if some of this information is found in other heavenly books, we can see that their Qur'anic equivalents differ in many aspects and are sometimes quite the contrary. As for information about the time period when the Qur'an descended, or that of later periods, there are many facts that would have been impossible for a human being to know revealed in the Qur'an. God Himself states that each of these is a miracle of the realm of the unseen:

> With Him are the keys to the Unseen; none knows them but He. And He knows whatever is on land and in the sea; and not a leaf falls but He knows it; and neither is there a grain in the dark layers of earth, nor anything green or dry, but is (recorded) in a Manifest Book. (An'am 6:59)

An evaluation of Qur'anic information pertaining to the Unseen under three headings, past, present, and future, will help us to better understand this matter.

a. Information pertaining to the past: Life stories of many Prophets, starting with Prophet Adam, the first man and ending with Prophet Muhammad, the seal of the Messengers, and the incidents that occurred between them and their communities, the stories of tyrants who lived in the past and the people who were tortured by them are all narrated in the Qur'an. God Almighty informs us in the following verses that the majority of such narrations were not known by those who lived in the Arabian Peninsula before the revelation of the Qur'an:

> Those are accounts of some exemplary events of the unseen (a time and realm beyond any created's perception) that We reveal

to you, (O Messenger). Neither you nor your people knew them
before this. Then (seeing that there is no substantial difference
between the conditions in which the Messengers carried out
their missions and the reactions they encountered) be patient
(with their reactions and their persistence in unbelief). The
(final, happy) outcome is in favor of the God-revering, pious.
(Hud 11:49)

(All that We have told you about Moses and the Book granted
to him is a Revelation We reveal to you, O Muhammad, for)
you were not present on the spot lying to the western side (of
the valley) when We decreed the Commandment (the Torah) to
Moses, nor were you a witness (to what happened there). But
(after them) We brought into being many generations and long
indeed were the ages that passed over them. (The information
you give about them is also that which We reveal to you, just as
what you tell about what happened concerning Moses in Midian
is also a Revelation. For) neither did you dwell among the people of Midian so that you are conveying to them (the Makkan
people) Our Revelations (about what Moses did in Midian).
Rather, We have been sending Messengers (to convey Our
Revelations). And neither were you present on the side of the
Mount Sinai when We called out (to Moses), but (We reveal all
this to you) as a mercy from your Lord so that you may warn a
people to whom no warner has come before you, so that they
may reflect and be mindful. (Qasas 28:44-46)

(O Messenger:) that is of the tidings of the things of the unseen
(the things that took place in the past and have remained hidden from people with all their truth), which We reveal to you,
for you were not present with them when they drew lots with
their pens about who should have charge of Mary; nor were you
present with them when they were disputing (about the matter). (Al 'Imran 3:44)

The information which the Qur'an provides concerning the
past is only the kind of information that can be known by way of
oral tradition over the generations, but not through reason or
intelligence. Such narration is something that can only be attempted by literate people. The Prophet to whom the Qur'an was
revealed could neither write nor read, but what he recited sounds

as if he had participated in these events and was well acquainted with all these incidents. In fact, these incidents were all narrated by God with Whom all secrets of the realm of the Unseen reside and they were not the personal knowledge of Prophet Muhammad, peace and blessings be upon him.

b. Information pertaining to the present: The Qur'an provides information about some facts that pertain to the time period of its revelation. These are regarded as unknowable for both the Prophet and his people. Matters pertaining to God Himself, the angels, jinn, Paradise, and Hell may be considered to be examples in this regard. The Qur'an speaks of matters like the Attributes and deeds of God Almighty, His Essence, the features of the angels and the characteristics of Paradise and Hell. All these matters cannot be comprehended with the eye or the senses, but are rather realities conceivable only via Revelation.

In addition, we can see that the Qur'an relates certain incidents that pertain to the time of the Prophet. Such incidents were perceptible only after being mentioned in the Revelation. The following verse, which discloses some secrets of the hypocrites, is an example of this:

> Among the people there is he whose conversation on (the affairs of) the present, worldly life fascinates you, and he calls on God to bear testimony to what is in his heart, yet he is most fierce in enmity. When he leaves (you) or attains authority, he rushes about the land to foment disorder and corruption therein and to ruin the sources of life and human generations. Surely God does not love disorder and corruption. (Baqara 2:204-205)

This verse is said to have been revealed about Ahnas ibn Sharik. This hypocrite was a person with whom the tribe Banu Zuhra had made an alliance. He came to the Prophet declaring that he had converted to Islam. He spoke politely to the Prophet, in a kind and affectionate manner, swearing that he had converted to Islam. But, after he had left the presence of the Prophet, he went to the farm of some Muslims and burned their harvest and destroyed their animals.

Similarly, the Masjid al-Dhirar (the small mosque near Medina built by the hypocrites at that time to distract the early Muslim community; it was demolished on the order of the Prophet) is another example of this. We find the following statements in the Qur'an about these hypocrites and their mosque, which was used as a base for fifth-columnist activities:

> Some among the hypocrites – who have adopted a mosque out of dissension and unbelief, in order to cause division among the believers, and use as an outpost to collaborate with him who before made war on God and His Messenger – will certainly swear: "We mean nothing but good (in building this mosque)", whereas God bears witness that they are surely liars. Do not stand in that mosque to do the Prayer. The mosque that was founded on piety and reverence for God from the very first days (in Madinah) is worthy that you should stand in it for the Prayer. In it are men who love to be purified (of all spiritual and moral blemishes). God loves those who strive to purify themselves. (Tawba 9:107-108)

The strong warnings in the Qur'an informed the Prophet about the hypocrites' intentions and their actions were prevented.

c. Information pertaining to the future: Many predictions concerning important future incidents are one of the miraculous aspects of the Qur'an; whatever is predicted in the Qur'an either has come true or will come true when its time is due. This means that the one who is relating the words must be the All-Knowing Supreme Being. The following samples related to this matter clearly show this:

1. The prediction that the Byzantine Romans would be victorious:

> The Byzantine Romans have been defeated in the lands close-by, but they, after their defeat, will be victorious within a few (nine) years – to God belongs the command (the absolute judgment and authority) both before and after (any event) – and at the time (when the Romans are victorious), the believers will

rejoice because of God's help leading them to victory. He helps whom He wills to victory. He is the All-Glorious with irresistible might, the All-Compassionate (especially towards His believing servants). (Rum 30:1-4)

The Eastern Roman and Persian empires were the two super powers during the early years of the Revelation. The Eastern Romans were People of the Book and the Persians were fire-worshippers. In 614, the Roman lands of Jerusalem and Palestine had been occupied by the Persians and they had even come down to Alexandria and advanced as far as the capital city of Constantinople, present-day Istanbul. Due to this victory, both the Persians and the Meccan polytheists were extremely pleased. Since the Persians' victory had been so great no one thought it possible that the Byzantine Romans could turn defeat into victory in only nine years. Now, the above verse predicted not only the victory of the Byzantine Romans over the Zoroastrian Persians in just a few years, but it also predicted that the Muslims would be victorious over the polytheists and would consequently be pleased.

When the above verses were revealed, Abu Bakr told the polytheists who were pleased by the defeat of the Byzantine Romans: "God's Messenger has informed us that God will not enlighten your days. I swear by God that within a couple of years the Byzantine Romans will certainly be victorious over the Persians." Ubayy ibn Khalaf bet Abu Bakr ten camels that the Byzantine Romans would not be victorious within three years. When the Prophet came to know of this, he said: "The Qur'an has used the word *Bidh*, which applies to a number up to ten. Therefore, make the bet for ten years and increase the number of camels to a hundred." When Abu Bakr met Ubayy ibn Khalaf once more, he asked Abu

Bakr: "I presume you are unhappy with your bet." Upon this Abu Bakr bet a hundred camels for ten years. And Ubayy accepted the deal. Finally, the Byzantine Romans became victorious over the Persians, and this was the very year when Muslims had achieved a decisive victory against the Meccan polytheists at Badr. Later, Abu Bakr demanded and received those 100 camels from the heirs of Ubayy and took them before the Prophet who ordered, "Give them away in charity."

2. **The narration that the Prophet would be guarded against his enemies:** Many people, primarily the Meccan polytheists, were ferocious enemies of the Prophet after he announced his Prophethood. All of them wanted to kill him. They soon began laying traps and making plots against him. However, none of these plots, traps or attacks yielded any result, as the Prophet was under the custody of the Supreme Creator and because God had guaranteed the Prophet's safety. The polytheists could not harm the Prophet and could not touch him with their evil intentions. The following verse explains this fact:

> O Messenger (you who convey and embody the Message in the best way)! Convey and make known in the clearest way all that has been sent down to you from your Lord. For, if you do not, you have not conveyed His Message and fulfilled the task of His Messengership. And God will certainly protect you from the people. God will surely not guide the disbelieving people (to attain their goal of harming or defeating you). (Maeda 5:67)

3. **The narration that the Muslims would be victorious:** The Qur'an declared that Muslims, even though they were very weak and few in number, particularly in the early periods, would eventually become stronger and finally become victorious over their enemies. Such Qur'anic dec-

larations were made in a period during which the majority
of the early Muslims were exposed to a number of forms
of torture, while others were forced to migrate from
Mecca or their property was confiscated by the polytheists. In fact, under normal circumstances to tell people
who find themselves in such a position that they would
soon be victorious would be nothing less than ridiculing
them. But, God, with His all-encompassing Knowledge,
informed the believers of the consequence and of this
Qur'anic miracle that would occur in the future; events
turned out exactly as written. The following verse predicts
and declares the soon-to-be future state:

> God has promised those of you who believe and do
> good, righteous deeds that He will most certainly
> empower them as vicegerents on the earth (in the
> place of those who are in power at present), even as
> He empowered those (of the same qualities) that pre-
> ceded them, and that, assuredly, He will firmly estab-
> lish for them their Religion, which He has (chosen
> and) approved of for them, and He will replace their
> present state of fear with security (so that they can
> practice their Religion freely and fully and in peace).
> They worship Me alone, associating none with Me as
> partners (in belief, worship, and the authority to order
> their life). Whoever turns ungrateful after that, such
> indeed are the transgressors. (Nur 24:55)

4. **The narration that the Qur'an will never be challenged:**
    As far as the issue of having something similar to itself
    created, as seen above, the Qur'an laid out a challenge for
    all times and places, openly discussing this matter in its
    verses. The Qur'an displays its miraculous authenticity in
    the following verse:

    > Say: "Surely, if humankind and jinn were to come
    > together to produce the like of this Qur'an, they will

never be able to produce the like of it, though they backed one another up with help and support. (Isra 17:88)

5. **The narration that the Prophet and the Companions will peacefully enter Mecca:** Both the Prophet and his Companions who migrated to Medina never were able to forget Mecca, the city where they had been raised. But, the dangerous circumstances made them despair of returning there one day. Moreover, they were not able to even imagine being able to safely return there or to be able to circumambulate the Ka'ba to their hearts' content. Yet, the Qur'an informed them that even under such extremely unpromising circumstances that one day they would enter Mecca in great serenity and safety. The prediction became a reality with the Treaty of Hudaybiya, which in time proved to be a manifest victory. The Prophet's vision came true when Muslims entered Mecca and completed their minor Pilgrimage in full security:

> God has assuredly confirmed the vision for His Messenger as true (and will certainly fulfill it) in reality: you will certainly enter the Sacred Mosque, if God wills, in full security, with your heads shaven or your hair cut short, and you will have nothing to fear. But He always knows what you do not know, and (therefore, without allowing you to enter the Mosque this year,) granted you a near victory before this. (Fath 48:27)

6. **The narration that the corpse of the Pharoah would be found:** The Qur'an declares in the following statement that the body of the Pharaoh, who drowned pursuing Prophet Moses, would not be lost forever, but rather would be found later:

> So this day (as a recompense for your belief in the state of despair which will be of no avail to you in the Hereafter), We will save only your body, that you may

be a sign for those to come after you. Surely, a good many people among humankind are heedless of Our signs (full of clear warning and lessons). (Yunus 10:92)

This prediction is an explicit Qur'anic miracle, yet at the time of the Prophet there was no knowledge about this matter. As mentioned in the Qur'an, the body of the Pharaoh was found prostrate beside the Nile towards the end of the 19th century. The Pharaoh is now displayed in the hall of royal mummies in the Museum of Egypt.

CHAPTER 8

Preservation of the Qur'an

PRESERVATION OF THE QUR'AN

57 | Other Holy Books have been altered over time; is this the case for the Qur'an?

God Almighty sent down all the Scriptures with His Messengers. Though the basic message of all the Prophets, and thus the basic message of all the Books they brought, is one and the same message from God to human-kind, it is quite natural that new and different principles and laws would be needed, depending on the social and intellectual level of the people and in answer to new and different problems and needs. During the time of Prophet Adam, for instance, there were not many people and the means of meeting their needs were rather limited. Hence, God sent them a Scroll of ten pages which con-tained principles that were sufficient to meet their needs. In keep-ing with the developments in human communities and societies, the increase in human population and the diversification of their needs, the message of each and every Prophet contained changes and diversifications to a certain extent.

In the same way that there is an inclination towards perfec-tion in the universe and everything in it is subject to laws of change, divine Revelations correspond to man's position on earth and in history and the level they have reached in their develop-ment. There is a correlation between the ultimate perfection of the Holy Books and amendments made to constitutions in the sense that when constitutions are amended, partly or wholly, over time and in accordance to social need, the Holy Books were also gradu-ally modified and improved according to the material, spiritual and intellectual developments that the human race had achieved at a particular time; this was done not because the Holy Books were trying to keep up with human development but rather so that the Books addressed the intellectual and spiritual level of the people at that time.

The Qur'an, as the culmination of a series of divine messages, is the last of the Holy Scriptures. It applies for all times, those in the past and those to come and has been preserved by Divine authority. It is impossible for any falsehood or alteration of any part of the Qur'an to be made and not noticed.

When we think of God's promise that the Qur'an will be preserved, we see a miracle which bears witness that it came from God; it is impossible for any book that has been exposed to such a number of circumstances and influences throughout the ages to preserve its authenticity, remaining unchanged. So, it would not have been possible for the Qur'an to have stayed the same if the Supreme Being had not protected it against all circumstances and conditions.

Throughout history hostile and opposing groups have had no opportunity to add to or delete any verses from the Qur'an due to its divine guardianship. Its verses have remained exactly as they were at the time of revelation. There have been many difficult and calamitous periods in the history of Islam, times which have left Muslims unable to safeguard their lands, social order, or values. At times their enemies have maintained absolute control over them. Nevertheless, the enemies of Islam have been unable to do one thing; they have not been able to cause any harm to this divinely preserved Book. This too proves the divine Authorship of the Qur'an.

The promise of: *"Indeed it is We, We Who send down the Reminder (i.e. the Qur'an), and it is indeed We Who are its Guardian"* (Hijr 15:9) is not valid only for the time of the Prophet, it is an eternal divine promise. After all these great calamities and many centuries this promise today has remained intact, miraculously proving that it comes from God. With this promise God has undertaken to preserve the Qur'an from all forms of alterations. This preservation can be understood in a number ways.

God's preservation of the Qur'an is, first of all, seen in the form of His making it a particular miracle that has been set aside from the human word and which renders all humanity unable to make any addition to or deletion from the Qur'an. Should someone add or delete something from the Qur'an, the harmony of the wording changes and such an attempt would promptly be noticed by all. God has also ensured that a group of people have been raised in every age to guard the Qur'an; people read it, memorize it and spread it among the public. No other book has been preserved as the Qur'an has been. The reason for this is that all the other heavenly books were sent as temporary sources of guidance, not as eternal ones. The Qur'an was sent in order to complete the previous books, to correct the verses that had been altered by human beings and to be a criterion for them. God willed that the Qur'an be a proof of authenticity that will remain with us until the Doomsday; whenever He wills something to be He facilitates its causes for being, for He is absolutely the All-Wise, the All-Knowing.

58   Is it possible that the Qur'an is the word of the Prophet?

There are great differences between the styles of the Qur'an and of the Prophet. Arabic speakers of both the Prophet's own time and of later periods noticed the obvious differences between these two styles. Thus, they could not hide their admirations towards the Qur'an. Captivated by the eloquence of its words, literary geniuses like Umayya ibn Khalaf prostrated before it, even though they did not believe in it. Such a thing would never have happened if the word of the Prophet was involved.

Moreover, the Prophet was totally unaware that the Revelation would come, he had never ever thought about it. In addition,

God's Messenger could not have known of the accounts of past Prophets and their people.

> (All that We have told you about Moses and the Book granted to him is a Revelation We reveal to you, O Muhammad, for) you were not present on the spot lying to the western side (of the valley) when We decreed the Commandment (the Torah) to Moses, nor were you a witness (to what happened there). But (after them) We brought into being many generations and long indeed were the ages that passed over them. (The information you give about them is also that which We reveal to you, just as what you tell about what happened concerning Moses in Midian is also a Revelation. For) neither did you dwell among the people of Midian so that you are conveying to them (the Makkan people) Our Revelations (about what Moses did in Midian). Rather, We have been sending Messengers (to convey Our Revelations). And neither were you present on the side of the Mount Sinai when We called out (to Moses), but (We reveal all this to you) as a mercy from your Lord so that you may warn a people to whom no warner has come before you, so that they may reflect and be mindful. (Qasas 28:44-46)

> Those are accounts of some exemplary events of the unseen (a time and realm beyond any created's perception) that We reveal to you, (O Messenger). Neither you nor your people knew them before this. Then (seeing that there is no substantial difference between the conditions in which the Messengers carried out their missions and the reactions they encountered) be patient (with their reactions and their persistence in unbelief). The (final, happy) outcome is in favor of the God-revering, pious. (Hud 11:49)

It should not be forgotten that the Qur'an declared that the Prophet's source of information about various Prophets was purely the divine Revelation. The following verses explicitly indicate this fact:

> (O Messenger:) that is of the tidings of the things of the unseen (the things that took place in the past and have remained hidden from people with all their truth), which We reveal to you, for you were not present with them when they

drew lots with their pens about who should have charge of Mary; nor were you present with them when they were disputing (about the matter). (Al Imran 3:44)

That is an account of some exemplary events of the unseen (a realm and time beyond the reach of any created being's perception) that We reveal to you, (O Messenger). You were not with them when those agreed upon their plans, and then were scheming (against Joseph). (Yusuf 12:102)

The repetitive narration of such stories in the Qur'an indicates that the source of information for an illiterate Prophet, a source that enabled him to go into great detail about historical facts that took place thousands of years ago, was the Revelation.

We can see that the Qur'anic narrations that are concerned with nations and Prophets of the past are sometimes quite informative. Some of this information was not known by the community at that time, and some was contrary to what was known or found in the Old and New Testaments. However, Prophet Muhammad, peace and blessings be upon him, was able to disclose all such details without any hesitation; in addition, the fact that the Qur'an describes them in particular as information about the Unseen indicates that the Revelation was not something created by the Prophet, but rather it is the Word of God. The Prophet's ability to convey the histories of bygone nations via the Revelation and his supreme confidence in his mission is a challenge to all ages and peoples as well as being one of the undeniable proofs of the Prophethood.

Another proof that the Qur'an is not the words of the Prophet was his anxiety that he would not be able to commit it to memory. At the beginning of his mission, the Prophet was greatly concerned when receiving the Revelation to commit it to the heart and it was this anxiety that caused him repeat it immediately and to memorize the revealed verses. He had no such habit before the Prophethood and there was no custom like this among the Arabs. Their poems were improvised and not committed to memory. Had the Qur'an been the creation of the Prophet, then his style of

preaching would also have been similar to his individual and community traditions; this would have required that he underwent
long sessions of meditational silence to mature his ideas. However,
this was not the case. The following verses depict this state of the
Prophet during the revelation:

> Absolutely exalted is God, the Supreme Sovereign, the Absolute
> Truth and Ever-Constant. Do not show haste (O Messenger)
> with (the receiving and memorizing of any Revelation included
> in) the Qur'an before it has been revealed to you in full, but say:
> "My Lord, increase me in knowledge." (Ta.Ha 20:114)

> (O Prophet!) Move not your tongue to hasten it (for safekeep-
> ing in your heart). Surely it is for Us to collect it (in your heart)
> and enable you to recite it (by heart). So when We recite it, fol-
> low its recitation; thereafter, it is for Us to explain it. (75:16-19)

These verses prohibit the Prophet from rushing to read the
revealed portions or from moving his tongue before the Revelation
was completed; he is reassured that God will enable him to memorize the Revelation and understand its meaning. This is powerful
proof that the Prophet was consciously aware of the arrival of the
Revelation and thus hastily repeated it, moving his tongue so that
he would not forget even the smallest part.

Another proof that the Qur'an was not the Prophet's own
words is the fact that the Revelations used to come to him suddenly
and in places and at times when he was not prepared; this occurred
both in the early and later periods. Before the Prophethood, God's
Messenger did not say anything about receiving a revelation. He
never expected that such a thing might happen one day. The first
revelation suddenly came to him, as did the later revelations. The
following verse clearly verifies that the Prophet did not have any
expectations about receiving the revelation: *"You did not expect that
this Book would be revealed to you; but it is being revealed to you as a
mercy from your Lord, so do not lend any support to the unbelievers"*
(Qasas 28:86).

59　Is it possible that the Prophet was taught the Qur'an by others?

Such a thing is neither possible nor probable; all of history is witness that God's Messenger was never a student to anyone nor had he ever been taught by anyone. As a matter of fact, it is extremely well-known that he could neither read nor write.

The Meccan polytheists sometimes attributed the Qur'an to God's Messenger himself and sometimes to some other person whom they claimed had imparted it to the Prophet. But, in fact, they themselves did not believe in these lies. The Qur'an reproaches them for their slander as follows:

> Those who disbelieve say: "This (Qur'an) is but a fabrication which he (Muhammad) himself has invented, and some others have helped him with it, so they have produced a wrong and a falsehood." They also say: "(It consists of) only fables of the ancients which he has got written. They are being read to him in early mornings and evenings (while people are at home)." (Furqan 25:4-5)

> Certainly We know that they say, "It is but a human being that teaches him." But the tongue of him to whom they falsely hint is outlandish, while this (Qur'an) is in clear Arabic tongue. (Nahl 16:103)

60　It has been narrated that the Prophet had met with certain individuals from the People of the Book. What is the significance of this?

God's Messenger met with a priest named Bahira in the Busra market near Damascus when he was a child. He also met Waraqa ibn Nawfal in Mecca just after the first Revelation. In later years he met some Jewish and Christian scholars. However, all such meetings were not covert gatherings, but rather short and public. It has never been suggested that anything was taught or instructed either to the Prophet or to the other parties in these meetings.

The priest in Damascus saw Prophet Muhammad when he was young and, relying on the attributes described in the Bible, noticed in him the signs of the final Prophet. The priest turned to Prophet Muhammad's uncle Abu Talib and said: "This child is destined for greatness!"

A similar reaction was given by Waraqa ibn Nawfal. The Prophet could not, at first, fully comprehend the significance of the first Revelation that had occurred during one of his visits to the Hira Cave on Mount Nur, where he retreated for meditation and contemplation. He told Waraqa ibn Nawfal about the first visitation by the Angel of Revelation. After having listened to the Prophet, Waraqa said that this was the same angel of Revelation which had been sent to Moses, and he accepted Muhammad's Prophethood, adding that, should he live enough, Waraqa would support and help him.

Not only does the above show that it is highly unlikely that Prophet Muhammad, peace and blessings be upon him, was learning from others, we can also see that these learned religious scholars quickly recognized the Prophet and accepted that he was a Prophet because of the very attributes that they had seen.

61 | During the time of the Prophet was the Qur'an committed to memory and writing down?

The Qur'an was revealed to an illiterate Prophet who grew up in a society that was for the most part illiterate. Thus, the Prophet's primary concern was to commit the Revelation to memory and to convey it to others. The following verse sheds light onto this fact:

> He it is Who has sent among the unlettered ones a Messenger of their own, reciting to them His Revelations, and purifying them (of false beliefs and doctrines, and sins, and all kinds of uncleanness), and instructing them in the Book and the Wisdom,

whereas before that they were indeed lost in obvious error. (Jumu'a 62:2)

The Prophet was eager to memorize and preserve the Revelations that came to him. He would hastily repeat the Revelation, worried that he might forget that which Archangel Gabriel had brought him. As indicated above, the Prophet was later assured that God would enable him to memorize the Revelations.

As the Qur'an conveys to us below, among the many false objections raised by the Meccan polytheists was also the claim that some scholarly people in Mecca were secretly reciting from some old books to the Prophet, giving him these ideas that were later written down: *"They also say: '(It consists of) only fables of the ancients which he has got written. They are being read to him in early mornings and evenings (while people are at home)'"* (Furqan 25:5). The Prophet, however, received the Divine Revelation in its precise meaning and wording through Archangel Gabriel and committed it to his memory. He dictated it to his scribes and conveyed it to people in strict accordance with God's command. He also recited it during the prayers and on other occasions, whether they were during the day or at night. In addition, he recited and presented to Archangel Gabriel those verses and chapters he had received every Ramadan. In the year of the Prophet's death this happened twice.

In the following verses, the Qur'an speaks of itself as the Book that has been written down or recorded:

> Most certainly it is a Qur'an most honorable in a Book well-guarded. None except the purified ones can reach it (to obtain the knowledge it contains. And none except those cleansed of material and spiritual impurities should touch it). (Waqia 56:77-79)

> No indeed! It surely is a reminder and an admonition (that suffices for all who come to it with an open heart). So whoever wills receives admonition and takes heed. (It is recorded) in scrolls greatly honored, exalted (in God's sight) and perfectly purified (of falsehood, vanity, and inconsistency). (Abasa 80:11-14)

The incident described below, which was the cause of Umar's conversion to Islam, also indicates that the Companions had kept private records of some portions of the Qur'an from the very beginning.

Umar, in accordance with a decision made by the Meccan poly-theists at Dar al-Nadwa, was to assassinate the Prophet. On his way to carry out this task, Umar met Nu'aym ibn Mas'ud, one of the early Muslim converts and learned from him that Umar's sister and her husband had also become Muslim. So, Umar decided to go to kill them first. Upon arriving at their house, Umar heard the Qur'anic verses being recited inside. The people in the house quick-ly hid the Qur'anic pages when they heard Umar come in. He asked them what they had been reciting and, without waiting for their answer, he hit his brother-in-law. Umar's sister was angered by her brother's behavior and told him that they had become Muslim. They then showed Umar what they had been reciting. Umar impa-tiently started to read the pages, but quickly became fascinated by what he was reading. He suddenly turned to Islam, went to the Prophet to declare that he had become Muslim.[22]

God's Messenger had the whole text of the Divine Messages, from the beginning to the end, committed to writing by the scribes of the Revelation. The Revelation scribes recorded the revealed verses on leather or scraps of parchment, palm leaves, flat and wide stones, wooden plates, pieces of bone, or whatever other suitable material they could find. The names of some of the scribes of the Revelations are: Abu Bakr, Umar, Uthman, Ali, Zayd ibn Thabit, Ubayy ibn Ka'ab, Muawiya ibn Abu Sufyan, Khalid ibn Walid, Ab'an ibn Said, and Thabit ibn Qays. The Prophet, as can be under-stood from relevant narrations, demanded that the Revelation scribe read the Revelation that had just been recorded to check its accura-cy. After this, a large number of Companions who could write would make a copy of the text of the Qur'an, and would satisfy themselves that their record was correct by reading it out to the Prophet. Consequently, the preservation of the Revelations was not solely dependent on the compilation of verses that remained only in the memories of some people; it was also preserved in a written form so that even one change to one word would be noticed.

62 | Is there any *naskh* (abrogation) in the Qur'an?

The term *naskh* literally means to abolish, destroy, abrogate, nullify or to transcribe or copy out. When pertaining to the Qur'an it refers to the abrogation of a previous religious injunction by a latter injunction. Abrogation, or *naskh*, occurred not only in Islam, but also in the former divine religions.

Proofs of the existence of abrogation

a. The following verses are examples of the abrogation of certain injunctions in the laws of former Prophets: "*So, because of the wrong committed by the Jews We made unlawful for them many pure, wholesome things which had (hitherto) been lawful for them, and because of their barring many from God's way*" (Nisa 4:160). As can clearly be understood from this verse, certain deeds that had previously been allowed to the Jewish people had now been rendered unlawful to them due to their mischievous actions. Similarly, certain deeds, primarily hunting, was prohibited to the Jews on the day of Sabbath; previously there had been no difference in the days of the week in Judaism: "*We raised the Mount to tower above them to secure their promise (to hold firmly to the Book), and (on another occasion when We guided them to a town) We commanded them, "Go into it through its gate prostrating (humbly in utmost submission to God)"; and again We once commanded them, "Do not exceed the bounds with respect to the Sabbath," and We took from them a most solemn pledge*" (Nisa 4:154).

b. Not only was there abrogation in the laws of past Prophets; there are certain Qur'anic verses which the injunctions contained were later abrogated. Therefore, there is abrogation in Islam. Issues like the changing of the *qibla* (the direction of prayer) and later the abolishment of compulsory almsgiving for those who would like to consult the Prophet are a few examples of such situations.[23]

c. It is generally agreed that the following verse defines the meanings of *naskh*:

> (Though they would exploit the abrogation of some rules of secondary degree to challenge your authority, the truth is that) We do not abrogate any verse or omit it (leaving it to be forgotten) but We bring one better than it or the like of it (more suited to the time and conditions in the course of perfecting religion and completing Our favor upon you). Do you not know (and surely you do know) that God has full power over everything? (Baqara 2:106)

Accordingly, some verses were abrogated or annulled by God, either with the injunctions they contained and the wording preserved or with both their wording and the commandments. The following verses are also evidence for *naskh*, or abrogation:

> When We put a Revelation in place of another Revelation (in the course of perfecting the Religion and completing Our favor upon you), – and God knows best what He sends down – they say: "You are but a forger!" No, rather, most of them do not know. (Nahl 16:101)

> God effaces what He wills (of things and events He has created, and laws He has established), and He confirms and establishes (what He wills): with Him is the Mother of the Book. (Rad 13:39)

d. There are also certain rulings in the Sunna which were later abrogated. For instance, the Prophet prohibited visiting graveyards in the early period of Islam. But, he later abrogated the prohibition of visiting graveyards and even encouraged it, since the cause of the prohibition ceased with the widespread practice of Islam within the Muslim community and visiting graveyards now reminded Muslims of life in the Hereafter.

In every era, if there are misguided non-Islamic customs and superstitious behavior like using graveyards for places of worship, lighting candles, or tying pieces of cloth to make wishes, then people should be discouraged from visiting tombs and graves. Thus, there may be a temporary prohibition for such people until they give up such acts. As far as *naskh* is concerned, it is important to take all the conditions of the human situation into consideration, for example, or the characteristics of people, the time, state and condition of their Islamic practices in the society. Hence, this process of *naskh* contributes a great deal to the dynamism of Islam, accompanied by its applicability for all times and under all conditions and its ability to provide answers for all humanitarian and social issues.

63 | What is the divine wisdom behind abrogation?

Abrogation is a divine Providence which God disposes via His absolute will, as far as orders and prohibitions are concerned. He establishes whatever He will and effaces whatever He will from the laws He has established. Nevertheless, His commands and prohibitions are always connected to divine wisdom.

Many remarkable things happen around us and human needs are diversified according to the time, place, and individuals. A doctor, for instance, may prescribe a certain medicine to their patients according to the patient's needs. In the first stages of the illness the dosage is high, and then as the patient regains health the amount of medicine would be reduced. Similarly, a mother breastfeeds her baby at first and gradually introduces the baby to bland and easy to digest solids. She gradually adds new and more solids into the baby's diet as the baby develops and grows. This is a gradual process that is in keeping with the development of the child.

God, with His eternally All-Encompassing Knowledge, knows that the abrogated injunction is a temporary one, but not a permanent one. He also knows that such temporality is limited to the announcement of the abrogating injunction. God's eternal Knowledge covers the new injunctions that have substituted the previous ones (*nasikh*) and the abrogated ones (*mansukh*) altogether. This shows that *naskh*, in fact, is the announcement of the latter injunction in God's Knowledge whereas it is an abrogation in human comprehension. Our limited knowledge and comprehension recognize the announcement of the latter rule as an abrogation, since the time of expiry of the former rule has not been announced. There is no way that Omnipotent God cannot know that some of His commands will be substituted. He had the knowledge of both those that will be abrogated and the new ones that will take their place before He created the world. Also, by His Supreme Divinity and wisdom, the Transcendent Being, Who wills good for humankind and Who has knowledge of all things and events beforehand, knows that the abrogated injunction is limited only due to a good reason and a divine wisdom that expires at a certain time.

64 — What is the divine wisdom for the letter *alif* not being used in the *basmala*?

With respect to the omission of the Arabic letter *alif* from the *Bismillah*, or "*In the Name of God*", we can consider the following factors: First and foremost, *Bismillah* is the most frequently recited of all Qur'anic phrases, occurring 114 times in the Qur'an. It is due to this great frequency of the phrase that the *alif* is not used here. However, the letter *alif* is omitted in no other words in the Qur'an, but only in *Bi.smi. llah*. The letter *alif* appears in "*Iqra' bi (i)smi Rabbikallaziy khalaq*" ("*Read in the Name of your Lord, Who has created*") (Alaq 96:1).

Such a practice with respect to the exceptional omission of the letter *alif* in the *basmala* is yet more evidence that the Qur'an has reached us without any alterations. If this were not the case, scholars of Arabic would have opposed this usage, saying: "Such use is contrary to the grammar of the Arabic language" and would have changed this usage. The fact that such an alteration did not occur indicates that the Qur'an has been written in this way from the very beginning and that it was written under the supervision of God and His Messenger.

65 | Has there been any external interference in the Revelation?

The very basic foundations of the heavenly religions are the Revelations and the Prophethood. Messengers have a degree of sublimity; to them are sent Revelations and they are made examples in trustworthiness, virtues, and good deeds. They are far removed from any accusation.

God Almighty provided full support and protection to the Messengers so that they would be able to fully commit the Revelations to memory, without forgetting any part and thus convey them accurately to human beings:

> We will establish the Qur'an in your heart and have you recite (it to others), so you will not forget (anything of it). (A'la 87:6)

> (O Prophet!) Move not your tongue to hasten it (for safekeeping in your heart). Surely it is for Us to collect it (in your heart) and enable you to recite it (by heart). So when We recite it, follow its recitation; thereafter, it is for Us to explain it. (Qiyama 75:16-19)

> Those who disbelieve say (by way of yet another false argument for unbelief): "Why has the Qur'an not been sent down on him all at once?" (We send it down in parts) so that We may (impress it on your mind and) establish your heart with it, and We are conveying it distinctly and gradually, (one part supporting the other, and providing guidance and instruction for emerging occasions). (Furqan 25:32)

These verses assure the Prophet that God will enable him to memorize the Revelations and understand their meaning. Thus, with such a divine assurance, it is unthinkable that any external interference in the Revelation by others would be possible.

> Never did We send a Messenger or a Prophet before you but that when he recited (God's Revelations to the people) Satan would make insinuations (about these Revelations, prompting people to misconstrue them in many wrong senses, rather than the right one). But God abrogates whatever insinuations Satan may make, and then He confirms and establishes His Revelations. God is All-Knowing, All-Wise. (Hajj 22:52)

The above verse may also be interpreted as follows: "O Muhammad! Whenever We raised a Prophet or Messenger from a nation, with clear commands and proofs of the truth to guide their people, some wicked persons opposed the Prophets and tried to prevent people from listening to the Revelations. These wicked persons also claimed that the Messengers and Prophets said things that they had never even considered, so that people would be alienated against them and so that they would be deviated from the right path along which the Messengers and Prophets trod. However, God has established the truth and has totally eliminated falsehood. The Prophets did not abandon their efforts but were patient until truth defeated falsehood, despite all such refusals and hardships. God clearly eliminates any suspicions and firmly establishes His signs and verses."

On the other hand, each and every Messenger is, in a way, concerned with how they are to perform their duty. Every Prophet has conveyed God's Message to their respective communities so that the community will accept the Message they have brought, follow the admonitions and abandon sins. All Prophets are keen that their communities accept the Revelation and that they are obedient. Prophet Muhammad, peace and blessings be upon him, was the most desirous of all in this respect. These verses clearly indicate that he was very concerned with the guidance of the people and physically pained by unbelief, tormented by the fear that they might not believe:

> Yet it may be that you (O Muhammad) will torment yourself to death with grief, following after them, if they do not believe in this Message. (Kahf 18:6)

> Yet, be you ever so eager, most people will not believe. (Yusuf 12:103)

> If your Lord had so willed (and, denying them free will, compelled humankind to believe), all who are on the earth would surely have believed, all of them. Would you, then, force people until they become believers? (Yunus 10:99)

Therefore, as every Prophet had such strong feelings for their communities, it would be easy for Satan to erect barriers, throw secret fears into the hearts of people and cause them to fight against their Prophet. But indeed, God certainly does whatever He will, erasing all unfounded suspicions and misgivings that Satan can place in the heart of human beings, clearing all the barriers between them and the Message, thus firmly establishing His Message.

God can secure and preserve His Message from Satan's tricks in the same way that He secures and preserves His Message against lies and from obstacles. Prophets are exempted by God from all sorts of satanic temptations. God communicates the Divine Message to His Prophets while eliminating Satan's tricks. He firmly establishes His verses and signs and removes all forms of suspicion or worry. Thus, there is no chance for Satan to interfere with the Revelation coming to the Prophet or of him misleading the Prophet in this respect. The Prophet never fell into any sort of confusion or suspicion about the Revelations; he never fell under the influence of either Satan or any persons of evil character, nor did he succumb to any temptations.

The following verse is similar in context and it clearly indicates that such wicked and ill-willed persons have no chance to mislead the Prophet as he was completely protected against such attempts:

> But for God's grace and favor upon you and His mercy, one
> party of them determined to mislead you, yet they mislead
> none but themselves, and cannot harm you in any way. (How
> could they do so, seeing that) God has sent down on you the
> Book and the Wisdom, and taught you what you did not
> know. God's grace and favor upon you is tremendous indeed.
> (Nisa 4:113)

Human beings are essentially prone to desires, whims and fancies. But Prophets are pure personalities and are exempt from any such weaknesses that are apparent in other humans. The strongest desire in their hearts is to invite humanity to the Ultimate Truth. They eagerly desire that people instantly take to the path of faith; they display no behavior that is contrary to this, as this would be against the divine purpose. Thus, God has completely eliminated all sorts of false desires from their hearts that might exist in other humans. As a matter of fact, God's Messenger, who was rewarded and supported with both the Prophethood and Messengership and who was to be universally recognized by all of humanity never suffered any satanic attacks during his mission. As he was under Divine supervision, no one could cause him to doubt or make him utter incorrect things as part of the Revelation.

The Prophet suffered much from his community. His heart experienced a great deal of pain due to their frivolous demands. But, he never abandoned his mission and he never altered the divine commands, even when they persistently demanded that he do so; it was his obligation to convey these commands in full to the people. The following verse makes clear the oppressive and tyrannical demands that the Prophet was subjected to by the unbelievers:

> Now it may be that you (O Messenger) are drawn to abandon
> some part of what is revealed to you (such as the verses concerning your Messengership), and your breast is constricted
> thereby, on account of their saying: "Why has a treasure not
> been sent down upon him, or an angel accompanying him
> (visible to us)?" But you are only a warner. It is God Who has
> everything in His care and under His control. (Hud 11:12)

Here, the proclamation of "Will you then abandon as you feel pain in your heart, some of what we have revealed to you?" means that, despite all such serious hardships the Prophet faced, he was able to convey the Revelation to them without wearying or feeling any doubts.

The communication of the Divine Message is the most essential characteristic of Prophethood; the Prophet was ordered to continue conveying the Divine Message without paying any attention to the conceit or mocking of the unbelievers. He never abandoned this duty nor did he become weary of conveying all the Revelations; in this way he proved that he was pure and free from sin.

66 What evidence is there that the Qur'an is the Word of God?

The Qur'an itself is the most outstanding proof that it is the Word of God; a brief and basic search is sufficient to prove that the Qur'an resembles no other book, even in the language and expressions used. The Qur'an is inimitable in its style, wording, meaning, and content and thus, it cannot be the word of human beings. As a matter of fact, its expressions can have emanated only from a Supreme Being, Who holds absolute control of the whole universe at His disposal; they could not have been created by a human being, even a Prophet, as indicated in the following verses:

> Do they not contemplate the Qur'an (so that they may be convinced that it is from God)? Had it been from any other than God, they would surely have found in it much (incoherence or) inconsistency. (Nisa 4:82)

> You did not (O Messenger) read of any book before it (the revelation of this Qur'an), nor did you write one with your right (or left) hand. For then those who have ever sought to disprove the truth might have a reason to doubt (it). (Ankabut 29:48)

> Or do they say that he (the Messenger) has fabricated it? Say:
> "(If it is possible for a mortal to fabricate it) then produce a
> surah like it and call for help on anyone you can, apart from
> God, if you are truthful (in your doubt and the claim you base
> upon it)." (Yunus 10:38)

God's Messenger could neither write nor read; he was challenged with the Divine Revelation he received; since that time, educated people, great scholars and literary persons have faced the same challenge. The Prophet, the perfect bearer of God's final Revelation to all humanity, invites men of science and literature, including physicists, chemists, astronomers, doctors, sociologists and men of letters, to the Qur'an and he says to them "Hurry up and unite! And if you can bring forth something, be it ever so brief, something that is similar to a single Qur'anic verse." The fact that this humble challenge has not been met is sufficient witness and proof that the Qur'an is the Word of God, not of that of an illiterate Prophet.

It is quite easy to differentiate Prophet's style of expression from that of the Qur'an. In fact, no human being can attain the utmost eloquence and rhetoric of the Qur'an. The Prophet was raised among the Meccans and they were aware that he was illiterate and never dealt with poetry or prose. Indeed, the inimitable style of the Qur'an resembles neither the style of the Prophet nor that of his contemporaries. It is neither poetry nor prose. In the face of the eloquence and manner of expression of the Qur'an even the most eloquent of the Arabs, the first to be addressed by the Revelation, were amazed. Even though the Qur'an employed the very same letters and words they themselves used, it astonished them with its style, which was beyond the words of man. They were so amazed by supremacy of the Qur'an that they could not help approaching the Muslims at night to secretly listen to the recital of the Qur'an. The Qur'an made the most famous literary men, unrivalled preachers, and public speakers of the time kneel down in front of its inimitable miraculous style. Famous poets like

Hansa and Labid abandoned poetry after converting to Islam. When they were asked to recite or write a poem they would write a verse from the Qur'an, stating that it was not right for them to write poetry after having read the Qur'an.

Although poetry was extremely developed and had reached a high level at that time, Arabic, as a language, lacked metaphysical, scientific, religious, or philosophical concepts and expressions. This language, which enabled the desert Bedouin to express their ideals and sentiments and their desert-bound lifestyles, suddenly gained through the Qur'an great value and high prosperity; suddenly the language could discuss all manner of scientific, economical, legal, social, political, administrative and metaphysical matters. Such an event never occurred anywhere else in the history of linguistics. Not only could this great a revolutionary philological development which embraced all times and places have been achieved by the individual efforts of an illiterate person, but it would not have been possible with the joint and orchestrated efforts of hundreds of linguistic scholars. This was not a gradual development of the Arabic language. It was rather a giant leap forwards, achieved by a revolutionary development process; it was rather a sudden jump, from a primitive level of logic to a point where the ideological and sentimental expression of a brand new culture and civilization was possible. And it is as clear as day that such an improvement could not have been the achievement of an individual. Is there any other book that is understood and shared by people of all age groups, educational levels and capacities, including those who are literate and those who are illiterate, graduates of primary schools and those of universities, philosophers, laborers, physicists, chemists, and shepherds? The only book that is read and benefited from, which is regarded as a path to follow and as the basis for the principles of a lifetime, which is seen as a solution to all problems, as a cure to ailments and as an agent to polish ideals by poets, musicians, preachers, sociologists, economists, jurists, administrators and politicians, educators, teachers, and mystics, which shines like a bright star at everywhere, including the remotest villages is only the Qur'an.

There is no other book like this; the Qur'an can be read a number of times without there being any weariness. It is only the Qur'an that can be read repeatedly, which is recited everyday at all the daily prayers and on all occasions, never producing any feelings of boredom or disgust. Many an exceptional work, essay or poem loses its value and originality; many a work can only survive for a couple of years or even a couple of months. These works quickly lose their value both in their accuracy and usefulness and are soon discarded. But, with every new day the Qur'an sends fresh breezes to our souls, to our consciences, intellects, hearts, and minds; it presents ideals, sentiments, and knowledge at more advanced levels and it survives by preserving and by increasing the freshness and vigor. It never pales, shrivels up or becomes faded in its wording, meaning, language, or contents; its originality, practicality, and accuracy remain always fresh.

It is also obvious that the Qur'an cannot be the word of humans due to its portrayal of human beings in all their material and spiritual aspects; it mentions subjects that are related to every aspect and category of life, it imposes problem-solving principles in social, economical, legal, political and administrative areas and promises human prosperity in the Hereafter as well as in this worldly life with the imposition of principles that satisfy the soul as well as the intellect. It is not possible for a person to be a guide and an expert in every field. Therefore, an individual would be unable to provide the principles to solve all problems of human beings on every level, in every century, or under all conditions. No humanitarian principles can provide peace and prosperity in all places at all times. No man-made system that is not based upon the divine Revelation can survive, not even for 50 years, without being revised or changed.

Man-made principles, systems, ideals, and ideologies become old and insufficient, needing to be amended or even replaced.

However, it is not possible to find any inconsistency, deficiency, or mistake in the Qur'an. Whoever created man and the universe sent down the Qur'an, because the Qur'an clearly explains the reality of man while also commenting on the book of universe. The Qur'an reads and interprets human beings with all their virtues and weaknesses while contemplating the universe with all its mysteries. Therefore, an entity that does not have the power of the universe at their disposal cannot utter such words.

It is extremely difficult for a person to fully express themselves in their works or put all their ideas and sentiments fully into their writing. Even if we presume, for a moment, that one is able to do so, it would be next to impossible for them to maintain all their ideals and sentiments, keeping their morals and behaviors unchanged. However, God's Messenger throughout the twenty-three years of his Prophethood did not change even one of his words, mode of behavior, morals, or ideals. During this period of Prophethood we can also see that each and every command and prohibition of the Qur'an found their full reflection in his life; on the last day of the Prophet on this earth he said the same as what he had been saying on the first day. Assuming the impossible to be fact, if he had invented the Qur'an himself, he would have never have been able to display the power and capability to repeat the same thing he had said on the first day of his mission in his final days; he would have been unable to keep all his words and acts in agreement with his writing. He would have had to struggle greatly to remain unchanged throughout his lifetime, a time of great struggle. Thus we can conclude that he was a Prophet who spoke and acted under Divine guidance. He is the best of all creation and the seal of the Prophets and the Qur'an is the Divine Book that was revealed to him by God.

Authors are generally influenced by the conditions that they experience in their life time and this shows in their works; the incidences that they have been exposed to and the environment in which they live are reflected. They cannot extricate themselves from the relatively narrow span of time and space in which they live, and even if they are able to do so to some extent, this would be a form of utopia or science-fiction. However, we can see the clear expressions that are utilized by the Qur'an concerning the beginning and the end of the universe and the creation of life, as well as the future of human beings; willingly or not, in the end we must admit that "this cannot be the word of a human being."

An author most often produces works in their particular field of expertise. At such a time of expertise as today, there are fewer and fewer "Renaissance Men" and people are becoming more and more narrow in their fields of expertise. But, the Qur'an lays down principles in fields of anthropology, economics, law, psychology, politics, the military, medicine, physics, biology; in short, it is concerned with every field and describes the very basic reality of each particular field while mentioning both the future and the past. How could a person who was illiterate and who had none of the techno-scientific knowledge we have today, have written such a Book? What author can assert that the realities contained in their works will last for centuries without becoming outdated; how can they guarantee that no other book in any field will be able to surpass it at any time? Any human endeavor cannot help but become obsolete or outdated and thus lose much value. It is only the Qur'an, despite all hostile efforts and attempts to find weak points, which becomes fresher and fresher every day, firmly conquering minds and hearts. Even in our present time when the sciences are fairly advanced, no intelligent person can put absolutely certain theories about topics like the creation of heavens, earth, stars, mountains, trees, animals and humanity or about life. They may attract a few supporters, but their words never last long. There have been cases of false prophets and of scientists who produce theory after theory; these are obvious examples of what is being stated above.

The following forms of address in the Qur'an are clear samples of God's addressing His Prophet. Such Divine addresses as, "O Prophet, say!" are frequently employed and the imperative form, *qul*, or "say" is repeated 332 times in the Qur'an. At times the Prophet was asked questions and he used to remain silent and wait for the Revelation to come before answering such questions. In about 15 different places in the Qur'an there are questions in the form of *yas'alunaka*, or "They ask of you," directed to the Prophet; these, too, are given replies in the imperative form, beginning with *qul*, ("say!"). It is clear in the Qur'an that no one but God replies to questions about what is permissible and what is impermissible, such as the sharing of the gains of war, the new moon and crescent, Judgment Day, and almsgiving. No human being would be able to come up with the most suitable and fair solution to these problems, nor would he be able to create the most fitting verse for every incident.

In most such forms of address in the Qur'an there are answers to questions that come from outside; matters of education, advice, the formation of principles of canonical jurisprudence and solution to problems are all found here. There are invitations to polytheists and to People of the Book in some cases, whereas at other times they are silenced; there are examinations of the true nature of humankind, our sentiments and abilities and an analysis of the structure of the soul. There are signs from the realm of the unknown, warnings for the realm of eternity; there are attempts to prevent bad morals and encourage good morals. Matters related to women, encouragement to worship and warnings of torment are here as well as explanations, signs, and symbols that pertain to the future and indicate scientific facts. Who would be able to speak on God's behalf and bring all this, addressing the Prophet with the imperative *qul*?

Could an author ever address his own self as "You are *ummi*," (you do not know how to read or write), thus denying and contradicting his own contribution to the work, while speaking of matters that pertain to the past and the future, speaking about life and the creation, the beginning and the end, placing general rules and principles related to every aspect of life, drawing attention to scientific and technical inventions that will be disclosed hundreds of years later and, in short, speaking better than any intelligent educated man could ever speak?

Suppose, for a moment, that you are able to speak with confidence about certain incidents in the remote past and a future in which extensive historical research will be carried out in front of a historically literate audience; you tell your audience that you have not witnessed these past incidents nor read any information about them at all. Would such a thing be possible? Should such an audience listen to you and heed your words? How can the comparison and expression that we find in the Qur'an, for instance in verse 125 of Sura An'am, originate from the imagination and genius of a man who was raised illiterate in the desert? This verse as a Qur'anic miracle alludes to a scientific fact which would be discovered centuries later: *"He causes his breast to become tight and constricted, as if he were climbing towards the heaven..."* Despite the scientific advances of today if we are deprived of the proper apparatus when one climbs to the mountain peaks one suffers from breathlessness, and their chest is constricted due to the lack of oxygen. This fact is clearly understood and noticed only when one rises in a balloon or climbs very high mountains. Traveling with a balloon was not even imaginable during the lifetime of the Prophet and there are no high mountains in the Arabian Peninsula; so how did the Prophet know of the feeling of constriction on one's chest? Such a comparison can only be that of the All-Knowing God.

An author writes when they are inspired and it is at times like this when their mental concentration is at its peak. They bring forward events that worry or please them in their works. The most beautiful literary works were written at times when hearts were full of the most delicate and clearest emotions. Most such literary works speak of love, family, or important events. Suffering in a dungeon, memories of exile, experiences and bittersweet moments in one's professional life all find their reflections in literary works. It is not that easy to keep those experiences that have created deep impacts on the heart and soul out of one's work. In light of the above, let us look at the life story of the Prophet, which is full of suffering, misery, struggle, hardship, and grievances. Take into consideration how he raised and taught his exceptional community, while displaying fortitude against his opponents on the other. Finally, look at the Qur'an and see if you can find any verses in it that are concerned with his sufferings, calamities, and hardships or even any verses involving the lives and deaths of his own children! Also, see if you find any verses that mention his dear wife Khadija, who was his greatest supporter and fellow sufferer during his most miserable days, or any reference to the "Year of Sorrow," the year when both his uncle Abu Talib and his beloved wife passed away, or mention of the boycott to which the Prophet's close relatives from Banu Hashim were exposed for three years under the sun of Meccan desert, or mention of the assassination of his dear uncle Hamza, whose liver was carved out or finally, mention of the polytheist chiefs who deemed lawful every sort of cruel treatment. You will certainly not find any verses in the Qur'an mentioning these details. Thus, this Divine Book cannot be the work of the Prophet. He is merely a Messenger, the perfect bearer of the Divine Message for all humanity.

While writing a work an author might focus on feelings or considerations such as possessing wealth, becoming rich, gaining high positions or fame, communicating and exalting his ideals, or serving sacred or blasphemous thoughts. During the first era of the Prophethood in Mecca, God's Messenger was offered the leadership of Mecca, he was offered wealth the like of which no one else in Mecca had ever possessed, and he was offered the most beautiful girl of Mecca. But, he rejected all these proposals out of hand, merely saying, "Even if they were to place the sun in my right hand and the moon in my left, by God, I will never give up my mission." Would not a person fond of fame mention of himself in his own book? But, in the Qur'an, although the names of past Prophets are mentioned about 500 times, the name "Muhammad" is only mentioned 4 times in the entire Qur'an.[24] So, we cannot help bow down, once more, in front of Muhammad, the best of all creation and say, "We bear witness that you certainly are God's Messenger." These and thousands of similar signs prove that the Qur'an is not the word of humans, but rather that it is the Word of God, Who is the Creator and Lord of all the worlds.

67 | What does the divine guardianship of the Qur'an mean?

L et us first explain that, unlike other Holy Scriptures, the Qur'an has never been exposed to any alteration; both the Old and the New Testaments were written long after their revelation. They were also written by many different people and revised at many different times throughout history. Their scribes were also not the contemporaries of the Prophets witnessing the coming Revelation. The situation is totally different for the Qur'an. It should be noted first and foremost that the revealed verses and chapters were memorized by both the Prophet and his Companions and were committed to writing immediately by the scribes of the Revelation.

It should also be noted that the four Gospels of Matthew, Mark, Luke, and John were independently written. There were also many other gospels that were later not included into what became known as the Bible. Thus, the New Testament, which, in fact, came from a single source, became changed over time. In connection to this reality the Qur'an says that there can be no human interference with this Divine Book:

> Do they not contemplate the Qur'an (so that they may be convinced that it is from God)? Had it been from any other than God, they would surely have found in it much (incoherence or) inconsistency. (Nisa 4:82)

The process which earlier Holy Scriptures underwent has been clearly outlined in the Qur'an in the following verses:

Woe, then, to those who write the Book with their hands (interpolating into it their readings of the Scriptures and their explanatory notes thereto, stories from their national history, superstitious ideas and fancies, philosophical doctrines and legal rules) and then in order to sell it for a trifling price (such as worldly benefit, status, and renown), they declare: "This is from God." So woe to them for what their hands have written and woe to them for what they have earned (of the worldly income and the sin thereby). (Baqara 2:79)

They alter words from their context (in order to distort their meanings), and they have forgotten a (most important) portion of what they were admonished about. You will not cease to light upon some act of treachery from them, except a few of them. Yet pardon them, and overlook (their misdeeds). Assuredly, God loves those devoted to doing good deeds, aware that God is seeing them. (Maeda 5:13)

O Messenger! Let them not grieve you who would rush in unbelief, as if competing with one another in a race, such of them as say with their mouths, "We believe," but their hearts do not believe, and those of them who are Jews. They are eagerly listening out for falsehoods (especially about you) and eagerly listening out (spying) on behalf of other people who have never come to you (even to learn the essence of your Message); altering any words (whether pertaining to God or not) from their contexts to distort their meanings. They say (about matters referred to you for judgment): "If such and such judgment is given to you, accept it; but if it is not given to you, then beware!" (Maeda 5:41)

Due to the reliability of its origin the Qur'an has a unique status that no other heavenly Books possess. God Almighty has guarded it against any corruption:

Indeed it is We, We Who send down the Reminder in parts, and it is indeed We Who are its Guardian. (Hijr 15:9)

Falsehood can never have access to it, whether from before it or from behind it (whether by arguments and attitudes based on modern philosophies or by attacks from the past based on earlier Scriptures); (it is) the Book being sent down in parts from the One All-Wise, All-Praiseworthy (to Whom all praise and gratitude belong). (Fussilat 41:42)

68 | What is the evidence that the Qur'an has remained exactly the same, without even the smallest change?

The greatest proof that the Qur'an has never changed since the time of its revelation and that it will not be changed until the Last Day is the promise of God in the verse, *"Indeed it is We, We Who send down the Reminder in parts, and it is indeed We Who are its Guardian"* (Hijr 15:9). This is not just an empty claim, it is the absolute truth. The fact that there is not even the slightest difference between the Qur'an which was recited during the earliest period of Islam and any other copies printed or recited now in any part of the Muslim world is another proof that the Qur'an has not changed since its revelation.

As a matter of fact, there is no difference at all between the Qur'an manuscript that carries the signature of the third Caliph Uthman, dated 30 A.H., No. 457 in the Museum of Turkish and Islamic Arts in Istanbul, Turkey, or manuscript No. 557 in the same museum, which carries the signature of the fourth Caliph Ali, or the Qur'an copy No. 458 in the same museum which is believed to have been hand-written by the fourth Caliph Ali himself and all the other historical Qur'an manuscripts that are scattered throughout the Islamic world.

Should there be any least of difference between the old and the new copies of the Qur'an the enemies of the Qur'an and Islam, who have been doing their best to find any errors in it, would have utilized this as a golden opportunity for their purposes. This is more clear evidence of the Qur'an's authenticity that they did not, or in fact, could not find any such opportunity.

CHAPTER 9

_____

Themes and Basic Purposes
of the Qur'an

THEMES AND BASIC PURPOSES
OF THE QUR'AN

69 | Does the Qur'an contain knowledge pertaining to different branches of science?

If we examine the Qur'an we can see that it contains answers to those issues about which everyone desires a solution; in short we are presented with a multi-dimensional treasury of knowledge. It must be added, however, that the Qur'an does not contain detailed information about the various branches of sciences, but only speaks of the basic laws and basic principles of sciences. The Qur'an is not a book of sciences and is not concerned with subjects like physics, chemistry or mathematics. Such a thing would indeed be impossible. The Qur'an mentions scientific facts only parenthetically and uses them as evidence for the truths it conveys. Whatever knowledge it provides can be regarded only as informative at an introductory level. After mentioning the basic rules and principles, the Qur'an does not go into details. The reason for doing so is that man is regarded as an entity that has will power, and not as a dry leaf that is dragged hither and thither by the wind. That is, the Qur'an does not just give us a fish to eat, it teaches us how to fish. This is how the assertion that the Qur'an comprises all sciences should be approached. Otherwise, one would expect the Qur'an to classify all sciences throughout the history of humanity and those of the future. But this is something that is beyond the purpose of the Qur'an and beyond its being a divine word.

What is meant by the fact that the Qur'an comprises all the sciences is that it shows the truest of all things to humankind at all times and in all locations with the rules and principles it puts forth. It enlightens humankind, announcing the existence of a life in the Hereafter by emphasizing the necessity of believing in God, His angels, His books and His Prophets and guiding them to the truest of ways and the best of behavior; it warns and prevents them from indulging in superstitious or deviant ways. The Qur'an directs humans towards acts of worship which are performed easily and which purify and equip them with will power.

By ordering high morals and virtues and by putting forth personal and social principles by which man can abide, the Qur'an directs every human towards being God's vicegerent on earth. By doing so, it also aims to keep societies safe from violence and confusion and to provide peaceful, secure and happy living conditions. The religion brought by the Qur'an is one that is best suited to the natural human disposition, and satisfies all the needs of both the mind and the soul while maintaining a perfect balance between this world and the next. The religion of Islam also displays the greatest level of moderation and provides convincing and satisfying solutions, far removed from apathy and excess when responding to human needs.

Likewise, the procedure that should be followed when two people break with one another and ways of solving family-related problems are explained. Matters like the status and rights of non-Muslim subjects, relations between Muslim and non-Muslims in times of war and peace, steadfastness and courage on the battle-field, the treatment of prisoners of war and the provisions of peace treaties are all dealt with in the Qur'an.

A person may be specialized and have some things to say in one or a couple of different subjects. But, the Prophet, who was illiterate, may not always have things to say and provide solutions on every issue which interests everybody and from all aspects. And, it is absolutely impossible for a person's deeds to be totally perfect. But, as we look at the Qur'an, we notice that there is not almost any matter which it did not say anything on or which it deals explicitly or alludes to. More importantly, as whatever it said could not have been falsified, they, on the contrary, all have been proved to be true and to be excellently suitable for humanity until now, although so long a time has passed since its revelation. This clearly indicates that, although the Qur'an speaks over such a large and diverse field, it is not a human word, but the Word of God.

In addition, many other subjects pertaining to everyday life are also dealt with. For example, how one should behave towards one's relatives, how we should receive bad treatment with kindness and forgiveness, encourage good deeds and justice, safekeeping things left in one's trust, humility and abstention from pride, abstention from mockery, suspicion, backbiting and prying out the secrets of others, respect and care for the privacy of others in their homes, the importance of honesty and chastity, as well as the principles for receiving guests are all laid out. In short, the Qur'an has a vast diversity and variety of subjects related to our everyday lives.

70 | What are the main purposes of the Qur'an?

For the most part, throughout all the verses the Qur'an aims to establish and confirm four basic, universal truths: the existence and Oneness of the Maker, the necessity of the institution of the Prophethood, the Resurrection, and worshipping God as an indication of our servitude. We can notice either all or some of these major purposes in every chapter, every verse and even in every word of the Qur'an.

The first and primary purpose of the Qur'an is to properly teach humankind about God's existence and Oneness, or Divinity. As a matter of fact, the divine purpose for creation and God's sending humankind to this worldly life is, the Qur'an teaches us, that we recognize and worship our Creator. The following verse clearly explains this: *"I have not created the jinn and humankind but to (know and) worship Me (exclusively)"* (Dhariyat 51:56). Accordingly, knowledge of God is the ultimate cause for creation. The Supreme Being wills to be known and recognized in the correct way, to be believed and worshipped.

As history clearly witnesses, human beings have forgotten the Divine purpose of their creation. Even during the periods between the Prophets who were sent, people went on committing excesses, and betraying the Divine trust they fell again to worshipping many deities and displayed servitude to many idols, lifeless creatures, celestial stars, none of which could provide benefit or harm. Believing in God is, in fact, a natural need that exists in human disposition. Every person feels a need to believe in a being who is more powerful and stronger than themselves. If, however, for some reason this inner need is not satisfied by belief in God, the Maker of the universe, then people will attempt to satisfy this need with incorrect solutions and fall prey to misconceptions about the Deity. Some might conceive of this supreme entity as forces of nature, while others will see it to be contained in idols they have produced. Thus, the very first and primary aim of the Qur'an is to teach humankind the correct belief in God.

The second purpose of the Qur'an is to provide true guidance to humankind through the Messengers. Divinity demands that there is a person who will make God known to others and teaching humankind how to perform their servitude to their Lord. God Almighty appointed Prophets and Messengers one after the other, and all Prophets expended great efforts to tell their communities of the One God and invited them to recognizing Him and submit only to Him.

The third purpose of the Qur'an is to tell and describe the reality of the bodily Resurrection and the existence of the Hereafter. As this world is transient, since Heaven and Hell and the events which humans are to encounter after death are of immense importance to them, and because belief in the Hereafter affects behavioral modes of human beings positively and favorably, the Supreme Creator frequently emphasizes in various chapters and verses of the Qur'an the reality of the bodily Resurrection and the existence of the Hereafter.

Finally, the fourth primary purpose of the Qur'an is to inform humanity that they need to serve and worship God. Such matters as why we have to worship, how we have to worship, and the forms and extent of our worship are among subjects that have frequently been dealt with in the Qur'an.

---

71 | Who are the Prophets whose names are mentioned in the Qur'an? Are there Prophets who are not mentioned?

The Qur'an speaks about a number of distinguished Prophets God has sent to humanity since the time of Prophet Adam. Some of them are recounted in detail while others are mentioned only briefly. God's honorable Prophets and Messengers are not, however, limited only to those whose names are mentioned in the Qur'an. The following verses disclose that only some of the many Prophets are mentioned in the Qur'an:

> And Messengers We have already told you of (with respect to their mission) before, and Messengers We have not told you of.... (Nisa 4:164)

> Indeed We sent Messengers before you; among them are those (the exemplary histories of) whom We have already related to you, and among them are those (the exemplary histories of) whom We have not related to you.... (Mu'min 40:78)

In some hadiths it is reported that God sent 124,000 Prophets at different times and to different locations. The following are the Prophets whose names are mentioned in the Qur'an: 1. Adam, 2. Enoch, 3. Noah, 4. Hud, 5. Salih, 6. Abraham, 7. Lot, 8. Ishmael, 9. Isaac, 10. Jacob, 11. Joseph, 12. Shu'ayb, 13. Job, 14. Dhu'l-Kifl, 15. Moses, 16. Aaron, 17. David, 18. Solomon, 19. Elijah, 20. Elisha, 21. Jonah, 22. Zachariah, 23. John, 24. Jesus, and 25. Muhammad, may peace be upon them all.

There is disagreement regarding whether Luqman, Dhu'l Qarnayn and Ezra, whose names are mentioned in the Qur'an, were Prophets. Some scholars are of the opinion that they were Prophets while others believe that they were not Prophets, but rather God's righteous servants who were given a special mission.

72 | Why are the narratives of bygone nations mentioned in detail in the Qur'an?

The narratives of the Prophets, or *qisas al-anbiya*, constitute almost half of the Qur'an. The Arabic word *qissa* literally means tracing or narrating something. Terminologically it means relating a past event to people in later periods. The term *qissa*, in this sense, is different from a story or parable. While the event told in a story or in a parable does not have to have actually occurred, the *qisas* are the actual history of past nations. Thus, every *qissa* related in the Qur'an actually happened.

As for the Qur'an's frequent mention of the *qisas* (narratives), we can say that the Qur'an uses them as a method to establish and confirm its purposes. As explained above, the Qur'an pursues the establishment of four cardinal truths: the existence and Oneness of the Maker, Prophethood, bodily Resurrection, and worship. So, the Qur'an utilizes the narratives of the Prophets and their people so that it can relate these important truths. By recounting the narratives of bygone nations, the Qur'an is not aiming at literary art in the narratives. However, the fact that the narratives in the Qur'an are intended for religious purposes does not prevent them containing literary artistry. The Qur'anic expressions have both religious purposes and literary artistry; they address the human soul with the beauty of such literary artistry. The understanding of the audience and the pleasure they receive from such supreme artistry influences them religiously. It is not always easy to convey the intended message(s) to an addressee, as during any intellectual encounter the audience may adopt a defensive or reactionary attitude. Ideas are better grasped when presented accompanied by emotions and this is the reason why the greatest works of literature present their intended messages in poetical or artistic manners. In this way, the ideals presented can be better understood by the audience.

The Qur'anic narratives or *qisas*, in this context, should be regarded as a history of the faith of unity and to a great extent they relate the Prophets' messages and the attitudes of the respective communities to these messages. The narratives of the Prophets Adam, Noah, Abraham, Joseph, Moses, Jesus, and Muhammad are mentioned more frequently in the Qur'an than the other Prophets.

The Divine reasons behind these narratives in the Qur'an can be given as follows:

a. To prove the Prophethood of Muhammad; the depiction of events that were experienced and buried in the depths of the past by an illiterate Prophet shows that these narrations can be nothing but Divine Revelation.

b. To notify that the Truth which was unanimously propagated by all Prophets is "Islam", a word that literally means submission to the One and only God, the Creator of all universes.

c. To help human beings learn certain lessons; learning lessons from the narratives involves a couple of aspects. By temperament, human beings are strongly opposed to the wicked people and their deeds which are narrated here and this encourages them to abstain from doing similar things. In this regard narratives provide a number of lessons and give examples of what should and should not be done. Another way that these narratives provide a lesson is that the Prophets and their miracles that are narrated in the Qur'an illuminate the path of humanity towards scientific explorations and encourage scientific study.

d. To strengthen the hearts of the Prophet, his Companions and the following generations; the terrible end that these tyrants meet after having acted rebelliously against the Prophets and forcing them to migrate from their own lands was a good means to encourage the heart of the Prophet and that of other righteous people.

| 73 | Does the Qur'an clearly mention the five daily prayers and how to perform them? |

We have previously mentioned that the Revelation which came to the Prophet was more than what is included in the Qur'an. In the Qur'an, God, sometimes openly mentions the obligations of human beings, sometimes only pointing them out, sometimes just referring to their names, or sometimes not mentioning them at all. He taught their applications and how to perform them via the Sunna. Although the Qur'an commands the believers to *"establish the Prayer in conformity with its conditions"* (Ankabut 29:45), it does not specify how the prayer is to be performed with all its conditions. Thus, how to establish the daily prayers is laid out in the Practice of the Prophet. In a related hadith God's Messenger said: "Establish the prayer as you see me establish it."

God Almighty taught His Messenger through Archangel Gabriel how to perform the five daily prayers and the time of each prayer. The Prophet, in one of his traditions, said: "Archangel Gabriel led me twice in all five daily prescribed prayers nearby the Ka'ba. The first day, he led me in the noon prayer, after midday immediately after the sun had left the highest point and just when the shadows were the shortest. He later led me in the afternoon prayer just at the time when the shadows were the same as their actual height. He led me in the evening prayer at the time of breaking the fast, the night prayer when twilight had disappeared and the sunrise prayer when it is forbidden to eat and drink anything for those who want to fast. The following day, he led me in the noon prayer at the time when the shadows were equal to their height, the afternoon prayer at the time when the shadows were twice as high as their own height, the evening prayer at the same time as the previous day, the night prayer after one third of the night had passed and the sunrise prayer when the daylight had appeared. He later turned towards me and said: 'O Muhammad! These are the times of prayers which the previous Prophets performed and the best time of any prayer is that which is in the middle of the two prayer times (that I have shown you).'"

We find references to the times of daily prayers in the following verses of the Qur'an:

> Establish the Prayer (O Messenger) at the beginning and the end of the day, and in the watches of the night near to the day. Surely good deeds wipe out evil deeds. (Hud 11:114)

> Therefore, be patient (O Messenger) with whatever they say and glorify your Lord with praise before sunrise and before sunset, and glorify Him during some hours of the night – as well as glorifying (Him) at the ends of the day – so that you may obtain God's good pleasure and be contented (with what God has decreed for you). (Ta.Ha 20:130)

> So glorify God when you enter the evening and when you enter the morning; and (proclaim that) all praise and gratitude in the heavens and on the earth are for Him – and in the afternoon and when you enter the noon time. (Rum 30:17-18)

74 | How does the Qur'an prescribe the behavior of believers in the context of inter-personal relations?

Matters concerning the interrelations of human beings are dealt with in various Qur'anic chapters. Sura Hujurat, for instance, is one of the Qur'anic chapters in which the divine ordinances pertaining to the manners and behaviors of believers in their social life are dealt with.

The aspect of religion that pertains to how believers relate to one another and how Muslims should behave toward the Prophet and each other is of great importance; this is mentioned in the Qur'an in many aspects. For instance, people would come and stay for a long time when visiting the Prophet; he would show merciful tolerance to this behavior despite the difficult position they put him. The Qur'an warned these people, but such admonitions for causing others inconvenience are valid for people of all times. Those who carry out their actions mindful of God should observe the etiquette of social interaction that is laid out in the Qur'an. The Prophet faced difficulties because some people, merely because they enjoyed his conversations, would never consider that he might be prevented from doing some important tasks. Thus, in Sura Ahzab Muslims were warned to leave after their business was done:

> O you who believe! Do not enter the Prophet's rooms (in his house) unless you have been given leave, (and when invited) to a meal, without waiting for the proper time (when the meal is to be served). Rather, when you are invited, enter (his private rooms) at the proper time; and when you have had your meal, disperse. Do not linger for mere talk. That causes trouble for the Prophet, and he is shy of (asking) you (to leave). But God does not shy away from (teaching you) the truth. When you ask something of them (his wives), ask them from behind a screen. Your doing so is purer for your hearts and for their hearts. It is not for you to cause hurt to God's Messenger as it is unlawful for you ever to marry his widows after him. That (marrying his widows) would be an enormity in God's sight. (Ahzab 33:53)

The ethical principles enunciated here is not restricted to a particular time or environment. By exhorting the Prophet's Companions to revere his person, the Qur'an reminds all believers, at all times, certain rules of behavior bearing on the life of the community. Believers are taught be mindful of mutual consideration and respect for the sanctity of each other's personality and privacy. For instance, one should not enter others' houses and have a meal without the host's consent. However, the Qur'an, in order to secure and maintain a comfortable social life, declared that it is permitted to eat without seeking permission in houses of such people as the spouses, children, parents, brothers, sisters, uncles, aunts, friends and those who left keys of their houses to us for safeguarding and protection as there is nothing wrong for us to eat in houses of such kith and kin.

75 | Why is the Prophet's wedding to Zaynab mentioned in the Qur'an?

The Prophet's marriage to Zaynab after her divorce from Zayd, the Prophet's emancipated slave whom he called "my son" in accordance with the customs of the time before adoption was legally abolished, is another initiative towards the nullification of the misguided practices of the Age of Ignorance. Zaynab bint Jahsh, a lady of noble birth and descent, was the daughter of the Prophet's aunt. When she came of age, the Prophet made known to her parents that he wished her to marry Zayd, his adopted son, to show that people should not judge others by their color or social status.

By virtue of Zaynab's marriage to Zayd, a number of new practices were introduced to the community and a number of the practices of the Age of Ignorance were nullified. Among the many reasons of this marriage, we can mention the following:

During the Age of Ignorance, the attitudes behind racism were prevalent in Mecca in the guise of tribalism; slaves had long been regarded as despicable and second class. Due to this perception they were unable to tackle the barrier of class difference even when they had been emancipated. Islam, a religion that defended absolute equality, did not tolerate such unjust treatment. The criteria of the supremacy or inferiority of a person in Islam is not whether they are free or a slave. Rather, Islam's criteria of supremacy is only related to how good one is:

> O humankind! Surely We have created you from a single (pair of) male and female, and made you into tribes and families so that you may know one another (and so build mutuality and co-operative relationships, not so that you may take pride in your differences of race or social rank, and breed enmities). Surely the noblest, most honorable of you in God's sight is the

one best in piety, righteousness, and reverence for God. Surely
God is All-Knowing, All-Aware. (Hujurat 49:13)

It was not, however, an easy task to erase such a deep-rooted and
long-standing social tendency. The Prophet aimed to abolish first
slavery, eliminating feelings of inferiority and to change the despicable and mean image of slaves in people's mind. He attempted to solve
this issue with his close relatives and wed his aunt's daughter Zaynab
to his freed slave Zayd. By this initiative, he wanted to show that a
man freed from slavery and a free and noble person are equal in social
status and thus there was nothing wrong in their marriage.

Zaynab's family, at first, was hesitant to accept such a proposal and the following verse was revealed upon this hesitation:
"*When God and His Messenger have decreed a matter, it is not for a
believing man and a believing woman to have an option insofar as they
themselves are concerned…*" (Ahzab 33:36). Finally, Zaynab and her
family all consented to this proposal even though they had hoped
to marry their daughter to the Prophet. However, Zaynab's marriage with Zayd did not last long and they soon divorced.

As indicated above, Zaynab belonged to a noble family and was
a kind and fine-spirited young woman. She could not regard Zayd
as equal to herself in social status and did not want to marry a freed,
ex-slave. She accepted this marriage merely because the Prophet
wanted her to. But, this marriage did not bring happiness to either
party. Their situation was repeatedly reported to the Prophet, but,
he always advised them patience and not to divorce. In particular he
told Zayd: "Keep your wife with you and fear from God, for, the
ugliest of permissible deeds in God's view is divorce."[25]

The Prophet knew, as God had informed him, that Zaynab
would one day be his wife. But, this seemed to be extremely difficult for the Prophet, because, according to the prevailing customs,
"adopted" children were treated as if they were real children in
matters of inheritance, divorce, or prohibition of marriage. But
God willed that this custom be abolished and first put it into effect

through His Messenger. The Prophet thought that people might draw incorrect conclusions and think negative things about him if he were to carry out such an action, and this would therefore harm their faith. The following verse refers to this fact:

> You were hiding within yourself what God (had already decreed and) would certainly bring to light: you were feeling apprehensive of people (that they might react in a way harmful to their faith), while God has a greater right that you should fear Him (lest you err in the implementation of His commands). So, when Zayd had come to the end of his union with her (and she had completed her period of waiting after the divorce), We united you with her in marriage, so that there should be no blame (or legal impediment) for the believers in respect of (their marrying) the wives of those whom they called their sons (though they really were not), when the latter have come to the end of their union with them. And God's command must be fulfilled. (Ahzab 33:37)

The misguided custom of the pre-Islamic era was to be abolished by the Prophet's marrying Zaynab after she was divorced from Zayd. Moreover, by marrying a woman who had divorced a freed slave, slaves were shown to be human beings who were equal to other people and that there was no problem with marrying their divorced wives. The Prophet thus completely abolished this deep-rooted tradition by marrying Zaynab according to the clear injunction of the Qur'an: "*We have married her to you.*" This announces the Prophet's marriage to Zaynab as a bond that has already been contracted. Such a move could have been achieved only by Prophet Muhammad, peace and blessings be upon him.

76 | Why does the Qur'an mention personalities like Abu Lahab?

The divine ordinances in the Qur'an are for the most part general. Although there are ordinances that address particular matters this does not challenge the universality of the Qur'an. That is to say, addressing particular persons or matters does not mean that the ordinance pertaining to them is limited only to this time period. The particularity of the circumstances and causes of a Revelation does not necessarily mean that the divine ordinance is also particular. The ordinance is general. But, due to certain divine reasons, God has declared His ordinance by mentioning particular persons and matters in certain suras. Abu Lahab, Zayd's divorce, and a woman's complaint to the Prophet are all examples of this. In this way God draws our attention towards certain facts. Let us look at the case of Abu Lahab for instance:

Despite the fact that he was very close to the Prophet, Abu Lahab could not benefit from his guidance and he soon became the most resolute enemy to the Prophet. Hence, the most terrible punishment and the severest treatment were prepared for him, both in this world and in the Hereafter. His wife was a rich woman of noble birth. She took great pleasure in participating in committing the most ill-mannered and shameless acts against the Prophet.

Abu Lahab was an extremely stubborn man. When speaking about him, Abu Jahl used to say: "Never make him angry. If he takes to the other side, no one will ever be able to bring him back to our side." In solidarity with his wife, he honored and worshipped the idols that were then kept inside the Ka'ba, never trying to understand and benefit from the great personality of the Prophet.

Abu Lahab constantly tried to cause the Prophet harm. He joined forces with Abu Jahl, who had organized a total embargo and boycott against the Prophet and Muslims; this embargo lasted three years and was a time during which Muslims suffered greatly and many elderly persons and infants died. Abu Lahab never felt any sympathy towards the Prophet or the Muslims. Khadija, the wife of the Prophet, could not bear this treatment and passed away in the Year of Sorrow due to the tyranny and injustice which the Muslims were exposed to. Abu Talib, the Prophet's elderly uncle, also passed away in the same year. Though he was not a Muslim, his love and affection for his nephew caused him to bear the same tyrannies and injustices the Muslims were subjected to.

While Abu Talib, the Prophet's elderly uncle, was safeguarding him, the Prophet's younger uncle, Abu Lahab, was inflicting every type of brutality on him. The Prophet visited a number of tribes, telling them of the true religion of Islam and inviting them to it. Abu Lahab followed every step of the Prophet and tried to convince the people he had visited not to believe in what he was preaching. It is because of this boundless enmity that the Qur'an designated Abu Lahab, the Father of the Flame, signifying that he was one who would be destined to be among those suffering the greatest torment in Hellfire.

The Qur'an announces the punishment to be inflicted on him as: *"May both hands of Abu Lahab be ruined, and is ruined himself!"* The chapter which takes its name from the verb *Tabba*, or ruined, in the first verse promises and foretells the destruction of Abu Lahab and his wife, thus implying the perdition of similar enemies of Islam.

77 How should we understand and interpret the Qur'anic verse that refers to the permission to beat one's wife?

God made all of humankind, both male and female, honorable. The Qur'an treats women as individuals, just as it treats men:

> Surely all men and women who submit to God (whose submission is attested by their words and deeds), and all truly believing men and truly believing women, and all devoutly obedient men and devoutly obedient women, and all men and women honest and truthful in their speech (and true to their words in their actions), and all men and women who persevere (in obedience to God through all adversity), and all men and women humble (in mind and heart before God), and all men and women who give in alms (and in God's cause), and all men and women who fast (as an obligatory or commended act

of devotion), and all men and women who guard their chastity (and avoid exposing their private parts), and all men and women who remember and mention God much – for them God has prepared forgiveness (to bring unforeseen blessings) and a tremendous reward. (Ahzab 33:35)

The Qur'an provides clear instructions on what a husband should do during times of disagreement when the wife is behaving in an un-Islamic manner. If we keep in mind that the reason for chastising a woman must be very serious, the reasons why such corrective and educative measures have been laid out in the following verse can be better understood:

Men (those who are able to carry out their responsibilities) are the protectors and maintainers of women inasmuch as God has endowed some of people (in some respects) with greater capacity than others and inasmuch as they (the men) spend of their wealth (for the family's maintenance). Good, righteous women are the devoted ones (to God) and observant (of their husbands' rights), who guard the secrets (family honor and property, their chastity, and their husband's rights, especially where there is none to see them and in the absence of men) as God guards and keeps undisclosed (what should be guarded and private). As for those women from whose determined disobedience and breach of their marital obligations you have reason to fear, admonish them (to do what is right); then, (if that proves to be of no avail), remain apart from them in beds; then (if that too proves to be of no avail) beat them (lightly without beating them in their faces). Then if they obey you (in your directing them to observe God's rights and their marital obligations) do not seek ways against them (to harm them). (Be ever mindful that) God is indeed All-Exalted, All-Great. And if you fear that a breach might occur between a couple, appoint an arbiter from among his people and an arbiter from among her people. If they both want to set things aright, God will bring about reconciliation between them. Assuredly, God is All-Knowing, All-Aware. Nisa 4:34-35)

Islam, as a religion, does not passively tolerate the disruption of marital harmony; if the wife is behaving in a way that is disruptive to the family and, therefore, to the society the problem must be dealt with in a resolute way. If this is not the case, the family would one day disappear. Beating, as stated in this verse, is to be employed as the last resort after exercising a number of preliminary corrective efforts, including discussion and reasoning. Thus, it is an exceptional action and would only be applied to those who are not open to reason. Although Islam permits light physical chastisement, the conditions under which this is permissible and the degree are clearly defined. In line with the purpose of the Qur'an to guide the affairs of humans, this Qur'anic passage aims to provide a means for resolving disharmony between husband and wife.

It is needless to say that, if there is harmony between partners in such an important social institution, then there is no need for any such measures. In fact, a believing woman should be respectful to her husband as part of genuine faith and this respect should be mutual. A really obstinate and disobedient person is one that is so obvious in rebellious deeds. The term *nashaz* which has been used to describe such people in this verse means "to rise up." Once signs of any such obstinacy and rebellion would become evident, the gradual precautionary measures should promptly be implemented to eradicate the state of disorder between the couple. The Qur'an is thus authorizing the husband with implementing certain corrective and educative methods which are playing a favorable role in most cases. It is not, surely, aimed, by such methods, to take revenge from the obstinate wife, to belittle or to hurt her. Instead, it is aimed to prevent any potential damage in the family union at this very early stage. The purposes of such precautionary measures in the Qur'an are to heal the souls and to solve problems before they take root without destroying the heart or will or causing them to be filled with hatred or feelings of revenge or giving rise to feelings of inferiority.

What is intended in the verse is not to encourage a struggle between men and women in which the honor of the woman would be injured. Such a purpose has nothing to do with Islam. "*As for those women from whose determined disobedience and breach of their marital obligations you have reason to fear, admonish them to do what is right.*" So, the first step to be followed in the sequential manner suggested by the Qur'an is to admonish the wife; this is also a frequently applied means of education and training, as God says in another Qur'anic verse, "*O you who believe! Guard yourselves and your families (through the enabling discipline of Islamic faith and worship) against a Fire whose fuel is human beings and stones. Over it are angels stern and strict (in executing the command to punish), who do not disobey God in whatever He commands them, and carry out what they are commanded (to carry out)*" (Tahrim 66:6).

The purpose of such an admonition would be to prevent arguments and thus save the marriage. In certain cases such a step might not be enough, for example, if the woman has indulged in great selfishness or self-pride. Depending on her beauty, wealth, nobility, or any sort of a private concession or privilege, she might forget that she is an equal partner in the family. In such cases, the second remedy should be applied; the aim of this is to save the woman from unnecessary and unjustified self-pride. If open discussion or verbal solution fails, then the Qur'an suggests a more drastic solution: "*...then, (if that proves to be of no avail), remain apart from them in beds.*" The bed is a place of sexual pleasure. An arrogant woman is at the peak of sovereignty here. If a man can limit his desires against such incitement, he would disarm an arrogant wife. The display of such a powerful will at such a critical moment generally causes the woman to retreat and become humble. However, the husband should refrain from apathy or access at this most sensitive time as it is not possible to obtain the desired results thus. Man should continue to share the bed, but turn his back on his wife, thus keeping a distance from her. He should neither leave the room and nor make a second bed for himself; this is not as meaningful. In addition, such an action should be kept within the secrecy of the bedroom and the children or strangers should not be aware of the situation. This is a type of cooling off period during which it is possible to regain marital harmony without taking the final step mentioned in the verse.

If this second remedy is not successful what then? Is the family to fall apart? No. There is a final measure to take in such extreme cases: light chastisement is permitted. This may look a bit more drastic than the other two measures, but it is certainly much less risky and much easier to apply. After taking the common purpose of the two remedies above into consideration, we can see that the said "beating" is not some sort of sly method of abusing one's wife or gaining revenge, nor is it an act intended to hurt or dishonor a woman. This act of beating is permissible only if a motive of correction is intended, like that of a loving mother towards her children or a teacher towards their students.

The matter of this physical chastisement should be considered in connection with the above-mentioned three aspects. Otherwise, sticking to only the subject of beating, whether in support of it or opposed to it, one cannot hope to arrive at a balanced approach. First of all, beating is not the primary act. Beating one's wife was the norm at the time of the Revelation and Muslims would come to the Prophet and complain him about the caprices of their wives. He responded, saying "pat them gently without causing any harm", and told them not to strike their wives on the face. After a short while, the women who had been beaten by their husbands came to the Prophet's wives and complained about their husbands. When the Prophet's wives reported this situation to him the Prophet came to the mosque and brought together his Companions and said: "I have heard that you are beating your wives. Beat not your wives anymore."

There are a number of traditions from the Prophet about not beating women. These traditions elaborate on certain matters that are treated briefly in the Qur'anic verse. Some traditions discuss the unnaturalness of abuse, strongly criticizing those who beat their wives during the day and approach them at night. He once advised a Muslim woman, Fatima bint Qays, not to marry a man who was known for beating women.

The Prophet gave great care to the rights of women. One of his Companions asked him, "O God's Messenger! What is my duty to my wife?", the Prophet replied: "That you give her to eat what you eat yourself, and clothe her as you clothe yourself; and do not slap her in the face or abuse her, or separate yourself from her in displeasure." Another time the Prophet said: "The best of you are those who treat their wives the best. And, I am the best amongst you to my family."

While implementing the gradual measures that are aimed at saving a marriage from collapse, if the application of the measures mentioned in the verse do not yield any favorable results, then the Qur'an suggests another precautionary measure:

> And if you fear that a breach might occur between a couple, appoint an arbiter from among his people and an arbiter from among her people. If they both want to set things aright, God will bring about reconciliation between them. Assuredly, God is All-Knowing, All-Aware. (Nisa 4:35)

In order to prevent divorce, Islam suggests a mechanism for resolving the problem through extended consultation and arbitration. The verse proposes two arbiters to be selected and agreed upon, one from the side of each spouse, to deal with the problem. These two arbiters would try to mediate the offended spouses. If both spouses would have desires of reconciliation in their hearts, but would abstain from doing so just because of their mutual angers, then, God would grand this couple reconciliation and agreement due to positive approaches of both arbiters: being free from the psychological restraints that are involved in marital relations, these arbiters are able to calmly meet and discuss the matter. The arbiters of both sides can avoid defamation to their respective families and they are both full of affection and sympathy to the children of the family in question. They are also not interested in scoring points off one another. All they want is to achieve what is beneficial to both sides, the happiness of their children and the safety of a home that has been faced with the threat of collapse.

The spouses should not hesitate to share their problems with them for solution. *"If they both want to set things aright, God will bring about reconciliation between them."* The arbiters desire to reconcile the couple and God will accept their wishes and succeed them. However, human beings can take initiative. Developments beyond this point are at the disposal of God, Who is the All-Knowing and the All-Aware.

78 | In the Qur'an it is stated that heavenly rewards and blessings are greater for men. Is this true?

Nowhere in the Qur'an does it assert that only men will be rewarded in Paradise and that women are to be presented to them as a reward. For believing men and women there will be pure spouses in Paradise:

> Give glad tidings to those who believe and do good, righteous deeds: for them are Gardens through which rivers flow. Every time they are provided with fruits (of different color, shape, taste, and fragrance and that are constantly renewed) therefrom, they say, "This is what we were provided with before." For they are given to them in resemblance (to what was given to them both in the world, and just before in the Gardens, familiar in shape and color so that they may not be unattractive because unknown). Furthermore, for them are spouses eternally purified (of all kinds of worldly uncleanliness). They will abide there (forever). (Baqara 2:25)

There is nothing that is opposed to women in the Qur'anic verses or in the Prophetic traditions that are related with Paradise and Hell, or reaching eternal happiness. On the contrary, these sources declare that there is equality among the sexes for rewards and penalties in the afterlife. It is not only men that have their palaces in Paradise; rather both men and women are sultans of their own palaces in Paradise.

Nothing that human beings do not desire will be offered to them in Paradise. Everything that they desire will be given to them there. Everyone will be happy and pleased with their spouses. Paradise is a place of endless happiness. Although they resemble those which we know from this mortal worldly life, the rewards are unique only to Paradise: "*No soul knows what joyous means of happiness are kept hidden (reserved) for them as a reward for what they have being doing*" (Sajda 32:17).

Pursuant to what we have been notified by God in the Qur'an, we have faith in the Unseen and believe in that there will be *houris*, or pure maidens in Paradise who will be previously untouched by neither men nor jinns. They will also be totally free from such worldly defects and weaknesses.

However, the pious believing women of this world will be more virtuous and valuable than the *houris* in Paradise. It is reported of Umm Salama, one of the wives of the Prophet, that she said: "I said, 'O God's Messenger! Are the women of this world supreme or the *houris* in Paradise?' He replied: 'No. The women of this world are certainly more supreme than the *houris* in Paradise, just as the cloth is more valuable than its lining.' I asked, 'Why O God's Messenger?' He replied: 'It is because the women of this world perform the prayers, observe the fast of Ramadan, and worship God Almighty.'"

It is obvious that sexuality occupies an important place in human life, and as emphasized in Sura Rum, the opposite sexes reach sensual and spiritual satisfaction by uniting their lives: "*And among His signs is that He has created for you, from your selves, mates, that you may incline towards them and find rest in them, and He has engendered love and tenderness between you. Surely in this are signs for people who reflect*" (Rum 30:21). A similar type of satisfaction will also be attained in the life of Hereafter. Both Qur'anic verses and Prophetic traditions which depict life in Paradise express that worldly women will exist along with the *houris* in Paradise. The expression of *"eternally purified wives"* that we see in Qur'anic verses includes worldly women in addition to the *houris*. We can also understand from Qur'anic verses and Prophetic traditions that, following the physically and spiritually purifying process which the believers will go through prior to entering Paradise, the people of Paradise will be totally and absolutely freed from their worldly physiological defects, weaknesses and from any psychological depression that might negatively effect their happiness.

On the other hand, it can reasonably be argued that in the depictions of Paradise found in the Qur'anic verses and Prophetic traditions, that while features such as beauty, attraction and etc. are reserved for women, the encouraging advantages and benefits of all such depictions have been reserved for men and that women have been mostly depicted as means and instruments of satisfaction for men. We can see that the Qur'an mentions women as being among the greatest blessings of Paradise for men, rather than vice versa. The fact that while the man will be rewarded with at least two wives, one being a woman destined to Paradise and a *houri*, the woman will be rewarded with only one husband in the paradisical life, where no one will stay single, should also be bound to the same theme. Indeed, in all psychological studies women have unanimously demonstrated that they have been created with monogamous tendencies and prefer to devote their hearts to one man.

79 Why is the testimony of a woman not regarded as being equal to that of a man?

The Qur'anic verse that is concerned with requiring witnesses is as follows:

> O you who believe! When you contract a debt between you for a fixed term, record it in writing. Let a scribe write it down between you justly, and let no scribe refuse to write it down: as God has taught him (through the Qur'an and His

Messenger), so let him write. And let the debtor dictate, and let him avoid disobeying God, his Lord (Who has created him and brought him up with mercy and grace) and curtail no part of it. If the debtor be weak of mind or body, or incapable of dictating, let his guardian dictate justly. And call upon two (Muslim) men among you as witnesses. If two men are not there, then let there be one man and two women, from among those of whom you approve as witnesses, that if either of the two women errs (through forgetfulness), the other may remind her. Let the witnesses not refuse when they are summoned (to give evidence). And (you, O scribes) be not loath to write down (the contract) whether it be small or great, with the term of the contract. Your doing so (O you who believe), is more equitable in the sight of God, more upright for testimony, and more likely that you will not be in doubt. If it be a matter of buying and selling concluded on the spot, then there will be no blame on you if you do not write it down; but do take witnesses when you settle commercial transactions with one another, and let no harm be done to either scribe or witness (nor let either of them act in a way to injure the parties). If you act (in a way to harm either party or the scribe and witnesses) indeed it will be transgression on your part. (Always) act in due reverence for God and try to attain piety. God teaches you (whatever you need in life and the way you must follow in every matter); God has full knowledge of everything. (Baqara 2:282)

This verse states that any record of a debt requires witnesses. The verse instructs those believers who are engaged in financial transactions to secure two male witnesses or one male and two female witnesses. The reason why the Qur'an calls for two women in the place of one man in commercial transactions is straightforward.

It should be noted first that there are differences between men and women; indeed it is these differences that help to create harmony. The Qur'an has been sent to us also to ensure that those tasks which are necessary in society are fulfilled in the best way. Men and women are complementary to one another, and are not equally effective in every situation. Typically, across the diverse cultures in the world, men are generally more conversant with financial transactions and are directly responsible for providing materially for the family.

Islam imposes the financial maintenance of the family on the husband, and the wife is under no obligation to help him. Again men tend to have better powers of recall while a woman can be swayed by emotions. There may be women who are conversant with financial matters, who are emotionally removed, and have a more powerful memory than men. However, general principals are made in accordance with general temperaments rather than the exceptions. Thus, two women witnesses are required to ensure that errors, for whatever reason, are not made.

The forgetting or mistake mentioned in this verse may originate from a number of causes; the woman witness might not have the necessary knowledge about agreements and contracts or she might not be aware of all the critical details of such matters. In addition, her sensitive nature might as well be a cause for her possible erring, since a woman tends to be more easily moved by emotions. The condition requiring two women in this verse is thus a kind of guarantee to ensure accuracy in testimony and remove all doubts concerning the terms of the transaction, thus reducing the potential for future disagreement.

Finally, the requirement of witnesses in this verse is specific to financial transactions. The testimony of two women is not sought in place of a man in the matters in other fields where perhaps women have greater knowledge or specialty than men.

80 In the Qur'an are there any differences between the rights of man and woman?

The Qur'an makes no distinction between men and women in their basic natures:

O humankind! Surely We have created you from a single (pair of) male and female, and made you into tribes and families so that you may know one another (and so build mutuality and co-operative relationships, not so that you may take pride in your differences of race or social rank, and breed enmities).

> Surely the noblest, most honorable of you in God's sight is the
> one best in piety, righteousness, and reverence for God. Surely
> God is All-Knowing, All-Aware. (Hujurat 49:13)

> O humankind! In due reverence for your Lord, keep from dis-
> obedience to Him Who created you from a single human self,
> and from it created its mate, and from the pair of them scattered
> abroad a multitude of men and women. In due reverence for
> God, keep from disobedience to Him in Whose name you make
> demands of one another, and (duly observe) the rights of the
> wombs (i.e. of kinship, thus observing piety in your relations
> with God and with human beings). God is ever watchful over
> you. (Nisa 4:1)

The Qur'an considers the birth of a girl or a boy to be a blessing from God: *"To God belongs the sovereignty of the heavens and the
earth. He creates whatever He wills. He grants to whom He wills daughters and grants to whom He wills sons"* (Shura 42:49). It severely criti-
cizes the brutal pre-Islamic treatment of daughters and condemns
the heinous practice of female infanticide:

> When any of them is given news of the birth of a girl, his face
> becomes overcast, and he is (as if choking inwardly) with sup-
> pressed anger. He hides himself from the people because of
> the evil (as he wrongly supposes it) of what he has had news
> of. (So he debates within himself:) Shall he keep her with dis-
> honor or bury her in earth? Look now! how evil is the judg-
> ment they make (concerning God, and how evil is the decision
> they debate)! (Nahl 16:58-59).

The idea that the birth of a daughter is something to be
ashamed of can be seen in other faiths. In the Bible, for instance,
the birth of a daughter is seen as a loss and the girl is considered a
potential source of shame for the father.[26]

In contrast to the Biblical Eve, who led Adam to be deceived
by Satan, the Qur'an mentions Adam and Eve together while narrating the reason for Adam and his wife being expelled from the
Garden for their sin; thus it is emphasized that there is no difference between men and women:

Then Satan made an evil suggestion to both of them that he might reveal to them their private parts that had remained hidden from them (and waken their carnal impulses), and he said: "Your Lord has forbidden you this tree only lest you should become sovereigns, or lest you should become immortals." And he swore to them: "Truly, I am for you a sincere adviser." Thus he led them on by delusion; and when they tasted the tree, their private parts (and all the apparently shameful, evil impulses in their creation) were revealed to them, and both began to cover themselves with leaves from the Garden. And their Lord called out to them: "Did I not prohibit you from that tree, and did I not say to you that Satan is a manifest enemy to you?" (A'raf 7:20-22)

But Satan (tempting them to the forbidden tree despite Our forewarning,) caused them both to deflect therefrom and brought them out of the (happy) state in which they were. And We said, "Go down, all of you, (and henceforth you will live a life,) some of you being the enemies of others. There shall be for you on the earth a habitation and provision until an appointed time." (Baqara 2:36)

Due to the belief that Eve had seduced Adam to follow her in sin while in the Garden, in medieval Christianity women were regarded as temptresses and sinful, and were thus humiliated. On the other hand, the Qur'an regards Adam as being the first to act in this matter, *"(Aware of his lapse and in the hope of retrieving his error, rather than attempting to find excuses for it,) Adam received from his Lord words that he perceived to be inspired in him (because of his remorse, and he pleaded through them for God's forgiveness). In return, He accepted his repentance. He is the One Who accepts repentance and returns it with liberal forgiveness and additional reward, the All-Compassionate (especially towards His believing servants)."* (Baqara 2:37) and mentions that they both paid repentance together: *"They said (straightaway): 'Our Lord! We have wronged ourselves, and if You do not forgive us and do not have mercy on us, we will surely be among those who have lost!'"* (A'raf 7:23).

The Qur'an also emphasizes that both genders are God's creatures whose goal on earth is to worship their Lord, do righteous deeds, and avoid evil, and then be judged accordingly. Both are promised the same reward for good conduct:

> Whoever does good, righteous deeds, whether male or female, and is a believer, most certainly We will make him (or her) live a good life, and most certainly We will pay such as these their reward in accordance with the best of what they used to do. (Nahl 16:97)

> And thus does their (All-Gracious and Generous) Lord answer them: "I do not leave to waste the work of any of you (engaged in doing good), whether male or female. (As males and females following the same way) you are all one from the other. Hence, those who have emigrated (in My cause) and been expelled from their homelands and suffered hurt in My cause, and have fought and been killed, indeed I will blot out from them their evil deeds and will admit them into Gardens through which rivers flow, as a reward from God (with infinite Mercy and Power to fulfill whatever He promises)." With God lies the best reward. (Al Imran 3:195)

The above verses plainly indicate that God makes no distinction between the sexes as far as their rights or responsibilities are concerned; on the contrary, God declares that both sexes are equal.

Moreover, women's rights are emphasized in Sura Nisa ("Women") in the Qur'an. Sura Mujadila ("The Pleading Woman") takes its title and subject matter from the woman who came and complained about her husband to the Prophet; here it is stated that God has protected her and with her case a misguided pre-Islamic custom against women has been abolished.

The Qur'an provides both spiritual dignity and material rights for women. They are honorable and worthy in all aspects of life, whether they are a daughter, a sister, a wife, a mother, a relative, or a neighbor. The Qur'an gives great value to women, particularly as mothers, commanding us to respect them. The 15th verse of

Sura Ahqaf, for instance, describes how important mothers are as they undergo great difficulties during pregnancy, give birth to us in pain, suckle and care for us. Also, another chapter in the Qur'an urges us to treat parents with kindness and affection:

> Your Lord has decreed that you worship none but Him alone, and treat parents with the best of kindness. Should one of them, or both, attain old age in your lifetime, do not say "Ugh!" to them (as an indication of complaint or impatience), nor push them away, and always address them in gracious words. Lower to them the wing of humility out of mercy, and say: "My Lord, have mercy on them even as they cared for me in childhood." (Isra 17:23-24)

The Qur'an also regards women as one of the signs of God's existence and power and advises humankind to reflect on this fact: *"And among His signs is that He has created for you, from your selves, mates, that you may incline towards them and find rest in them, and He has engendered love and tenderness between you. Surely in this are signs for people who reflect"* (Rum 30:21). It again regarded spouses as garments for one another: *"It is made lawful for you to go in to your wives on the night of the Fast. (There is such intimacy between you that) they are a garment for you (enfolding you to protect you against illicit relations and beautifying you) and you are (in the same way for the same reasons) a garment for them"* (Baqara 2:187). Each of the sexes are mutual complementary halves. The Prophet also said that women and men are the two halves of a whole. As each of these halves has features that are peculiar to itself, the rights and responsibilities of a woman are, thus, equal to those of a man, but they are not the same.

The fact that the Qur'an does not make any differentiation between women and men, and provides women with equal, but not identical, rights shows that it recognizes the important characteristics that make women different, and gives proper respect to both the difference in constitution and personality as well as the need for equal dignity.

In different places in the Qur'an there are different statements about what human beings have been created from; is this not contradictory?

T he question of what humanity has been created from is described with different words and terms in the Qur'an. However, the fact that the words and terms are different does not necessarily mean that the Qur'an is providing information that is contradictory in itself, but rather it draws our attention to a different stage of human creation. If we look at these different substances from which humanity is made, we see that they are; "*a humble fluid*,"[27] "*earth*,"[28] "*a drop of seminal fluid*,"[29] "*clay*,"[30] "*a clot clinging*,"[31] "*molded dark mud*,"[32] and "*he was nothing*."[33]

The reason for the differences between the related verses is that each of these verses places an emphasis on a different stage of the creation of human. While dealing with the creation of Adam in one section, the creation of Eve is referred to in another, the creation of their children in yet another, and the creation of all other human beings in another.

God first created Adam when he was a "mere nothing." Prior to this Adam's existence was only within the Divine Knowledge, as clearly referred to in the following verse: "*Does human not bear in mind that We created him before when he was nothing?*" (Maryam 19:67). As for the stages of Adam's creation, God first made him of soil (*turab*), later adding water to this soil (*ma'*). Then, this mixture became a kind of mud (*tin*) and later this mud was converted into another black and odorous substance (*hama'in*) through a process of transformation (*masnun*). This mud dried, without being heated by any of fire, was converted into a form of *salsal*, that is something which "produces a sound due to its dryness." And finally, God breathed a soul into this substance, making it human and calling him Adam. Thus, there is no contradiction in this sequence of divine processes. Everything starts with the pure soil: "*He Who makes excellent everything that He creates; and He originated the cre-*

ation of humankind from clay" (Sajda 32:7). This is the stage where
water meets soil. As the water dries out and evaporates within the
mud, the matter becomes sticky clay (*tin al-ladhib*): "*Indeed, We
have created them (human beings) from a sticky clay*" (Saffat 37:11).

Later, as this sticky clay is converted into the form of a human
being, it starts to change in color and odor and is described as molded dark mud (*hama'in masnun*). This stage is described as follows:

> Assuredly We have created humankind from dried, sounding clay,
> from molded dark mud. And the jinn We had created before,
> from smokeless, scorching fire penetrating through the skin. And
> (remember) when your Lord said to the angels: "I am creating a
> mortal from dried, sounding clay, from molded dark mud. When
> I have fashioned him in due proportions and breathed into him
> out of My Spirit, then fall down prostrating before him (as a token
> of respect for him and his superiority)." So the angels prostrated
> themselves, all of them together, but *Iblis* did not; he refused to be
> among those who prostrated themselves. (God) said: "O *Iblis*!
> What is the matter with you that you are not among those who
> have prostrated?" (*Iblis*) said: "I am not one to prostrate myself
> before a mortal, whom You have created from dried, sounding
> clay, from molded dark mud." (God) said: "Then get you down
> out of it; surely You are one rejected (from My mercy). "And
> cursing is upon you until the Day of Judgment." (Hijr 15:26-35)

These are the stages of the creation of human beings. The following verses also bring the first creation to our attention and then
all the stages of the development of the human embryo, from the
male sperm and female egg:

> O humankind! If you are in doubt about the Resurrection, (con-
> sider that) We created you from earth (in the beginning while
> there was nothing of your existence as humankind, and the mate-
> rial origin of every one of you is also earth). Then (We have cre-
> ated you) from a drop of seminal fluid, then from a clot clinging
> (to the womb wall), then from a lump in part shaped and in part
> not shaped, and differentiated and undifferentiated, and so do We
> clarify for you (the reality of the Resurrection).... (Hajj 22:5)

> We created humankind (in the very beginning) from a specially sifted extract of clay. Then We have made it into a fertilized ovum in a safe lodging. Then We have created of the fertilized ovum a clot clinging (to the womb wall), and (afterwards in sequence) We have created of the clinging clot a (chew of) lump, and We have created of (a chew of) lump bones, and We have clothed the bones in flesh. Then We have caused it to grow into another creation. So Blessed and Supreme is God, the Creator Who creates everything in the best and most appropriate form and has the ultimate rank of creativity. (Mu'min 23:12-14)

> Did We not create you from a humble fluid? Then We placed it in a firm, secure place (to remain) for a known, pre-ordained term (of gestation). Thus have We determined (everything related to your existence), and how excellent We are in determining! (Mursalat 77:20-23)

> We have surely created human from a small quantity of mingled fluids, moving him from one state to another, and (finally) We have made him one hearing and seeing (so that he may hear God's Message and see His signs). (Insan 76:2)

Accordingly, the human being has been created from humble beginnings – a drop of semen, a blood clot, an embryo. That a being with consciousness, with the ability to discern right from wrong, has developed from such beginnings is yet another sign to be mediated upon: "*Let human, then, consider from what he has been created. He has been created from some of a lowly fluid gushing forth. It proceeds (as a result of incitement) between the (lumbar zone in the) vertebra and the ribs*" (Tariq 86:5-7).

The above verse refers to both the mechanism of the ejection of the seminal fluid and the area from which it is emitted. This is a relatively recent biological discovery, yet the Qur'an taught us about it fourteen centuries ago; it also lays out the full stages of the development of the human embryo. So, the existence of humanity, which started with the miraculous creation of Adam and Eve, has continued with physical causes that function as a veil over God's divine activity.

The genuine and divine purpose of the creation of humanity, which, on the surface, has continued with the desires of humanity itself, but actually with the acts of God, is humankind's acknowledgment of and obedience to the Supreme Creator.

82   Why is Virgin Mary mentioned in the Qur'an as Prophet Aaron's sister?

The Qur'anic account of the immaculate conception of Jesus is given in Sura Maryam. When Mary was given the glad tidings of a son, Mary said: *"'How shall I have a son, seeing no mortal has ever touched me, and I have never been unchaste?'"* (Maryam 19:20). Mary is told in response to her query, *"'That is how it is,' he (the Spirit who appeared before her) said, 'God creates whatever He wills; when He decrees a thing, He does but say to it 'Be!' and it is"* (Al Imran 3:47). So, the birth of Jesus is brought about by the all-powerful word of God: *"when He decrees a thing, He does but say to it 'Be!' and it is."* God wished to create the child without a father, like Adam, who had neither father nor mother. After the birth of Jesus, Mary returned home with the baby:

> She came to her people, carrying him. They exclaimed: "O Mary! You have come for sure with an unheard of, mighty thing! O sister of Aaron, your father was never a wicked man, nor was your mother unchaste." Mary pointed to him (the infant, signifying that they should ask him). They cried: "How can we talk to one in the cradle, an infant boy?" (Maryam 19:27-29)

The verse above addressing Mary, reads: *"O sister of Aaron."* However, Mary and Aaron were not contemporaries, not living in the same historical time period. So, why is Virgin Mary addressed this way?

The Arabic terms *abu* (father), *akh* (brother), and *ukht* (sister) are mostly used in a more comprehensive way than the narrow context of familial relationships. Accordingly, some take "sister of

Aaron" to mean a "descendent" of Prophet Aaron, since the term *ukht* is not limited to sisters; in addition Mary was of Jewish blood.

When asked about this matter, Prophet Muhammad, peace and blessings be upon him, said that it was a custom among the Children of Israel that they gave or linked their children to the names of renowned people or people who were connected with a renowned ancestor. Mary was a descendent of Prophet Aaron, so the people called her the sister of Aaron. Another time, Safiyya, the Prophet's wife who was of Jewish origin, complained to him about certain women calling her "Jewish daughter of a Jew!" He told her: "Why do you not reply to them by saying: 'How lucky am I! Aaron is my father, Moses is my uncle and Muhammad is my husband! Why should I envy anyone?'"

83   Does the Qur'an openly state when the end of the world will come?

The end of time is the peak of the knowledge of *ghayb*, or the unseen. Its knowledge is unattainable by any human, even the Prophets, for God kept its knowledge only for Himself:

> With God alone rests the knowledge of the Last Hour (when it will come).... (Luqman 31:34)

> They ask you about the Hour, when it will come to anchor. Say: "It is my Lord alone Who knows it; none will disclose it in its time but He. It weighs heavily on the heavens and the earth. It does not come to you except unawares." They ask you as if you (being a Messenger required or meant that you) were well-informed of it. Say: "It is indeed God alone Who knows it, but most people have no knowledge (of this)." (Araf 7:187)

> They ask you (O Messenger) about the Last Hour: "When will it come to anchor?" But how could you have knowledge about its time, with your Lord alone rests (the exact knowledge) of its term. (Naziat 79:42-44)

Although the Qur'an does not provide us with any knowledge about the occurrence of the Day of Judgment, it provides us with detailed depictions about the catastrophes that precede the Judgment: on that Day those things that seem secure and lasting – the skies, the stars, the sun, the seas, the mountains, the reality of death as contained in the graves – are torn away. Various verses refer to the day when the sky will be flayed open and the mountains slide away, the seas boiling over and pouring forth, the earth opening up to reveal its secrets, the heaven being split, the stars slipping out of place and falling away, the sun being extinguished and overturned, the sky being ripped apart, the earth unfolding, and the mountains being moved like so many pieces of fluff. In addition to the cosmic unveiling that will occur on the final day, the Qur'an also tells of the day of reckoning on which the tombs will be burst open, when humanity, with eyes downcast, will come forth from their graves like moths scattered before the wind, the girl who was buried alive will be asked what she did to deserve infanticide, the scrolls containing the evidence of human beings' deeds are unrolled, Hell is set ablaze, and the Garden is brought close. A number of *suras* introduce the contrast between the resplendent appearance of those destined for Paradise and the grimy appearance of those destined for Hell; there is a comparison between those who are given the account of their deeds in their right hand and those who are given it in their left, or those whose scales are heavy with good deeds and those whose scales are light. The Qur'an also gives detailed accounts about Archangel Israfil first blowing the Trumpet to announce the end of the world, the cosmic catastrophes on the Last Day, the second Trumpet call for gathering on the Plain of the Supreme Gathering, the arising of people at the Resurrection, their looking around in shock and terror and rushing toward God's Presence utterly humbled, the Judgment, Paradise, and Hell. Depicting the horror at the end of time, the Qur'an reminds people about the certainty of the coming Day:

> We did not create the heavens and the earth and all that is
> between them save with truth (meaningfully, and with definite
> purpose, and on solid foundations of truth); and the Last Hour
> is surely bound to come. So, overlook (the faults of the people,
> O Messenger) with a gracious forbearance. (Hijr 15:85)

The Qur'an also mentions some clear signs that signal the final destruction of the world: Near the end of time the sky will bring forth a visible smoke, which will engulf the people as a punishment; a moving creature will be brought forth from the earth. The aggressive nations of Gog and Magog will attack the civilized world before the end of time. God's Messenger regards this invasion as one of the signs of the approach of the Last Hour.

One day when the Prophet was sitting with the Companions Archangel Gabriel openly asked the Prophet about the time of the Last Hour. The Prophet replied to the Archangel in the disguise of a man by saying: "The questioned person has no better knowledge than the questioner."[34] With this answer the Prophet showed and taught the Companions that nobody knows the time of the Last Day, including the Prophets or angels.

84 | What is the accursed *zaqqum* tree?

God's Messenger related all that he had seen during his miraculous Night Journey from the Sacred Mosque in Mecca to the Masjid al-Aqsa in Jerusalem and his Ascension from there to the heavenly dimensions. One of these extraordinary things was the *zaqqum* tree. This accursed tree, that is, the *zaqqum* tree that is mentioned in the Qur'an as being absolutely excluded from God's Mercy, is an extremely bitter and thorny tree that will grow in Hell. This tree, of which the people of Hell will eat, is a trial for unbelievers to mend their ways. Certainly, this is a consequence of some deeds of the unbelievers and constitutes one of the forms of torment in Hell. Far from providing sustenance, it will give pain and cause torment as food for the people of Hell.

Upon returning from the Ascension, the Prophet mentioned this tree as one of the things he had witnessed during his miraculous journey. However, the Meccan polytheists did not accept any of the things which he had told them about and, going to another extreme, they ridiculed him. Mocking him, Abu Jahl, the chieftain of the polytheists, told the persons around him: "Go and get some dates and some clotted cream for us!" And when they brought them, he said as he was eating the blend of dates and clotted cream: "Eat your fill! We do not recognize any *zaqqum* other than this!" Added another chieftain, Ibn Ziba'ra, said: "For us *zaqqum* is a blend of date and clotted cream. Eat that *zaqqum!*"

The extremely bitter fruits of the *zaqqum* tree are likened to the heads of devils. This tree will grow from the seeds sown by the evil deeds committed by the people of Hell, deeds that were prompted by Satan. The Qur'an mentions deeds – such as taking intoxicants and playing games of chance – as the loathsome deeds of Satan. So, it is quite natural that such deeds will grow into satan-like trees and yield fruit that resembles the heads of devils.

The various aspects of this tree which grows right from the bottom of Hell are described in Qur'an:

> Is this what is good as a welcome or the tree of Zaqqum? We have made it (that tree) a means of trial and punishment for the wrongdoers (who associate partners with God). It is a tree growing in the heart of the Blazing Flame. Its fruits are like the heads of satans. So, most surely, they will eat of it and fill up their bellies with it. Then, for them will be boiling water (to mix with the zaqqum in their bodies). (Saffat 37:62-67)

> (Here is) the tree of Zaqqum, the food of him addicted to sinning, like molten brass; it will boil in their bellies, like the boiling of hot water. (Dukhan 44:43-46)

> Then: O you who have strayed (from the Straight Path), who deny (the afterlife), you will surely eat of the tree of Zaqqum;

and you fill up your bellies with it. Thereafter you will drink of hot, boiling water; you will drink as the camel raging with thirst drinks. This will be their welcome on the Day of Judgment. (Waqi'a 56:51-56)

The cursed people destined for Hell will have to feed their stomachs with the fruit of the accursed *zaqqum*, which is extremely bitter and thorny, as and when they feel hunger and their pain will thus grow deeper and deeper.

In a narration by Abu Said al-Khudry, one of the Companions, the Prophet commented on the term *zaqqum*, saying: "It is like the sediment of olive oil. When the person who drinks it brings it nearer to his face, the skin of his face will break and fall into it."

85	Why are there different injunctions in the Qur'an with respect to intoxicants?

The Qur'an is not a book which was revealed all at once, but it was revealed in parts over a period of twenty-three years. The gradualness, particularly in divine decrees and prohibitions, is the primary matter of concern in this means of Revelation, since a totally new society is being formed. Certain things which were previously prevalent within the community of that day were not suddenly, but rather gradually banned. For those who are not aware of this fact, certain verses which were revealed at different times and the gradual nature of their jurisdiction may seem to be contradictory; such verses remain in the Qur'an even though they were later abrogated. God willed these verses to be present in the Qur'an and thus the Prophet asserted their existence within the Qur'anic chapters following his final *muqabala*, or reciprocal recitation of the entire Qur'an with Archangel Gabriel.

The principle of gradual introduction is an important method in Islam as far as communication of responsibilities and human education and training are concerned. The shocking effects of a sudden prohibition of certain social practices, particularly of those which are deeply-rooted, are taken into consideration, and thus certain commands and prohibitions have been gradually communicated in order to enable the people to understand and digest better their purposes and widespread benefits. Aisha, the wife of the Prophet, very concisely expresses this delicate matter of a gradual approach in eradicating evil habits instead of forbidding them outright: "Should the Qur'an have initially brought forward the prohibitions as 'do not drink alcohol' and 'do not commit adultery', the people around the Prophet would soon have left him."

This gradual approach was adopted when informing a community in which addiction to intoxicants and gambling were widespread and deep-rooted; people were first to think and decide the negative aspects of such addictions by themselves.

Meanwhile, securing a strong and devout faith within the hearts of the community was given top priority and absolute and unquestioning obedience to divine commandments was thus achieved. Following these preliminary steps, alcohol and gambling were completely banned and an unprecedented success in human history was thus obtained.

If we compare attempts of prohibition of alcohol in the US between 1919 and 1933 and the huge expense that was incurred for this purpose with the voluntary self-prohibition carried out centuries before we can see how effective it was.

When we look at the gradual nature of the Qur'anic verses pertaining to the prohibition of alcohol, we can see that the total prohibition of alcohol was achieved in four consecutive stages: In the first stage, during the early Meccan period, the revealed verses drew the attention of the people to the fact that intoxicating drinks, in addition to delicious and mouth-watering food were obtained from dates and grapes and accordingly, the negative nature of alcoholic drinks is emphasized: "*And there are (among the produce that God brings forth as nourishment for you on the revived earth) the fruits of the date-palm, and grapes: you derive from them intoxicants and good, wholesome nourishment. Surely in this there is a sign for people who reason and understand*" (Nahl 16:67). By mentioning both intoxicants and delicious food side by side in this verse, the fact that the two are different things is emphasized. Here, we are told that they have two distinct features; one is good and wholesome and the other is intoxicating. By using the phrase "good, wholesome nourishment" after intoxicants, the fact that an intoxicant is neither good or wholesome nourishment is implied, while the decision to choose either the clean and healthy aspect or enjoy the intoxicating feature of the same fruit is left to the free will of humanity; at the same time this is an indication that intoxicants will be prohibited in the future.

In the second stage, the Revelations drew attention to the fact that while alcohol has some benefits, its negative aspects are greater than the benefits: "*They ask you about intoxicating drinks and games of chance. Say: 'In both there is great evil, though some use for people, but their evil is greater than their usefulness'*" (Baqara 2:219).

In the third stage, the coming Revelations command that believers not pray while drunk: "*O you who believe! Do not come forward to (stand in) the Prayer while you are in (any sort of) state of drunkenness until you know what you are saying…*" (Nisa 4:43). This commandment clearly prohibits Muslims from making any prayers while being drunk. Consequently, the Muslims started to establish their drinking times so that they would not coincide with their prayer times. The term *sakr*, or drunkenness, in this verse refers not only to alcohol, but any form of intoxication. If a Muslim approaches the prayer while drunk, since anything which leads to inebriation is, in fact, prohibited, then, they are presumed to have been guilty of twice the offense. In this verse, the times available for consuming intoxicants are limited and believers are being encouraged not to drink it.

In the fourth and last stage, the coming Revelations fully and completely prohibits consuming intoxicants and puts the final point on the matter: "*O you who believe! Intoxicants, games of chance, sacrifices to (anything serving the function of) idols (and at places consecrated for offerings to other than God), and (the pagan practice of) divination by arrows (and similar practices) are a loathsome evil of Satan's doing; so turn wholly away from it so that you may prosper (in both worlds). Satan only seeks to provoke enmity and hatred among you by means of intoxicants and games of chance, and to bar you from the remembrance of God and from Prayer. So, then, will you abstain?"* (Maeda 5:90-91).

With this gradual approach towards prohibiting alcohol, the Qur'an makes it easy for people to accept these principles, to give up old and negative habits and it thus succeeds in carrying out a significant social transformation. The Qur'an never stepped back from this and never abandoned any of the principles it had laid down after achieving the final point.

Finally, we can say that the appearance of seemingly contradictory verses in the Qur'an does not necessarily mean that there are contradictions; rather the presence of such verses indicates the gradual nature of the laying down of the principles necessary for a devout social formation and obedience to God's true religion.

86 | Does the Qur'an mention faith in destiny?

Belief in destiny is one of the essentials of Islamic faith. Just like a Muslim has to believe in God, His angels, His Books, His Prophets and resurrection after death, they also have to believe in destiny.

The Qur'anic word that has been translated as "destiny" is *qadar*, which literally means "determination," "giving a certain measure and shape," and "judging." It is terminologically defined as the Divine measure, determination, and judgment in the creation of all things in accordance with His Eternal Knowledge.

The Divine Destiny, accordingly, means God's knowing, planning, programming, determining, designing and creating all of existence, from subatomic particles to the universe, as a whole with all their pasts, presents, and futures, as well as God's control of all things, from planning, programming, and designing, to the realms of creation and existence and His registering all things within the *Kitab al-Mubin*, or the Manifest Book: in this Book the lives of all things and beings are recorded in detail before they have come into existence and His divine execution of all things with their predestination. His Eternal Knowledge encompasses all space and time and is inclusive of all things in the past, present, and future, while He Himself is beyond all time and space.

The following verses refer to the truth of destiny, the belief of which is one of the pillars of Islamic faith:

> With Him are the keys to the Unseen; none knows them but He. And He knows whatever is on land and in the sea; and not a leaf falls but He knows it; and neither is there a grain in the dark layers of earth, nor anything green or dry, but is (recorded) in a Manifest Book. (An'am 6:59)

> Say (O Messenger): "I have no power to harm or benefit myself, except by God's will. For every community there is an appointed term; and when the end of the term falls in, they can neither delay it by any period of time, however short, nor can they hasten it." (Yunus 10:49)

> God knows what any female bears (in her womb with all its traits from her conception of it until delivery), and what the wombs diminish and what they increase, (and by how much they may fall short in gestation, and by how much they may increase the average period), and everything with Him is by a determined measure. (Ra'd 13:8)

> He to Whom belongs the sovereignty of the heavens and the earth, and He has taken to Himself no child, nor has He any partner (in His dominion or any aspect of His being God), and He creates everything and determines its destiny. (Furqan 25:2)

> There is nothing hidden (from them as from all creatures) in the heaven or on the earth but is in a Manifest Book. (Naml 27:75)

> Surely it is We Who will bring the dead to life; and We record what they send ahead (to the Hereafter) and what they leave

behind (of good and evil). Everything We have written down and kept in a Manifest Record. (Ya.Sin 36:12)

No affliction occurs on the earth (such as drought, famine, and earthquakes) or in your own persons (such as disease, damage in your property, and loss of loved ones), but it is recorded in a Book before We bring it into existence – doing so is surely easy for God. (Hadid 57:22)

Destiny is the coalescence of one's deeds and of God's bringing these deeds into material existence. That is to say, a person desires or wishes something to be and God creates. Accordingly, destiny is one's willing to do something by their volition and God's creating that particular deed, if He, the Divine Power, wills it to be brought into material existence. So, Divine destiny or predetermination is God's knowing and determining all things with His Eternal Knowledge before their material existence.

It should be noted that Eternal Divine Knowledge is one of many aspects of destiny. While destiny denotes the All-Knowing God's determination and predestination, it also denotes such attributes of God as *Sami'*, or "The All-Hearing," *Basir*, or "The All-Seeing," *Irada*, or "Divine Decree" and *Mashi'a*, or "God's Absolute Will." So, the denial of Divine destiny also means the denial of such Divine Attributes.

The obvious order and harmony, as well as the exact measure and balance in the whole universe clearly show that everything is determined, measured, created, and executed by God Almighty. The infinite variety between species and individuals, in spite of their being formed from the same basic materials, proves that everything in the universe occurs according to God Almighty's absolute determination and that there is no human will or volition involved. This is the universal destiny and the human willpower has no part in it. Being the sole Creator of everything, God creates whatever He wills and never asks anyone what to create. We should keep in mind, however, that nothing He does is in vain and that there are many instances of wisdom in His decrees and acts. The earth, since the first day of creation, has been turning both around itself and around the sun, under the order of this absolute Divine destiny or determination. No one can say "stop!" to this turning. The sun and the earth have each been moving on their orbits and no one can put an end to this unremitting race. Everything is bound by the predetermination in the universe.

On the other hand, the existence of Divine Will does not mean that we do not have free will. As for our part and willpower in our acts, God creates our actions according to the choices and decisions we make through our free will. Accordingly, the real command and will belong to God, even though human beings have their own free wills. Nothing happens unless God wills and commands it to. No thing can come into existence unless He absolutely wills. Neither time nor space could exist if He had not willed them to. Whoever believes in the attributes of Divine Knowledge, Will, and Power, should also believe in Divine destiny and determination.

Let us now examine some Prophetic traditions concerning the truth of Divine destiny as one of the pillars of Islamic faith: When Prophet Muhammad, peace and blessings be upon him, was asked about faith, He replied: "It means that you should believe in God, His angels, His Books, His Prophets, and the Last Day, and that you should believe in Divine Destiny and the decreeing both of good and of evil."[35]

Ubada ibn Samit, one of the Companions, said to his son on his deathbed: "Oh my son! You will not taste of the reality of faith in your heart (i.e., you will not receive the spiritual pleasure of your faith in your heart) unless you accept that what has come to you could not miss you, and that what has missed you could not come to you. I heard God's Messenger saying: "The first thing God created was the pen (of destiny). He said to it, "Write!" The Pen asked, "What should I write, my Lord?" God said: "Write what was been decreed about everything until the

Last Hour!" And, then, the Prophet continued: "Whoever dies with a belief other than this is not from me."[36]

Abdullah ibn Abbas was riding behind the Prophet when the Prophet told him: "O, young man! I will teach you something. Pay attention to God's commands and prohibitions so that God pays attention to you. Respect for God's sake so that He guards you. Demand whatever you demand only from God. Ask only His help whenever you ask for help. Be aware that if all the people gather to help you, they can never help you with anything other than what God has predestined for you. And also, if all people gather to harm you, they can never harm you with anything other than what God has predestined for you, for the pens have already been removed and the pages have already dried."[37]

In conclusion, we can say that the issue of destiny has been clearly and repeatedly referred to in a number of Qur'anic verses and Prophetic traditions. Divine Destiny and human free will are two aspects of destiny. The actions of humankind are within God's Knowledge and Wisdom. Accordingly, whatever happens to humanity is from God as God's Will is absolute and encompasses human free will. However, we are confronted by the results of our intentions and deeds, whether they are good or bad. Thus, faith in destiny does not set human beings free from responsibility or lead them to negligence. One cannot and should not commit sins by simply saying "God has predestined this for me," nor should one argue or defend their innocence by saying "Thus was God's pre-destiny and my fate!" after having committed a sin. God never compels a person to do a particular deed; the human experience of free will is genuine, and everyone is responsible and accountable for their actions. God has established what causes bring about what results in this world, and humanity cannot escape this framework. And He will create the results of the causes as and when human beings fulfill them. Accordingly, all success depends on God's abso-lute Will. But He wills success for those who revere Him and act righteously and piously.

CHAPTER 10

The Universality of the Qur'an

THE UNIVERSALITY OF THE QUR'AN

87 It is claimed that the Qur'anic principle of retaliation is incompatible with modernity? Are Qur'anic jurisdictions always valid?

The Qur'an is a universal Book and its principles will hold their validity until the Day of Resurrection. Its peace-giving and morally-instructive principles, applicable to the whole of humanity, never lose their authority. As time progresses the Qur'an becomes more and more modern; after all it was sent by the One Who is the First and the Last, of Whom there is none preceding Him and Who eternally exists, while all other things and beings perish. God sent a book to humanity that has an eternal message; He knows all the past, present and future at once and He is totally and completely aware of all the needs of all the creatures He has created. If some people think that some of the principles of His Book are impracticable and tiresome, it is because these people misunderstand them.

Let us, for instance, look at the so-called impracticable and unacceptable Qur'anic principle of *qisas*, or retaliation. The following is the verse that pertains to retaliation:

> O you who believe! Prescribed for you is retaliation in cases of (deliberate, unjust) killing: freeman for freeman, slave for slave, female for female. Yet if he (the murderer) is granted some remission by his brother (any of the heirs of the victim), then what falls on the pardoning side is fulfilling in fairness what has been agreed on, and the other side is making the payment kindly enough to please the other side. This is a lightening from your Lord, and a mercy. Whoever offends after that, for him is a painful punishment. (Baqara 2:178)

Almighty God explains the divine reason lying behind retaliation in the following verse:

> There is life for you in retaliation, (if you understand,) O people of discernment, so it may be that you (will perceive it and fulfill God's command and in so doing) attain the desired piety and righteousness and deserve His protection. (Baqara 2:179)

The Qur'an decrees retaliation in cases of wrong as a requirement of justice and emphasizes that such a punishment is, in fact, the guarantee for the security of individuals and society. It is a great deterrent to potential murderers if the death penalty exists in a society. Such a penalty helps to prevent an offense and thus save the lives of both the potential criminal and the victim. In addition, such a strong deterrent also puts an end to feelings of revenge and thus saves the lives of other innocent people on both sides of the issue who could presumably lose their lives as a result of a long-running cycle of enmity and feuds.

Accordingly, the law of retaliation requires the punishment of an offense to be of the same nature as the crime. For instance, killing and stealing are two offenses of different natures. Modern law gives the same kind and nature of punishment for both, namely imprisonment. The difference is only in time. However, time never serves as a substitute for quality or nature. Today, for instance, people pay huge sums of funds to provide safety and security for their possessions. The reason for the allocation of such huge amounts of money is because the penalties for theft and robbery are lenient and symbolic rather than preventive. Considering the deterrent punishment the Qur'an imposes for stealing, an intelligent and wise person would certainly not attempt to commit a theft. Stealing the properties of others is forbidden in Islam. Anyone who commits such an impermissible act will certainly deserve punishment both in this worldly life and in the Hereafter. Regarding this matter, the Qur'an commands:

And for the thief, male or female: cut off their hands as a recompense for what they have earned, and an exemplary deterrent punishment from God. God is All-Glorious with irresistible might, All-Wise. But he who repents after having done wrong, and mends his ways, surely God accepts His repentance. For God is All-Forgiving, All-Compassionate. (Maeda 5:38-39)

The punishment the Qur'an introduces is based on justice and mercy. Although this is based on absolute justice, the Divine commandment also attaches great merit to forgiveness: "*...whoever remits (the retaliation), it will be an act of expiation for him*" (Maeda 5:45). Accordingly, one whose rights have been violated can either demand retaliation as a legal right or forgo that right. Also, by stressing and giving particular importance to repentance and reformation, the Qur'an approaches the matter as one of education and upbringing. It brings piety, reverence for God, and life to the forefront without limiting itself to legal sanctions alone. The law of retaliation was also prescribed in the Bible, without any injunction of remission.[38] The law of retaliation the Qur'an introduces decrees retaliation but also decrees that if the injured parties (or in cases of murder, the heirs of the deceased) pardon the guilty person either directly or in return for some compensation to avoid the retaliatory punishment.

In addition, the Qur'anic ordinance which lays down the cutting-off of a hand in punishment for theft is applicable just in the circumstances that the thief must have committed the crime purely with their own free will, without any compulsion; they must have taken possession of the thing stolen, thereby depriving its rightful owner of it; they must have stolen it from the place where it was kept, not in an open place where they could enter freely; they must not have had any right to it; and the stolen thing should be of the kind of thing that Islam regards as goods; the value of the goods should be above a certain amount; and it should not be fruit, vegetables, or grain that are not stored in a barn. There is another condition; the person who steals should not be constrained to steal out of dire necessity. Caliph Umar, for instance, did not enforce this punishment at times of famine. However, such exemptions do not mean that the person who steals will not be punished. Under these circumstances, the judge can determine a punishment for the thief, but cannot decide to have their hand cut off.

The penal law the Qur'an introduces is a collection of sanctions and cautions that help to maintain a healthy society; the deterring nature of such a law is extremely important. The severity or lightness of penalties demonstrates the degree of importance attached to the values that are being protected. The penalties the Qur'an decrees for the crimes committed against basic human rights, such as the right to life, personal property, belief, individual and public safety, as well those verses that legislate for crimes against mental and physical health show the importance the Qur'an attaches to these values and their protection.

88 | Is it mandatory that we accept all that which is mentioned in the Qur'an as the truth?

Whatever the Qur'an decrees is true and is for the benefit of humanity as we are all servants of God, Who knows best what is good or bad for us. There are many instances of wisdom in His decrees. What we must do is to accept them exactly as they are. As Islam is an indivisible whole, it is not possible to partially accept it. Those who do not accept or judge by God's commandments are unbelievers, wrongdoers, and transgressors. If they accept these laws, but do not judge by them if they are able to do so, they are both wrongdoers and transgressors. Thus, we cannot simply decide to accept some rulings of the Qur'an while denying others; such an approach destroys the entirety, harmony, and consistency of the religion. As a matter of fact, those who accept some parts of the Book while denying others are severely criticized and warned in the Qur'an: *"Then (like a people having no sense) do you believe in part of the Book, and disbelieve in part? What else, then, could be the recompense of those of you who act thus than dis-grace in the life of this world? On the Day of Resurrection, they will be consigned to the severest of punishment. God is not unaware and unmind-ful of what you do"* (Baqara 2:85).

89 | Is the claim that the Qur'anic prohibitions limit human freedom valid?

The Qur'an pays great attention to human liberty and free will and people are accountable in accordance with the freedom and free will that they have been given. Anyone who is not sane or free is not responsible to carry out religious duties. If there are impediments to freedom even war is then sanctioned. However, freedom does not necessarily mean that one can do whatever one desires; the freedom and security of others must be taken into account.

It would be wrong to conclude that there are limitations to human freedom by examining only certain commandments and prohibitions in the Qur'an. If there sometimes appear to be contradictions in the Qur'an to human nature, then this is because there has either been an incorrect approach to the Qur'an or there is a problem with the degree of knowledge of the religion.

Human beings are favored with being the vicegerent of God on earth; here we have been delegated to make use of all the resources that have been granted to us through this vicegerency. The following verses are evidence in this regard:

> It is He Who (prepared the earth for your life before He gave you life, and) created all that is in the world for you (in order to create you – the human species – and make the earth suit-able for your life); then He directed (His Knowledge, Will, Power, and Favor) to the heaven, and formed it into seven heavens. He has full knowledge of everything. (Baqara 2:29)

> He has also made of service to you whatever is in the heavens and whatever is on the earth, all is from Him (a gift of His

Grace). Surely in this there are (clear) signs for a people who reflect. (Jathiya 45:13)

Do you not see that God has made all that is in the heavens and all that is on the earth of service to you, and lavished on you His favors, outward and inward? And yet, among people are those who dispute about God without having any true knowledge or any true guidance or an enlightening Divine Book. (Luqman 31:20)

Accordingly, whatever is good or auspicious has been given to the service of humankind and whatever is bad or useless has been prohibited. God has endowed humanity with certain principal faculties that are fundamental to our survival and which help us to carry out our function as His vicegerent, such as reason or intellect and a desire for such things as the opposite sex, earning a livelihood, and gaining possessions. If these faculties remain undisciplined, they may drive people to pursue immorality, illicit sexual relationships, unlawful earnings, tyranny, injustice, deception, and other vices. Therefore, God has prescribed certain principles as commands and prohibitions; this is the result of His endless Mercy for humankind. He has not commanded anything other than what is good and auspicious and He has not prohibited anything that is not bad or ugly. In most cases the Qur'an explains these commands and prohibitions to help us understand the Divine wisdom behind them, as in the following verses:

O you who believe! Intoxicants, games of chance, sacrifices to (anything serving the function of) idols (and at places consecrated for offerings to other than God), and (the pagan practice of) divination by arrows (and similar practices) are a loathsome evil of Satan's doing; so turn wholly away from it so that you may prosper (in both worlds). Satan only seeks to provoke enmity and hatred among you by means of intoxicants and games of chance, and to bar you from the remembrance of God and from Prayer. So, then, will you abstain? (Maeda 5:90-91)

In fact, we can notice in the Qur'an that the number of prohibitions is limited when compared to those things that are permitted or encouraged. The prohibited deeds are limited in number, while many alternatives and options are offered. When interest is prohibited, for instance, many alternative profitable ways are permitted and even encouraged. Also, while adultery is prohibited, marital relations are advised and encouraged. Alcohol is banned, but many other drinks have been permitted. And although some food has been prohibited, there are plenty of foods that have been granted to us to enjoy. Therefore, the limits of the permissible are broad, and are quite adequate to fulfill one's desire.

God has not prohibited deeds and food to make things difficult for His servants, but rather to save them from suffering and falling into hardships. We should also keep in mind that God wills good for us, guides us to it, and enables us to do it. Though we must try to find the instances of wisdom in His decrees, there would still be – in fact, there are – a number of known and unknown divine wisdoms pertaining to this worldly life and also to the life in the Hereafter. The following verses are clear examples of this fact:

> Tell the believing men that they should restrain their gaze (from looking at the women whom it is lawful for them to marry, and from others' private parts), and guard their private parts and chastity. This is what is purer for them. God is fully aware of all that they do. And tell the believing women that they (also) should restrain their gaze (from looking at the men whom it is lawful for them to marry, and from others' private parts), and guard their private parts, and that they should not display their charms except that which is revealed of itself (Nur 24:30-31)

If we look only at the outer frame of any verse without making any effort to think about its Divine reason, it is possible that we can think that the particular verse is aimed to harm us. For example, God has created so much and so many beautiful things, He has equipped us with eyes to see them all, but He orders that we do not look at the opposite sex.

If we think about the verses in depth, we can notice that that the command of lowering our gaze is, in fact and in its essence, a divine mercy and grace for us. This divine command is aimed to set free and save humankind from the chains of corporeal slavery, but is not intended to exert any pressure on us or to put a burden on us. Looking is a means of affinity and attraction which, in turn, can lead to enslavement. When the eye sees a beautiful face, it renders both itself and the soul imprisoned. But God desires us to be free and emancipated. Emancipation from slavery can only be achieved when glances are diverted away from physical (corporal) beauty and focused on their Creator. And, when this focusing has been achieved, we have achieved proximity to God and are always in His company. This is, in fact, real freedom.

Another aspect of this issue is that this world is an arena of testing for us and God has created certain worldly attractions in order to test us: whether we will act in accordance with our primordial human nature and turn our faces towards the Divine Beauty or will imprison ourselves by adhering to simple worldly and transitory beauties. The focal point, here, is not whether we look at a beautiful face. The real motive is that other feelings soon follow the first look, then comes lust, then comes the attempt to satisfy this lust, and then comes the desire to attain that beauty or that attractive thing and so forth...

Now then, all such lustful desires seduce human beings and consequently we lose ourselves and our direction. We focus on that false attraction and thus forget our real goal. A person in such a mood has lost their freedom and has become a slave of bodily desires and lust.

Now we have reached the essence of certain prohibitions; things are prohibited because it is harmful. God based Islam on His Mercy and Love, not to oppress. In order not to suffer from harm, eyes should be secured and diverted from that which is prohibited. Also, in order to be on the safe side with regard to our selfish weaknesses, it is better to keep our eyes diverted from looking at prohibited things.

In conclusion, God has created the human being not only with the power to distinguish between good and bad, but also with a natural disposition to heed Divine prohibitions. God has made permissible all beautiful and clean things, which are much greater in number than the harmful things that are prohibited. If we can purify our nature, bringing them back to their original state we will be happy with whatever God chooses for us. Then, there would be no contradictions at all amongst what is in our hearts and what is in God's pleasure. And then, what a person desires for themselves is that with which God is pleased.

90 | What is meant when it is said that the Qur'an is universal?

We can define the concept of universality as an idea or belief that is appropriate and acceptable to all peoples, at all times, and in all places.

The following features of the Qur'an establish and prove its universality, in both time and space.

a. *The Qur'an is the Word of God:* It is God Who has created humanity and it is thus God Who knows human beings best. No matter how expertly ideologies that deal with human happiness and tranquility are developed and introduced, they cannot be perceived or accepted as universal since their sources are not Heavenly or Divine. But the Qur'an, which has been conveyed to the humanity by Prophet Muhammad, peace and blessings be upon him, was sent down by God. It is not the word of an ordinary person; it is the Word of God.

The religion of Islam is neither of a national character nor is it called after a person. Religions such as Judaism, Christianity, and Buddhism are all identified with personalities, but the principles introduced by the Qur'an are not identified with any one person or group. The term Christian means one who follows Jesus Christ, while Judaism refers only to the religion of the Jewish people. The labeling of Islam as Muhammadanism, which is used only by non-Muslims to refer to Islam, is the result of a false analogy with Christianity. The Qur'an's clear use of the term *Islam* can be seen in the following verse: "...*This day I have perfected for you your Religion (with all its rules, commandments and universality), completed My favor upon you, and have been pleased to assign for you Islam as religion*" (Maeda 5:3). It is to be noted that Muslims do not worship Prophet Muhammad, peace and blessings be upon him. He was neither a god, nor an incarnation, nor the son of God. He never claimed to be anything more than a man who had received Revelations from God. He did not make Islam; he simply received the Message of Islam to be conveyed to all humanity.

b. *The Qur'an is the authentic Word of God:* What is meant by the truthfulness of origin is that any faith that claims to have a divine origin should be free from any human interference throughout its existence, i.e., not only should it have an initial divine descent, but its authenticity must be preserved without undergoing any changes at all.

From the beginning of their existence on earth, humankind has received the Divine Message via Messengers. Each time people began to commit excesses, God Almighty purified the way of life through His Prophets. Each Prophet strove for the happiness and prosperity of the people, but not all of them were able to obtain their goals. Some of the Prophets were not recognized, even by their own people, while others were killed at the hands of their community or accepted only by a few people. Surely, it is the people to blame for not heeding the Prophets, and not the Prophets.

As far as the soundness of the origin, the Qur'an holds a unique position which none of the other heavenly Scriptures has enjoyed. It is under the guardianship of God Almighty, as expressed in the following verses:

> Indeed it is We, We Who send down the Reminder in parts,
> and it is indeed We Who are its Guardian. (Hijr 15:9)

Falsehood can never have access to it (the Qur'an), whether from before it or from behind it (whether by arguments and attitudes based on modern philosophies or by attacks from the past based on earlier Scriptures; (it is) the Book being sent down in parts from the One All-Wise, All-Praiseworthy (to Whom all praise and gratitude belong). (Fussilat 41:42)

Do they not contemplate the Qur'an (so that they may be convinced that it is from God)? Had it been from any other than God, they would surely have found in it much (incoherence or) inconsistency. (Nisa 4:82)

c. *The Messenger is the ideal communicator of the Qur'an:* In order for a teaching or a religion to be universally acceptable, its representative should, first of all, apply it and exemplify it in their own life so that those to whom it is addressed can see and believe that such a lifestyle is practicable and right and just. In addition, such a representative person should be able to shape the community with the relevant religious teachings and principles so that the system addresses not only individuals, but multitudes of people.

As we examine the history of humankind, we can see that it is only Prophet Muhammad, peace and blessings be upon him, who meets all these criteria. The Prophet was the perfect bearer of God's final Revelation to all people; he set a perfect example with his practices of the Divine Message in his own life. Through his life and teachings the Prophet encouraged the Companions to live an excellent, harmonious Islamic life.

d. *All aspects of the Messenger's life have been meticulously recorded:* Another precondition of the universality of a religious teaching is that the life of its Messenger should be known by the followers of the religion in the most detailed and reliable way possible. A person whose life is not known well or in detail cannot be thought to preach a universal teaching, for how can people learn from such a person principles that are related to all the aspects in their lives. In addition, human beings are keen to know all the details of the life of leaders. Again, there is only one personality in human history that can be said to possess such a life-history, that is, Prophet Muhammad, peace and blessings be upon him.

The life of no other Prophet or Messenger throughout the history of humanity is known as well as that of Prophet Muhammad, peace and blessings be upon him. When we examine any historical figure, it can be seen that there are many unknown aspects in their lives.

The life of the Prophet, from his words to his deeds, and even private moments, from what he approved of to what he disapproved of have all been reliably recorded and transferred from generation to generation, up until the present time. The Qur'an orders Muslims to emulate and follow the Sunna of the Prophet. In the Qur'anic verses obedience to the Prophet is deemed equal to obedience to God. Obedience to the Prophet is regarded as a prerequisite for obedience to God; refusing to obey or follow the example of the Prophet is regarded as a sign of non-belief.

Moreover, the exposition of the Prophet of certain Qur'anic chapters and verses, as well as his explanations on matters that were not dealt with in the Qur'an are all accepted as being fundamental to the religion, and therefore these have all been carefully transferred to the subsequent generations. This process of transmission to following generations has been carried out meticulously with great dedication. So much so that even the personal credibility and reliability of the narrators of Prophetic traditions was examined and classified with great care, leading to the creation of chains of Prophetic traditions.

The Prophet is the only person in all of human history to whom Divine revelations have been communicated and safeguarded; there is no parallel in any of the other Divine revelations. At the same time it is only Prophet Muhammad whose deeds, words, journeys, military expeditions, clothes and ways of dressing, routine daily behavior and his characteristic way of eating, drinking, even smiling have all been recorded and transmitted.

The Prophet delivered the Revelation during the last twenty-three years of his sixty-three years on this planet; he not only brought the final Divine Message from God to humanity, he also set a perfect example with his daily practices. Today, there is no difference in the practice of acts of worship like the daily prayers from what the Prophet performed. But, it is impossible to say the same thing for the followers of previous Prophets.

e. *The Prophet has been sent to all humankind:* In order for any ideology, teaching or religion to be universal, it should address and embrace not only one particular society, community, race, or nation, but also people from every walk of life and people throughout the world. Otherwise, such an ideology, teaching, or religion would be seen to be only local or national, and therefore, could not be regarded as universal.

The final Message was revealed to God's Messenger so that all of humanity would be guided to the objective of being prosperous in both worlds through acceptance of the faith and the performance of righteous deeds, and so that they would be guided to the right path in all acts at all times. We can observe this universality in many verses of the Qur'an:

> Say (O Messenger to all humankind): "O humankind! Surely I am the Messenger of God to all of you, of Him to Whom belongs the sovereignty of the heavens and the earth. There is no deity but He. He gives life and causes to die." Believe, then, in God and His Messenger, the Prophet who neither writes nor reads, who believes in God and His words (all His Books, commandments, and deeds); and follow him so that you may be rightly-guided. (A'raf 7:158)

> We have not sent you but to all humankind as a bearer of glad tidings (of prosperity for faith and righteousness) and a warner (against the consequences of misguidance). But most of humankind do not know (this, nor do they appreciate what a great blessing it is for them). (Saba 34:28)

> We have not sent you (O Muhammad) but as an unequalled mercy for all the worlds. (Anbiya 21:107)

The Prophet, who can be thought of as the mirror of God's man-ifestation of His All-Merciful favors reaching the whole of creation, is the first and foremost Universal Man. He is the means for all people to attain eternal happiness, and he is the owner of the most compre-hensive rank of intercession in the Hereafter. The Prophet declared that he was sent, not only to a nation, but to all of humanity: "I have been given five things that none of the Prophets and Messengers pre-ceding me were given. I have been given the characteristic of frighten-ing others from a distance of a month's journey. The whole earth has been rendered a mosque for me and for my community. Anyone from my community may perform their prayers anywhere on the earth. The gains of war have been rendered permissible for me. While the Prophets and Messengers preceding me were sent only to their own people, I have been sent to all of humanity. And, I have been reward-ed with the right and privilege of intercession."[39]

f. *The Qur'an meets and satisfies all the needs of humanity:* In order for any ideology, teaching, or religion to be universal, it must meet and satisfy the needs and demands of all the people it is addressing. Any ideology, teaching, or religion that cannot do so is not universal. We see that teachings and religions other than Islam, the religion of the Qur'an, deal with, address, and meet only certain aspects of human needs and desires; they are deficient in some aspects, overlooking some needs of humanity. But the Qur'an has no such defect. Nothing that humanity needs or desires remains unex-amined. From the least important aspect to the most crucial one, the Qur'an touches upon and deals with every matter that is of import to humanity.

Matters pertaining to faith, for instance, are things that humans can never withdraw or abandon. Detailed principles regarding faith have been mentioned in the Qur'an and the beautiful Names and Attributes of God are explained in detail. The fact that it is only God Who deserves to be worshipped is emphasized, while people are told to believe in His angels, Prophets and Messengers and the Books, as well as resurrection after death and being accountable for all deeds in the Hereafter. Principles pertaining to acts of worship, for example, the prayers, fasting during Ramadan, almsgiving, and pilgrimage to Mecca are explained and whatever rules humanity needs in their daily life have been laid down.

Moreover, issues of what is permitted or prohibited, as well as principles of financial matters are given; jurisdiction over orphans and their guardians have been fixed, issues such as marriage, dowries, divorce, alimony, and breast-feeding are clearly set out. Also, there are clear injunctions about the penalties to be applied for certain crimes, for example, retaliation for first degree murder, for second degree murder, the penalties for brigandage, for adultery and for false accusations of adultery. In addition, methods of solving disputes among people are explained, as well as the different ways to solve family problems; the principles to be observed in Muslim-nonMuslim relations, and relations during times of peace and warfare are set out. There are prohibitions of being afraid and retreating when meeting the enemy and principles are set out for the treatment of prisoners of war and the drawing up of treaties. Additionally, there are a number of topics about how to treat relatives, how to avoid bad treatment and how one should answer such treatment with good deeds; it is stated that forgiveness is the best thing to do; righteousness, trustworthiness, and humility are encouraged while pride and conceit are disparaged. The Qur'an tells us that denigrating others is bad, that we should avoid gossip and over-inquisitiveness while respecting the privacy of others; it outlines how we should behave when entering the private rooms of other people, warns women of how they should respect themselves and protect their chastity, as well as outlining the etiquette that pertains to visiting or hosting others.

In short, we can say that the Qur'an covers a vast portfolio of subjects that are of importance for all of humanity. All of these issues and matters that are dealt with in the Qur'an are issues and matters that human beings will encounter in their lives, sooner or later. Thus, it is easy for us to turn to the Qur'an when we need to find out how to behave in a certain situation. This again is one of the many proofs of the universality of the Qur'an and its timelessness.

g. *Whatever principles the Qur'an introduced are logically consistent and acceptable:* Many ideals, philosophical theories, and systems, since the earliest times of human history, have been developed and presented for humanity. However, none of them have been long-lasting, with even the most powerful ones sooner or later disappearing; only their names have remained, with the names of some having been forgotten. The primary reason for the disappearance of such systems or ideas is that they have no inner consistency and are not universally acceptable.

However, whatever tenets of faith and principles, moral or practical, the Qur'an has introduced have been acceptable. This is because God has created all these principles; God is the Creator of humankind and thus it is He Who knows best His creation and their limits. God Almighty would never force humanity to fulfill tasks that are too difficult nor would He put an unbearable burden on our shoulders. The verse concerned with fasting below is enough to show the importance Islam attaches to this issue:

> The month of Ramadan, in which the Qur'an was sent down as guidance for people, and as clear signs of Guidance and the Criterion (between truth and falsehood). Therefore whoever of you is present this month, must fast it, and whoever is so ill that he cannot fast or on a journey (must fast the same) number of other days. God wills ease for you, and He does not will hardship for you, so that you can complete the number of the days required, and exalt God for He has guided you, and so it may be that you will give thanks (due to Him). (Baqara 2:185)

Finally, we can say that all the basic features of the Qur'an that are mentioned above are indicators of its universality. The Qur'an is the culmination of a series of Divine Messages, and the commands and instructions by which it provides guidance for human beings are of a universal nature. These apply for all time to come, for all situations, and for all humanity.

CHAPTER 11

Interpretation and Exposition
of the Qur'an

INTERPRETATION AND EXPOSITION
OF THE QUR'AN

91 | Is it enough to read translations of the Qur'an to truly comprehend it?

S cientific, philosophical, and religious works should be explained by those who best understood them, for the audience is in need of such explanations to fully understand such works. As a matter of fact, we can see that various such works in historical sources have been footnoted many times in an attempt to explain the ideas contained. Such a necessity becomes more evident when we refer to the Divine Book of the Qur'an; this is a text that will save all of humanity from the swamps of heresy. Its principles are general. The Qur'an not only contains verses that are easy to understand, it also contains verses that require commentary. The Qur'an contains grand art, fine details, and deep meanings. Additionally, the Qur'an calls for reflection on its messages:

> This is a Book, which We send down to you, full of blessings, so that they (all conscious, responsible beings) may ponder its verses and that the people of discernment may reflect on it and be mindful. (Sad 38:29)

> Do they not meditate earnestly on the Qur'an, or are there locks on the hearts (that are particular to them so that they are as if deaf and blind, and incapable of understanding the truth)? (Muhammad 47:24)

The first Qur'an commentator was Prophet Muhammad, peace and blessings be upon him, and from his time onwards, commentators of the Qur'an have explained it according to the needs and scientific developments of their own time and community; this is a process that will also continue in the future.

As for translations, the Qur'an cannot be exactly understood from translation alone, as without the commentaries the translation cannot encompass all the grand art, literary subtleties, the circumstances of the revelation of various chapters or verses, the complicated meanings, the interrelation between the chapters and verses, or the hundreds of other matters that need clarification. The commentaries are necessary for Muslims otherwise they might merely be content with the translations alone and end up thinking (God forbid!): "This Qur'an does not seem to be as important as we thought." Thus, the commentaries are a necessary part of the Qur'an to understand it properly.

92 | Were there any Qur'anic commentaries during the time of the Prophet?

C ertainly; the first commentator of the Qur'an was Prophet Muhammad, who had brought the Divine Message from God to humanity. The Prophets and Messengers preceding him also used to both convey the Divine Messages and interpret them so that their people would better understand. The Prophets were commissioned to both convey and explain the Divine Messages to the people. The following verses confirm this:

> We have sent no Messenger save with the tongue of his people, that he might make (the Message) clear to them. Then God leads whomever He wills astray, and He guides whomever He wills. He is the All-Glorious with irresistible might, the All-Wise. (Ibrahim 14:4)

> O Messenger (you who convey and embody the Message in the best way)! Convey and make known in the clearest way all that has been sent down to you from your Lord. For, if you do not, you have not conveyed His Message and fulfilled the task of His Messengership. And God will certainly protect you from the people. God will surely not guide the disbelieving people (to attain their goal of harming or defeating you). (Maeda 5:67)

(We sent them with) clear proofs of the truth and Scriptures. And on you We have sent down the Reminder (the Qur'an) so that you may make clear to humankind whatever is sent down to them (through you of the truth concerning their present and next life), and that they may reflect. (Nahl 16:44)

God's Messenger used to interpret and expound Qur'anic verses in the following ways:

He would sometimes expound a verse after reciting it; sometimes he would read a verse and ask the Companions what they had understood from it. He would then explain it himself; sometimes he would be asked about various verses and he would answer the Companions and explain these verses. He would sometimes talk about an issue and later explain his words by reciting the relevant Qur'anic verses. At other times he would recite a verse and then clarify its meaning simply by adding a word or words to it.

93 | Can anyone interpret the Qur'an?

An interpretation of the Qur'an only has value in proportion to the interpreter's learning, knowledge, horizon of perception, and skills; there are some preliminary qualifications necessary in order to be able to interpret and expound the Qur'an, just as there are some preliminary qualifications and expertise to understand medical, engineering or other specialized texts. One who has not been properly trained cannot perform an operation, nor can anyone who is not qualified make furniture or cut hair; in the same way not everyone can interpret the Qur'an. In the same way that it is necessary to study and attend courses and training programs to carry out any of the professions mentioned above, it is necessary to be educated and to possess certain qualifications to expound and commentate on Qur'anic verses. We can briefly state the necessary qualifications as follows:

The language of the Qur'an is one of the essential, inseparable elements of the Qur'an. Thus, for the interpretation and exposition of the Divine Word, it is essential to be equipped with necessary, accurate knowledge of Arabic, the Qur'an's language. Without knowing Arabic, commentating on the Qur'an by merely studying various translations of the Qur'an would be a misguided, incomplete, and misleading approach. Due to its miraculous eloquence, the Qur'an has great depth and richness of meaning. One of the elements on which the eloquence of the Qur'an is based is its creative style, which is rich in artistry. The Qur'an frequently speaks in parables and adopts a figurative, symbolic rhetoric, using metaphors and similes. Also, the Arabic language is strictly grammatical and is rich in conjugation and derivation. All these and other features of the language make important contributions to the meaning and these must be given in a study of Qur'anic interpretation.

The second precondition that an interpreter of the Qur'an should possess is that they must adopt a holistic approach to the Qur'an. What we mean by this is that the main interpreter of the Qur'an is the Qur'an itself; the verses interpret one another and the Qur'an as a whole interprets each of them. A matter alluded to in a certain verse may be explained at length in another verse. Sometimes an aspect of one matter could be explained in one verse while another aspect of it could be explained somewhere else. Thus, a person who is unable to understand the Qur'an in its totality, but tries to explain only one verse by examining that specific verse would make an incorrect, incomplete, and misleading rendering.

The third precondition for the study of Qur'anic interpretation is that one should have a good knowledge of the Sunna, or the Practice of the Prophet; God's Messenger explained and interpreted the Qur'an with his words, deeds, and reactions to incidents and events. As has been explained, the most eminent and truest commentary of the Qur'an is the Prophet's commentary, i.e., his *Sunna*.

The fourth precondition for Qur'anic interpretation is that one should be conversant not only in religious sciences, but also other sciences, for example, sociology, psychology, and history, as this knowledge is necessary in the commentaries.

The fifth precondition for Qur'anic interpretation is that one should not expect any material gain. One should expect only God's pleasure. The following Qur'anic verse announces the good news to those who are sincere in this respect, stating that God will show them the right way: *"Those (on the other hand) who strive hard for Our sake, We will most certainly guide them to Our ways (that We have established to lead them to salvation). Most assuredly, God is with those devoted to doing good, aware that God is seeing them"* (Ankabut 29:69).

94 | Did the Prophet interpret the entire Qur'an?

The first and foremost interpreter of the Qur'an was the Prophet. However, whether he interpreted all of it is another question. There are three approaches of the scholars in this regard. Some scholars are of the opinion that God's Messenger interpreted the entire Qur'an. Some others state that the Prophet interpreted a small part of the Qur'an. Still others support the idea that God's Messenger interpreted the Qur'an as much as was necessary; the latter opinion is the most widely accepted approach.

Accordingly, the Prophet explained the *mujmal*, or concise, verses that pertain to faith, acts of worship, and practical matters in great detail, exemplifying what God wanted in both his sayings and deeds. There are also instances when the Prophet did not provide any explanation for certain other *mujmal*, or concise, verses; Muslim scholars in later eras provided explanations for these. That is why there are various interpretations and commentaries with respect to certain verses.

God's Messenger interpreted and gave details about the Hereafter, informed us about the world of the Unseen and the stories of bygone nations in the Qur'an by utilizing the literary arts of parable, metaphor and simile; thus he made it easy for people to understand the verses. He also explained subtle points and more complicated matters in the Qur'an.

Prophet Muhammad, peace and blessings be upon him, did not elucidate verses that were easy to understand. He did not interpret certain *mutashabih* verses of the Qur'an; these were to be better understood by humanity as their scientific levels progressed and as people become better acquainted with the Arabic language. However, when asked about such verses, he would provide an explanation to the person who had asked according to their level of understanding. By acting in this way, God's Messenger opened up the tradition of making commentaries and people were encouraged to use their reason and intellect to contemplate on the Qur'an until the Last Day, to find new insights and make fresh interpretations on the Qur'an.

As for those who wish to study how to interpret and make expositions of the Qur'an, they should, first of all, study how the Prophet interpreted the related verse. If the Prophet already interpreted that verse in a plain way that does not allow a variety of interpretations then the meaning given to the verse in the Traditions relating to it should be acted on and accepted. This is particularly true for verses on Islamic faith and practice which have been clearly elucidated and practiced by the Prophet and which do not allow for any other interpretation.

Finally, anyone can understand the Qur'an, particularly if they take the commentaries and explanations of God's Messenger into consideration. Although almost every individual who knows the language of the Qur'an can grasp something from it, a true and comprehensive understanding can only be achieved by experts of exposition and commentary who have attained the required level of knowledge. These experts take into consideration the linguistic rules, and pay attention to the methodology of exposition when trying to understand what is veiled, difficult, or abstruse. They expend great effort in reflection, contemplation, and meditation so that they can attain the correct understanding of the Divine purpose. They resort to the explanations of God's Messenger in order to expound the *mujmal*, or concise, verses and explore the depths of reported knowledge.

CHAPTER 12

The Etiquette of Recitation

THE ETIQUETTE OF RECITATION

95 | Is it difficult to learn how to recite the Qur'an?

The Qur'an is God's miraculous, peerless Book which has been sent to all of humanity. Learning how to read the Qur'an is not a difficult task, and memorizing it is so easy that every Muslim boy and girl easily learns to read the Qur'an within a month and memorize passages from the Qur'an, even before they know Arabic grammar. This is one of the miraculous aspects of the Qur'an. Every believer memorizes different passages from the Qur'an, and hundreds of thousands of believers throughout the world have committed the entire Qur'an to memory; thus they take it to heart, interiorizing the inner rhythms, sound patterns, and textual dynamics. This feature of is unique to the Qur'an.

As a divine favor to all humanity, God Almighty has made the Qur'an *"easy (to recite and understand)"* (Maryam 19:97). Its recitation, committing it to memory and fulfilling the principles of the Qur'an are not beyond human capability. Almighty God has never laid a burden that is too heavy to carry on the shoulders of humanity. Hence, He rendered the Qur'an easy to learn to read, recite, and practice.

96 | What should one pay attention to while reciting the Qur'an?

There are some points which one should pay attention to when reciting the Qur'an; this is the Word of the All-Merciful, Who embraces all beings. The more carefully it is recited the more the one reciting will benefit. The first point that one should pay attention to when reciting the Qur'an is what the Qur'an is and to Whom it belongs. The identity of the author has an important influence on the audience; thus it should be remembered that the Qur'an is not an ordinary word, but that it is a message that came from God Who is the Lord of all universe.

There are words which influence certain peoples and societies for some time, but then are forgotten due to a loss of power and influence. But there are also words which deeply influence the whole of humanity, never losing their deep impact. The words of the Qur'an fall into this second category. The Qur'an is the one and only Book that has challenged its opponents to bring forth something similar to itself; it is the only book to which its opponents could not help listen, despite their great enmity and it is the only book whose influence has encompassed and embraced all times and all places. God Almighty gives the following parable in the Qur'an to show what a great impact it will have on its audience and how they should approach it:

> If We had sent down this Qur'an on a mountain, you would certainly see it humble itself, splitting asunder for awe of God. Such parables We strike for humankind so that they may reflect (on why the Qur'an is being revealed to humankind and how great and important their responsibility is). (Hashr 59:21)

Accordingly, this Qur'anic parable reminds us that if a huge creation like a mountain were to have the sense and knowledge to make it responsible and accountable, as mankind actually is, before the Owner of the Book for its deeds, then it would be humbled, cracked, and trembling, in awe of God. So, the very first thing one should keep in mind when reciting the Qur'an is never to forget Who has sent it or one's accountability before Him.

Secondly, one should be physically and spiritually clean when approaching the Qur'an; this is a book of absolute purity and thus should be read in cleanliness. For this purpose, one should have ablution. One should also be spiritually prepared as they will soon be reading their Lord's words. These two points are important in maximizing the level and degree of benefit to be derived from reading the Qur'an.

There are also times and circumstances that are recommended for recitation. One should not attempt to recite the Qur'an when one is drowsy or mentally or physically exhausted; it is more likely that an error would be made at such times and one may become distracted due to preoccupation or an active environment or other such circumstances. It is at times like this that the Qur'an becomes unintelligible. Since the purpose of reciting and studying the Qur'an is to understand it and to meditate and ponder upon it ensuring contemplation and reflection under these circumstances would be difficult. Therefore, it is better to select times when our minds are clear and when there is no other important task waiting to be done. In addition, one should read as and when they are in the mood to read and stop when they feel that the mood has passed. The Qur'an should be approached without prejudice. If a person approaches the Qur'an and reads it with thoughts such as, God forbid, as, "This is an outdated book; there is nothing it can give me. It was revealed for a certain people at a certain time and in a certain geography; it has no factual bearing" or with similar considerations in their mind then they will not derive much benefit from the Qur'an. That is to say, it is unimaginable that the Qur'an would be able to open itself to the benefit of such people, since these considerations are the convictions of those who do not believe in it. The unbelievers cannot enjoy or derive any share of the benefits of the Qur'an, which was revealed as a source of guidance for all of humanity, and they cannot take advantage of its glory or brilliance; rather their backs are turned to it and they live without faith.

When one intends to begin reciting the Qur'an, they should say: *A'udhu billahi min ash-shaytan ar-rajim,* or "I seek refuge in God from Satan, who is eternally rejected (from God's Mercy)." This is a prayer for God's protection and help against evil suggestions from

Satan during the recitation. The influence of Satan on humankind cannot be underestimated or denied. He tries to divert humanity, whom he sees as the cause of his own decline, in a number of ways since he himself has gone astray and thus fallen away from God. One should seek refuge, especially when praying and reading the Qur'an, in God's protection from the evil whispers and deception of Satan; he can travel through the blood stream, like the blood cells. Satan approaches human beings through various ways, particularly when reading the Qur'an, throwing various suspicions into one's heart and planting negative thoughts in one's mind, encouraging us not to read it and trying his best to confuse us. The best thing to do at such times, as stated in the Qur'an, is to seek refuge to God's protection:

> So when you recite the Qur'an (as a good, righteous deed), seek refuge in God from Satan rejected (from His Mercy, because of his evil suggestions and whisperings during the recitation). (Nahl 16:98)

The Qur'an should also be recited calmly and distinctly, with pious reverence and in a meditative way. This slow and measured recitation of the Qur'an is known as *tartil*. It should also be noted that, no matter how good a deed it is to recite the Qur'an, the real purpose of reading it is to understand and meditate on it. Moreover, one should try to recite the Qur'an in a tone of *huzn*, or sadness. Such a tone of voice affects the heart more than a cheerful one. The way to achieve this is by bringing sadness to mind, thoroughly and carefully contemplating the warnings in the Qur'an, as well as the covenants and oaths contained in the Qur'an. Then, one should contemplate one's own shortcomings in obedience and submission to God's commands and prohibitions and feel sad about this. If this does not bring to mind *huzn*, or sadness and cry, then they should be saddened due to the lack of this emotion, since it is one of the greatest calamities. There is no greater or more serious misfortune or calamity than one who is insensitive to the Qur'anic verses and cannot shed tears in awe of God or due to a fear of giving account of their shortcomings.

Another important point that we should take into consideration when reading the Qur'an is that each and every verse of it should be thought of as addressed directly to ourselves, as if the events, parables, stories, personalities, etc. are also directly connected to us and as if there are warnings and lessons also for us in all of these. In this sense, for instance, when we read the verses about the story of Adam and Satan, we should realize that God is in fact and telling us about the mission of Satan, about how an insidious enemy he is, about how covertly he can approach us and deceive us, and about how we should not be careless and unmindful of his whispers and deception, even for an instant; in short, we should read these verses as if they were revealed for us.

When we read we should take also lessons from what we read, for instance the verses about the story of the nation of Prophet Noah; we should contemplate that the same thing might occur at any time and that God will help the righteous people and make them ultimately victorious; when we read the accounts of Prophet Abraham we should remember his struggles and realize that our tasks should be fulfilled without fear or trepidation; when reading the story of Prophet Joseph we should understand how evil jealousy is and thus should not lay traps for others; when reading about God's Messenger we should consider how he carried out his mission to a victorious conclusion and realize that even those people who tried to prevent the Prophet from fulfilling his mission at the beginning saw his compassion, mercy, patience, gentleness and Prophetic intelligence and then became united around him, becoming prosperous.

When reading the verses in which various aspects of human nature are related and where the weak points of humans are emphasized, we should understand that we need to be more careful and attentive, and say to ourselves: "This part applies to me and is concerned with my shortcomings."

While studying and reciting the Qur'an in different moods from that mentioned above, we may perhaps acquire information, learn the stories of the Prophets, understand better the characteristics of human nature, and comprehend what the life of Prophet Muhammad, peace and blessings be upon him, was like, but we cannot attain the real goal of reading the Qur'an, we cannot comprehend the true purpose behind its revelation, and we cannot benefit from it to the full.

97 | How can one best show respect to the Qur'an?

The Qur'an is a divine text that comes to us from our Lord, the Almighty; we should remember that it advocates a meaningful and profound interaction. We should read this divine communication in a state of humility and reflection and with the feeling that we are in His Presence as if we see Him; even if we do not see Him, surely God Almighty sees us. We should also keep in mind that the Qur'an is a cure for our diseases and sufferings. It is also the greatest and the most important trust that God has sent to us. Thus, the most proper way of showing our respect to it is to fulfill what it asks us to do in the best possible way.

The very first step in showing respect to the Qur'an is to read it carefully and with great humility. God says: *"This is a Book, which We send down to you, full of blessings, so that they (all conscious, responsible beings) may ponder its verses and that the people of discernment may reflect on it and be mindful"* (Sad 38:29) and thus encourages us to recite the Qur'an while pondering upon its verses.

Those who do not study and recite the Qur'an are described as having locks on their hearts and spiritual senses that are blind and deaf to the message of the Qur'an: *"Do they not meditate earnestly on the Qur'an, or are there locks on the hearts (that are particular to them so that they are as if deaf and blind, and incapable of understanding the truth)?"* (Muhammad 47:24).

Accordingly, respecting the Qur'an consists of not forgetting that it is the Word of the Lord of the worlds, reading it with full awareness, heeding its commands and prohibitions, and making it an indispensable part of our daily life.

98 | Is a reading of the commentary and translation of the Qur'an the same as a *khatma*, a complete recitation of the Qur'an?

First of all, an interpretation of the Qur'an is not the Qur'an. The Qur'an does not consist of meaning alone; its meaning on its own cannot be called the Qur'an. In order for a text to be considered to be the Qur'an, it should possess the features and characteristics which God calls the Qur'an. If we look at the Qur'an in this sense, we can see that there is an emphasis on the fact that the Qur'an was revealed in Arabic and therefore Arabic is an essential aspect of it:

> We send it down as a qur'an (discourse) in Arabic so that you may reflect (on both its meaning and wording) and understand. (Yusuf 12:2)

> And thus have We sent it down as a qur'an (a discourse) in Arabic and set out in it warnings in diverse contexts and from diverse perspectives, so that they may keep from disobedience to Us in reverence for Us and piety, or that it may prompt them to remembrance and heedfulness. (Ta.Ha 20:113)

These verses explicitly indicate that only the Divine Revelation in Arabic can be called the Qur'an and that no interpretation of the Qur'an can be thus called or regarded.

In addition, the following verses also clearly emphasize that the Qur'an is in Arabic:

> It is a Qur'an in Arabic with no crookedness (free from any contradiction and anything offensive to truth and righteousness and reason), so that they may keep from disobedience to God in reverence for Him and piety to deserve His protection. (Zumar 39:28)

> A Book whose communications have been spelled out distinct-
> ly and made clear, and whose verses are in ordered sequence, a
> Qur'an (Recitation) in Arabic for a people who have knowl-
> edge (and so can appreciate excellence in the use of the lan-
> guage). (Fussilat 41:3)

> And just so: (as We revealed these truths to the Messengers
> before you) We reveal to you a Qur'an (a Recitation) in Arabic
> so that you may warn the mother-city and all those around it,
> and warn of the Day of Assembly, about (the coming of) which
> there is no doubt. One party will be in Paradise, and one party
> in the Blaze. (Shura 42:7)

> We have made it a Recitation (a Qur'an) in Arabic so that you
> may reason (and understand it and the wisdom in its revela-
> tion). (Zukhruf 43:3)

What is clearly stated in all these verses is that the Qur'an is in
Arabic. As for its interpretations, they are, as the word "interpretation" itself implies, renderings of the Qur'an into other languages
with different words. Thus, an interpretation of the Qur'an can never
take the place of the Qur'an in Arabic. However, that does not mean
that such a reading is of no use and therefore is inadvisable. But,
what we call a *khatma*, i.e., a complete recitation of the Qur'an, means
a Qur'anic recital, which is an act of worship in itself. Thus, the *khatma* should be performed by reciting the entire Qur'an in Arabic. In
other words, one should recite the Qur'an in its original Arabic text
in order one to be able to say that they have recited it. Or else, what
one has read is not in itself the Arabic Qur'an, but the meaning of it
rendered into another language by someone in their own words.

99 | Can the Qur'an be read or touched without ablution?

It is not compulsory for one to have ablution to recite the
Qur'an from memory. However, if one is in a state of *jana-
ba*, or major ritual impurity, they should have a bath (*ghusl*)

before reciting the Qur'an. The most common causes of major ritual impurity are associated with ejaculation, intercourse, menses, or childbirth. In addition, one must have ablution when reciting the Qur'an if one is examining the actual written text. In relation to this issue, the Qur'an says:

> I swear by the locations of the stars (and their falling) – it is indeed a very great oath, if you but knew. Most certainly it is a Qur'an (recited) most honorable, in a Book well-guarded. None except the purified ones can reach it (to obtain the knowledge it contains. And none except those cleansed of material and spiritual impurities should touch it). It is a Book being sent down in parts from the Lord of the worlds. (Waqi'a 56:75-80)

Accordingly, none except those who have purified themselves from any physical impurity by taking ablutions or a bath, and those purified from the spiritual impurity of unbelief should touch the most honorable Qur'an.

According to a narration, Prophet Muhammad, peace and blessings be upon him, wrote a letter to the people of Yemen and said: "Only those who have ablution may hold the Qur'an in their hands."[40] Jurisdictions of such Islamic scholars as Abu Hanifa, Malik and Shafii are in keeping with this tradition.

It is reported of Caliph Ali that nothing kept God's Messenger from reciting the Qur'an except major ritual impurity. It is also reported of Caliph Umar that God's Messenger ordered those who were in a state of major ritual impurity or menses not to recite the Qur'an.

It should finally be noted that the Qur'an is the Word of God. It is thus a must to respect and to revere it. Refraining from holding the Qur'an without ablution is a token of respect and reverence to it.

ENDNOTES

1 See also the suras Maryam 19:97 and Dukhan 44:58.

2 Abu Dawud, *Sunna* 5.

3 Abu Dawud, *Sunna*, 5; Ibn Maja, *Muqaddima*, 2; Tirmidhi, *Ilm*, 10; Ibn Hanbal, *Sunan*, 4/132.

4 Ankabut 29:48.

5 Naml 27:6.

6 Bukhari, *Bad al-Wahy*, 7; Muslim, *Iman*, 252-254; Ibn Hanbal, *Musnad*, 6/153, 232.

7 Baqara 2:215, 217, 219-220, 222.

8 Haythami, *Majma' al-Zawaid*, 7/86.

9 Ibn Hanbal, 2/259.

10 Muslim, *Ashriba*, 102; Abu Dawud, *At'ima*, 15; Ibn Hanbal, 5/383, 398.

11 Abu Dawud, *Salat*, 122.

12 Abu Dawud, *Salat*, 122.

13 Hakim, *Mustadrak*, 1/356.

14 Bayhaki, *Shu'ab al-Iman*, 1/440.

15 The scholars who share and accept the views and jurisdictions of the early generations of Muslims.

16 Bukhari, *Wudu*, 10.

17 Edouard Montet, *Le Coran*, Paris, 1949, p. 53.

18 Georges Sale, *Sabil al-Rashad*, Issue 7, 1954, p.310.

19 Quoted in Omer Riza Dogrul's preface to *Tanrı Buyruğu*, (Divine Command).

20 Tirmidhi, *Ilm* 16; Abu Dawud, *Sunna* 6.

21 Bukhari, *Tayammum*, 3; *Salat*, 56; Muslim, *Masajid*, 3.

22 Ibn Hisham, *Al-Sirat al-Nabawiyya*, 1/342-350.

23 See Baqara 2:144; Mujadila 58:12-13.

24 See Al Imran 3:144, Ahzab 33:40, Muhammad 47:2 and Fath 48:29.

25 Abu Dawud, *Talaq* 3; Ibn Maja, *Talaq* 1.

26 Ecclesiasticus 22:3; 42:11; 26: 10-11.

27 Mursalat 77:20.

28 Rum 30:20.

29 Ya.Sin 36:77.

30 Sajda 32:7.

31 Alaq 96:2.

32 Hijr 15:26.

33 Maryam 19:67.

34 Bukhari, *Iman* 37.

35 Muslim, *Iman* 1; Abu Dawud, *Sunna*, 15; Ibn Maja, *Muqaddima* 9.

36 Abu Dawud, *Sunna*, 16.

37 Tirmidhi, *Qiyama*, 59; *Musnad* I, 293, 303/307.

38 See Exodus 21:12; Exodus 21:15-16.

39 Bukhari, *Tayammum* 1; *Salat* 56; Muslim, *Masajid* 3; Nasai, *Ghusl* 26; Darimi, *Siyar* 28; *Salat* 111.

40 Muwatta, *Mass al-Qur'an* 1; Darimi, *Talaq* 3.

BIBLIOGRAPHY

Abu Dawud, al-Sijistani, *Sunan al-Abu Dawud*, Istanbul: Çağrı Yayınları, 1981.

Abu Shahba, Muhammad ibn Muhammad, *Al-Sirat al-Nabawiyya Fi Daw al-Qur'an Wa al-Sunna*, Beirut: Dar al-Kalam, 1992.

Abu al-Suud, Muhammad ibn Muhammad al-Imadi, *Irshad al-Akl al-Salim ila Mazay al-Qur'an al-Karim*, Beirut: Dar al-Ihya al-Turas al-Arabi, undated.

Abu Zahra, Muhammad, *Al-Mujizat al-Kubra al-Qur'an*, Dar al-Fikr al-Arabi, undated.

Abbas Hasan, *Al-Nahw al-Wafi*, Cairo: Dar al-Maarif, 1987.

Abd ibn Hasan, Muhammad Yusuf, *Al-Munafiqun fi al-Qur'an al-Karim*, Cairo: Dar al-Tawzi' wa al-Nashr al-Islamiyya, 991.

Abdulhalim, Mahmud Ali, *Alamiyya al-Da'wat al-Islamiyya*, Cairo: Dar al-Wafa, 1992.

Akçay, Mustafa, *Çağdaş Dünyada İnsan ve Dîni Sorumluluğu*, İzmir: Işık Yayınları, 2000.

Akgül, Muhittin, *Kur'ân-ı Kerîm'de Hz. Peygamber*, Istanbul: Işık Yayınları, 2002.

Akiki, Najib, *Al-Mustashriqun*, Cairo: Dar al-Maarif, 1965.

Al-Muttaqi, Ali Husamuddin al-Hindi, *Kanz al-Ummal Fi Sunan al-Aqwal wa al-Af'al*, Beirut: Muassasat al-Risala, 1989.

Alusi, Mahmud Abu al-Fadl, *Ruh al-Maani fi Tafsir al-Qur'an al-Azim*, Beirut: Dar al-Ihya al-Turas al-Arabi, undated.

Aqq, Halid Abdurrahman, *Tarih al-Tawthik al-Nass al-Qur'an al-Karim*, Damascus: Dar al-Fikr, 1986.

———— *Al-Furqan wa al-Qur'an*, Damascus: Al-Hikma li al-Tibaat wa al-Nashr, 1994.

Ashkar, Umar Sulayman, *Al-Rusul wa al-Risalat*, Kuwait: Maktabat al-Falah, 1985.

Ateş, Süleyman, *Yüce Kur'ân'ın Çağdaş Tefsiri*, Istanbul: Yeni Ufuklar Neş-riyat, 1988.

Aydemir, Abdullah, *Hz. Peygamber ve Sahâbenin Dilinden Kur'ân-ı Kerim'in Faziletleri*, İzmir: Akyol Neşriyat, 1981.

Baghawi, Abu Muhammad al-Husayn ibn Mas'ud, *Maa'lim al-Tanzil*, Riyad: Dar al-Tayba, 1993.

Baqillani, Abu Bakr, *I'jaz al-Qur'an*, Cairo: Dar al-Amin, 1993.

Bardakoğlu, Ali, *İslam'da İnanç İbadet ve Günlük Yaşayış Ansiklopedisi*, Istanbul: İFAV Yayınları,1997.

Bayhaki, Abu Bakr Ahmad ibn Husayn, *Dalail al-Nubuwwa*, Beirut, 1985.

Biqai', Burhan al-Din Abu al-Hasan Ibrahim ibn Umar, *Nazm al-Durar fi Tanasub al-Ayat wa al-Suwar*, Beirut: Dar al-Kutub al-Ilmiyya, 1995.

Bucaille, Maurice, *The Bible, the Qur'an and Science*, (Translated as *"Kitâb-ı Mukaddes, Kur'an ve Bilim,"* by Suat Yıldırım), İzmir: T.Ö.V Yayınları, 1981.

Bukhari, Abu Abdillah Muhammad ibn Ismail, *Al-Jami al-Sahih*, Istanbul: Al-Maktabat al-Islamiyya, undated.

Buti, Muhammad Said Ramadan, *Min Rawai' al-Qur'an*, Damascus: Maktabat al-Farabi, undated.

Cerrahoğlu, İsmail, *Tefsir Usûlü*, Ankara: Elif Ofset, 1979.

———, *Garanik Meselesinin İstismarcıları*, Ankara: A. Ü. İlâhiyat Fakültesi Dergisi, issue 24, pp. 69-70, 1981.

Damaghani, Husayn ibn Muhammad, *Qamus al-Qur'an*, Beirut: Dar al-Ilm li al-Malayin, 1985.

Darimi, Abu Muhammad Abdullah ibn Abdurrahman ibn al-Fadl ibn Bahram, *Sunan*, Beirut: Dar al-Kutub al-Ilmiyya, undated.

Davenport, John, *Muhammad and the Qur'an*, (Translated as *"Hz. Muhammad ve Kur'ân-ı Kerim"* by Ömer Rıza Doğrul), Istanbul, 1926.

Demirci, Muhsin, *Vahiy Gerçeği*, Istanbul: İFAV, 1996.

Darwaza, Muhammad Izzad, *Asr al-Nabi*, Istanbul: Yöneliş Yayınları, 1995.

Draz, Muhammad Abdullah, *The Qur'an: An Eternal Challenge*, (Translated as *"En Mühim Mesaj Kur'ân"* by Suat Yıldırım), İzmir: Işık Yayınları, 1994.

Elmalılı, Hamdi Yazır, *Hak Dîni Kur'ân Dili*, Feza Gazetecilik A.Ş, undated.

Ertuğrul, İsmâil Fenni, *İzâle-i Şükûk*, Istanbul, 1928.

Fazlurrahman, *Islam*, Istanbul: Selçuk Yayınları, 1981.

Firuzabadi, Majduddin Muhammad ibn Yaqub, *Basaair al-Zawi al-Tamyiz fi Lataif al-Kitab al-Aziz*, Beirut: Maktabat al-Ilmiyya, undated.

———, *Qamus al-Muhit*, Beirut: Muassasat al-Risala, 1993.

Gülen, M. Fethullah, *Asrın Getirdiği Tereddütler*, İzmir: Nil Yayınları, 2001.

———, *Ölçü veya Yoldaki Işıklar*, Istanbul: Nil Yayınları, 2001.

———, *İnancın Gölgesinde*, İzmir: Nil Yayınları, 2001.

————, *Kur'ân'dan İdrake Yansıyanlar*, Istanbul: Feza Gazetecilik A.Ş, 2000.

Hamidullah, Muhammad, *İslâm Peygamberi*, Istanbul: İrfan Yayımcılık, 1991.

Haykal, Muhammad Husayn, *Hayat al-Muhammad*, Cairo: Dar al-Maarif, undated.

Himsi, Nuaym, *Fikrat al-I'jaz al-Qur'an*, Beirut: Muassasat al-Risala, 1980.

Hindi, Rahmatullah, *Izhar al-Haqq*, Riyad, 1994.

Ibn al-Arabi, Abu Bakr Muhammad ibn Abdullah, *Ahqam al-Qur'an*, Beirut: Dar al-Fikr, undated.

Ibn Faris, Abu al-Hasan Ahmad ibn Zakariyya, *Mu'jam al-Makayis fi al-Lugha*, Beirut: Dar al-Fikr, 1994.

Ibn Hanbal, Ahmad, *Musnad*, Beirut, undated.

Ibn Hisham, *Al-Sirat al-Nabawiyya*, Beirut: Dar al-Ihya al-Turas al-Arabi, undated.

Ibn Kathir, Abu al-Fida Ismail al-Dimashki, *Tafsir al-Qur'an al-Azim*, Istanbul: Dar al-Kahraman, 1992.

Ibn Maja, Abu Abdillah Muhammad ibn Yazid al-Kazwini, *Sunan*, Istanbul: Al-Maktabat al-Islamiyya, undated.

Ibn Manzur, Abu al-Fadl Jamaluddin Muhammad ibn Mukarram, *Lisan al-Arab*, Beirut, 1990.

Isfahani, Abu al-Qasim Husayn ibn Muhammad, *Al-Mufradat Fi Gharib al-Qur'an*, Beirut: Dar al-Ma'rifa, undated.

Jamal Umari, Ahmad, *Mafhum al-I'jaz al-Qur'an*, Cairo: Dar al-Maarif, 1984.

Jassas, Abu Bakr Ahmad ibn Ali al-Razi, *Ahkam al-Qur'an*, Beirut: Dar al-Ihya al-Turas al-Arabi, 1985.

Jawhari, Ismail ibn Hammad, *Sihah*, Cairo, 1950.

Jurjani, Ali ibn Muhammad, *Al-Ta'rifat*, Beirut: Dar al-Kutub al-Ilmiyya, 1988.

Karaçam, İsmail, *Sonsuz Mu'cize Kur'ân*, Istanbul: Çağ Yayınları, 1990.

Khalifa, Muhammad, *Al-Istishrak wa al-Qur'an al-Azim*, (Trns. by Marwan Abdussabur Shahin), Cairo: Dar al-I'tisam, 1994.

Köksal, Mustafa Asım, *Müsteşrik Caetani'nin Yazdığı İslam Tarihindeki İsnad Ve İftiralara Reddiye*, Ankara: D.İ.B.Y., 1986.

Kurtubi, Abu Abdillah Muhammad ibn Ahmad, *Al-Jami'li Ahkam al-Qur'an*, Beirut, 1985.

Qadi Iyad, Abu al-Fadl al-Yahsubi, *Al-Shifa bi Ta'rif Huquq al-Mustafa*, Beirut: Dar al-Fikr, 1988.

Qasimi, Muhammad Jamaluddin, *Mahasin al-Ta'wil*, Cairo: Dar al-Ihya al-Kutub al-Arabiyya, undated.

Qutub, Sayyid, *Fi Zilal al-Qur'an*, Cairo: Dar al-Shuruk, 1988.

Mahmud, Mustafa, *Understanding the Qur'an: A Contemporary Approach*, (Translated as *"Kur'ân'a Yeni Yaklaşımlar"* by Muhittin Akgül), İzmir: Işık Yayınları, 1999.

Mazi, Mahmud, *Al-Wahy al-Qur'aniyyu fi al-Manzur al-Istishraqiyyi wa Naqdihi*, Alexandria, Dar al-Da'wa, 1996.

Manna' al-Qattan, *Mabahith fi Ulum al-Qur'an*, Riyad: Maktabat al-Maarif, 1988.

Mawdudi, Abu al-Ala, *Tarih Boyunca Tevhid Mücadelesi ve Hz. Peygamberin Hayatı*, (Trns by Ahmed Asrar), Istanbul: Pınar Yayınları, 1992.

————, *Tafhim al-Qur'an*, Istanbul: İnsan Yayınları, 1996.

Muslim, Mustafa, *Mabahis fi I'jaz al-Qur'an*, Riyad: Dar al-Muslim, 1996.

Munawi, Abdurrauf, *Fayz al-Qadir*, Beirut: Dar al-Marifa, undated.

Muslim, Abu al-Husayn ibn Hajjaj, *Sahih al-Muslim*, Beirut: Dar al-Ihya al-Turas al-Arabi, undated.

Nursi, Said, *Sözler*, ("The Words"), Istanbul: Tenvir Neşriyat, undated.

Okiç, Tayyib, *Tefsir ve Hadis Usûlünün Bazı Meseleleri*, Istanbul: Nûn Yayıncılık, 1995.

Raghib, al-Isfahani, *Al-Mufradat*, Beirut: Dar al-Ma'rifa, undated.

Razi, Fahruddin Muhammad ibn Umar ibn Husayn ibn Hasan ibn Ali al-Taymi, *Al-Tafsir al-Kabir*, Beirut: Dar al-Kutub al-Ilmiyya, 1990.

Sabuni, M. Ali, *Rawai' al-Bayan Tafsir al-Ayat al-Ahkam Min al-Qur'an*, Istanbul: Dersaadet Kitabevi, undated.

Samin al-Halabi, Ahmad ibn Yusuf, *Al-Durr al-Masun fu Ulum al-Kitab al-Maknun*, Damascus: Dar al-Kalam, 1993.

Subayh, Muhammad, *Bahthun Jadidun An al-Qur'an al-Karim*, Cairo: Dar al-Shuruq, 1983.

Subhi, Salih, *Mabahis Fi Ulum al-Qur'an*, Istanbul: Dersaadet, undated.

Suyuti, Jalaluddin Abdurrahman, *Asbab al-Nuzul*, Beirut: Dar al-Ibn Zaydun, undated.

————, *Al-Hasais al-Kubra*, Beirut: Dar al-Kutub al-Ilmiyya, 1985.

————, *Al-Durr al-Mansur fi al-Tafsir bi al-Ma'sur*, Egypt, 1314 AH.

————, *Tartib al-Suwar al-Qur'an*, (ed. Sayyid Jumayli), Beirut: Maktabat al-Hilal, 1986.

Shahhata, Abdullah Mahmud, *Ulum al-Qur'an*, Cairo: Dar al-I'tisam, 1985.

Shawwah Ishaq, Ali, *Madha Hawla Umumiyyat al-Rasul*, Cairo: Dar al-Salaam, 1985.

Şimşek, M. Sait, *Garanik Rivâyeti'nin Târihî Değeri*, Bilgi ve Hikmet Dergisi, Spring issue, Vol. II, 1993.

Tabari, ibn Jarir, *Jamiu' al-Bayan al-Ta'wil al-Aya al-Qur'an*, Beirut: Dar al-Fikr, 1995.

Tabarsi, Abu Ali al-Fadl ibn al-Hasan, *Majma al-Bayan fi Tafsir al-Qur'an*, Beirut: Dar al-Ihya al-Turas al-Arabi, 1992.

Tabatabai, Muhammad Husayn, *Al-Qur'an Fi al-Islam*, 1982.

———, *Al-Mizan fi Tafsir al-Qur'an*, Beirut: Muassasat al-A'lami, 1997.

Tahir ibn Ashur, Muhammad, *Tafsir al-Tahrir wa al-Tanwir*, Tunisia: Dar al-Tunusiyya, 1984.

Tahiyya, Abdulaziz Ismail, *Al-Tafsir al-Ilmiyyu Li Huruf al-Awail al-Suwar Fi al-Qur'an al-Karim*, Cairo: Matabi' al-Ahram, 1990.

Tirmidhi, Abu Isa Muhammad ibn Isa, *Al-Jami al-Sahih*, Al-Maktabat al-Islamiyya, undated.

Ünal, Ali, *Kur'ân'da Temel Kavramlar*, İzmir: Nil Yayınları, 1999.

Wahidi, Abu al-Hasan Ali ibn Ahmad, *Asbab al-Nuzul*, Dammam: Dar al-Islah, 1991.

Yıldırım, Suat, *Kur'ân-ı Hakîm ve Açıklamalı Meâli*, Istanbul: Işık Yayınları, 2002.

———, *Peygamberimizin Kur'ân Tefsiri*, Istanbul: Kayıhan Yayınları, 1998.

———, *Kur'ân-ı Kerîm ve Kur'ân İlimlerine Giriş*, Istanbul: Ensar Neşriyat, 1983.

Yiğit, Yılmaz and Ergene, Mehmet, *Çağdaşlık mı? İnhiraf mı?* İzmir: Kaynak A.Ş., 1994.

Zahabi, Muhammad ibn Ahmad ibn Uthman, *Al-Sirat al-Nabawiyya*, Beirut: Dar al-Kutub al-Ilmiyya, 1982.

Zahabi, Muhammad Husayn, *Al-Wahy wa al-Qur'an al-Karim*, Cairo: Maktabat al-Wahba, 1986.

Zamahshari, Mahmud ibn Umar, *Al-Kashshaf al-Haqaiq al-Ghawamid al-Tanzil wa Uyun al-Aqawil fi Wujuh al-Tanzil*, Cairo: Dar al-Rayyan, 1987.

Zarkani, Muhammad Abdulazim, *Manahil al-Irfan Fi Ulum al-Qur'an*, Beirut: Dar al-Kutub al-Ilmiyya, 1988.

Zarkashi, Badruddin Muhammad ibn Abdillah, *Al-Burhan fi Ulum al-Qur'an*, Beirut: Dar al-Ma'rifa, undated.

Zuhayli, Wahba, *Al-Tafsir al-Munir*, Beirut: Dar al-Fikr, 1991.

INDEX

A

Aaron (Prophet), 12, 43, 189, 217, 218

Ab'an ibn Said, 162

Abdullah ibn Abbas, 229

Abdullah ibn Mas'ud, 80

Abdullah ibn Zubayr, 49, 81

Abdul Malik ibn Marwan, 83

Abdurrahman ibn al-Harith, 81

ablution, 261, 266, 267

Abraham (Prophet), 11, 12, 16, 35, 67, 73, 189, 191, 263

Absolute and All-Encompassing Knowledge of God, 138

Absolute Will of God, 227

Abu al-Aswad al-Dualy, 83

Abu Bakr (as-Siddiq), 22, 23, 48, 79-82, 146, 147, 162, 272, 273

Abu Jafar, 81

Abu Jahl, 17, 90, 129, 198, 221

Abu Lahab, 197-199; Father of the Flame, 199

Abu Musa al-Ash'ari, 81

Abu Said al-Khudry, 222

Abu Talib, 23, 115, 160, 179, 198, 199

Abu Ubayda, 22

accountability, 260

Adam (Prophet), 109, 121, 142, 153, 189, 191, 210, 211, 214, 216, 217, 263

Addas, 21, 22

adoption, 195

agreements and contracts, 209

Ahnas ibn Sharik, 144

Aisha bint Abi Bakr, 36, 47, 118, 223

Ala ibn al-Hadrami, 21

Alexandria, 146, 274

Ali ibn Abu Talib, 23

Amr ibn Rabia, 21

angels, 15, 16, 18, 19, 43, 70, 73, 106, 110, 111, 144, 186, 202, 215, 220, 225, 228, 246

Arabic, 3, 6, 11, 60, 67, 68, 73, 82-84, 87-89, 97-105, 109, 119-123, 155, 159, 166, 167, 173, 190, 217, 254, 256, 259, 265, 266; language of, 60, 97, 105, 167, 173, 254, 256; Arabic Qur'an, 99-101, 105, 266

Arabs, 60, 87, 89, 102-104, 119-121, 128, 129, 131, 157, 172

arbitration, 204

asbab al-nuzul (causes of revelation), 49; circumstances of the revelation, 49, 252

Ascension, the, 220, 221

authenticity of the Qur'an, 81, 82, 121, 131, 136, 148, 154, 155, 182, 242; Divine origin, 23, 30; Divinely preserved Book, 154, 155, 162; soundness of the ori-